ON CREATIVITY AND THE UNCONSCIOUS

ON CREATIVITY AND THE UNCONSCIOUS

Papers on the Psychology of
Art, Literature, Love, Religion

Sigmund Freud

Selected, with Introduction and Annotations by
Benjamin Nelson

HARPER TORCHBOOKS
Harper & Row, Publishers
New York, Cambridge, Hagerstown, Philadelphia, San Francisco
London, Mexico City, São Paulo, Sydney

The material in this volume, reprinted by arrangement with The
Hogarth Press Ltd., London, was originally published in 1925
under the title *Papers on Applied Psycho-Analysis* in the fourth
volume of Freud's COLLECTED PAPERS, translated under the
supervision of Joan Riviere, and included in The International
Psycho-Analytical Library edited by Ernest Jones.

First HARPER TORCHBOOK edition published 1958

Library of Congress catalog card number: 58-10153
81 82 83 22 21 20 19

CONTENTS

CONTENTS

INTRODUCTION TO
THE TORCHBOOK EDITION

I

Even ardent students of Freud are not likely to have encountered him in the roles in which he appears in these pages. For it is current fashion to insist on his single-minded concentration on establishing a psychological system anchored in scrupulous clinical observation. His lifelong absorption in exploring the roots of culture is, on the other hand, treated condescendingly as the pardonable hobby of a pure scientist, even though Freud repeatedly declared that his scientific activity was in a sense a detour from his original interests.

The title of the present Selection—ON CREATIVITY AND THE UNCONSCIOUS—is intended to establish the humane and cultural focus of these essays, indeed of his whole life work. To describe these papers as "essays in psychoanalysis", as was done in previous editions, permits, at least nowadays in this country, a misconstruction of Freud's underlying inspiration and his larger aims. Freud did not conceive of the realms of culture merely as "areas" in which to test the application of his theories. From boyhood he was haunted by the riddles and triumphs of culture and pondered them without cease, hoping to wrest from them basic clues to the understanding of man and his works. His interest in the lives, labors and lures of men's minds in all their tangled expressions was no less profound than that of the author of the *Phenomenology of Mind*, and his results readily bear comparison with such students of man's creativity as Simmel, Dilthey, and Santayana. Like Santayana, Freud sought to document both the animal basis and ideal ends of the fabric of culture, though he would doubtless have been reluctant to describe the odyssey of *The Life of Reason* as "phases in the story of human progress."

To know Freud only in the guise of a psychiatrist is to know hardly half the man. True, the word 'creativity' rarely figures in Freud's vocabulary. The reasons for this omission will quickly become evident to those who read his writings attentively. But can there be any doubt that he was as much obsessed by the passion for creativity as he was delighted by the marvels of creative achievement? In 1910 he confided to Ernest Jones:

> I could not contemplate with any sort of comfort a life without work. Creative imagination and work go together with me; I take no delight in anything else. That would be a prescription for happiness were it not for the terrible thought that one's productivity depended on sensitive moods. What is one to do on a day when thoughts cease to flow and the proper words won't come? One cannot help trembling at the possibility. That is why, despite the acquiescence in fate that becomes an upright man, I secretly pray:

no infirmity, no paralysis of one's powers through bodily distress. 'We'll die with harness on', as King Macbeth said."

In the very first of the essays, he declares himself to be one of those whose fate it was to rouse men from their slumbers. His blow to man's narcissism, he suggests, was perhaps even more damaging than the "cosmological" and "biological wounds" wrought by Copernicus and Darwin. Henceforth it would be impossible for man to regard himself as undisputed master in his own house.

A unique glimpse into Freud's own creativity is afforded by a recital of the circumstances of his preparations for the essay on "The Moses of Michelangelo." His interest in the statue began, Ernest Jones tells us, even before 1901, when in visiting the church of S Pietro in Vincoli he encountered the statue face-to-face for the first time. In September of 1912 he wrote his wife that he was visiting the Moses sculpture every day. At this time, for reasons he did not himself know, he threw himself without reserve into the most varied preparations for the study. Yet, in 1914, when his paper was completed, he refused to allow it to be presented under his own name in *Imago,* so diffident was he about regarding it as a scientific monograph!

Nineteen years later, however, in connection with the Italian publication of the essay, he wrote a letter to Edouardo Weiss, which is reproduced below in the Annotations, describing the work as a "love-child" which he only belatedly acknowledged (in 1924) as his very own. His description of his "three lonely weeks" of standing before the statue, sketching it again and again, is an unforgettable cameo of Freud in the throes of creativity. Posterity has not been ungrateful to him for this effort. In 1954 the distinguished student of Michelangelo, Charles de Tolnay, described Freud's essay and that of William Watkiss Lloyd as the two most brilliant interpretations in their genre.

He who needs evidences more material than these for Freud's artistic impulses has only to examine the photographs of his office and library in the second volume of Ernest Jones' comprehensive biography. There he will see veritable museums of antiquities. To feast his eyes on artifacts and art reproductions was indispensable to Freud's spirit.

Few men carried their learning as lightly as did Freud. It was, after all, for literature that the Goethe prize was awarded to him. So ingenious is he in concealing his craft that one hardly suspects the range and appositeness of his reading and study. (In the nature of the case, his extensive references could hardly be enumerated in the Index to the present volume, which was prepared originally for the limited circle of professional psychoanalysts.) At home in a number of languages, classical and modern, and a devoted collector of antiquities and *objets d'art,* Freud startles one by the bold leap of his synthetic imagination. Nor is it surprising to discover that he responded as creatively to fairy tales and "middlebrow" romances as he did to the outstanding works of the arts and sciences from preliterate days to his own. On any page, one is likely to find him alluding to an odd yet peculiarly appropriate assortment of sources; for example: Anzengrueber, Apuleius, Ariosto, St. Augustine, Grimm's Fairy Tales, Ernst Mach, Nestroy, Raphael, Shakespeare and Oscar Wilde. At every turn he avows himself humbled by artistic achievements which represented creative anticipations of his own plodding research.

II

Each of the essays is a little gem in its own right. And each needs to be read again and again as representing the best which psychoanalysis has yet had to offer in the interpretation of culture. It matters little that exceptions have been—and will continue to be—taken to details in the arguments. What is most striking is the contrast between the distinctive visions and modest claims of these papers and the arid neo-scholasticism which has marred so many of the writings of the epigones in the professional reviews. Occasionally one misses in Freud's style the dark profundities and eccentric scholarship of Jung, but one is grateful in the end for the unwavering light of his prose.

Two of the essays which appear in the closing section of the present edition should strike the contemporary reader with particular forcefulness. Freud's "Thoughts for the Times on War and Death" issued in 1915 will not these days seem an inexcusably grim pronouncement. The reader who has known the anguish of the last quarter-century will not regard Freud's remarks as pessimistic distortions to be explained by his allegedly blind belief in the fixity of impulse or by the torment of his own illness in the last year of his life. Few who read this essay with a fresh eye today will feel inclined to accept the charges endlessly reiterated by unsympathetic critics, such as John Dewey, Erich Fromm and others affected by the "liberal humanist" and "progressive democratic" outlooks of the 1930's and 40's, that Freud's insistence on the biological endowment and "constitutional determinants" made him miss the plasticity of culture. It is precisely the *plasticity* of culture which accounts for the precariousness of its foundations and makes the works of man susceptible to retrogression. Here, at the outset of his career, as in *The Interpretation of Dreams,* and again, at the acme of his life, in *Civilization and its Discontents* (1930) he exposes the myth that transcendence over primitive levels of feeling and thought are permanently achieved in individual and social development. It was this myth which underlay the evolutionary theodicies of the eras of the Enlightenment and the Victorian period. Who can say, after reading this essay, that he failed to overcome the illusions, rationalist and irrationalist alike, which were rife in the century of his birth? In no essay in the entire Freudian corpus are the accents of his realistic existentialism so clearly sounded as in this.

His study of the "Neurosis of Demoniacal Possession in the Seventeenth Century" is an excessively neglected contribution to the understanding of the vagaries of religious experience. The combination of close observation and imaginative power which were revealed in his outstanding report on the case of Justice Schreber reappear here in a setting which will be of the utmost interest to historians of art, literature, and religion as well as to psychiatrists. The sources available to him were the manuscript remains of the diary and paintings of Christoph Haitzmann, a possessed artist, who spent the last years of his life in the charge of the Fathers of Mariazell in lower Austria. The connections between the transactions of Haitzmann with the devil and the numberless variants of the Faust legend do not escape Freud, although he utterly resists the temptation to abandon the texts at hand for showy expeditions into comparative mythology and psychology. Almost at every turn in the paper's development one finds oneself

posing fresh questions concerning details of one or another instance of the
Faust story, whether it be Marlowe, Goethe, Lenau, or Thomas Mann.
At the paper's end one recognizes that one must think twice before depreci-
ating Freud's understanding and learning in the field of religion.

This is hardly the place to institute a full-scale review, which is badly
needed, of Freud's views on creativity, culture, and the unconscious. To
suppose, as some have, that the "most highly-valued products of our
civilization"—so he describes the realms of culture in his Preface to
Theodor Reik's *Ritual*—were simply a tissue of illusions and the efflux of
illness is to commit an elementary logical blunder and miss both the nuance
and force of his position.

Creativity, he knew, was a complex process requiring deeper explication
than that afforded by a psychology which construed all human action in
terms of deliberate behavior. The omnipresent unconscious worked
elusively, serving now as brake, now as spur to creative fulfillment in every
corner of man's conduct and culture—art, literature, love, even religion.
Regressive passions and phantasies might well be the goads to attempts at
creative integration, but it was less the illness than the power to engender
form and achieve completed embodiment in the work of art which characterized artistic fulfillment as distinguished from neurotic or psychotic
failure. In the case of the creator, regression served to mark out and light
up the path to reconstruction.

Perhaps we can best recapture the essence of Freud's vision by citing
the poet whose "Ode to Nature" first attracted him to the study of the
sciences. Goethe, whose autobiography, *Poetry and Truth*, is the subject
of an essay in the present selection is speaking to Eckermann in 1829:

> man is a confused creature: he knows not whence he comes or whither he
> goes; he knows little of the world and above all, little of himself.

Freud longed to add a grain to man's self-knowledge. Toward this end
he struggled to plumb the depths of the unconscious and scale the heights
of creativity. Midway on his journey he stumbled upon a clue: the road to
the heights was by way of the depths. Thus was begun his fateful odyssey,
on which we are all still engaged.

BENJAMIN NELSON

New York City
May, 1958

ONE OF THE DIFFICULTIES OF
PSYCHO-ANALYSIS [1]

(1917)

I WILL say at once that it is not an intellectual
difficulty I am thinking of, not anything that makes
psycho-analysis hard for the hearer or reader to
understand, but an affective one—something that
alienates the feelings of those who come into contact
with it, so that they become less inclined to believe
in it or take an interest in it. As may be observed,
the two kinds of difficulty amount to the same thing
in the end. Where sympathy is lacking, understanding
will not come very easily.

My present readers are, I take it, as yet unconcerned
with the subject and I shall be obliged, therefore, to
go back some distance. Out of a great number of
individual observations and impressions something like
a theory has at last shaped itself in psycho-analysis,
and this is known by the name of the ' libido-theory '.
As is known, psycho analysis is concerned with the
explanation and cure of what are called nervous disorders. A starting-point had to be found from which
to approach this problem, and it was decided to look
for it in the life of the instincts in the mind. Hypotheses
relating to the instincts in man came to form the basis,
therefore, of our conception of nervous disease.

The psychology that is taught in the schools gives
us but very inadequate replies to questions concerning
our mental life, but in no direction is its information
so meagre as in this matter of the instincts.

[1] First published (in Hungarian) in the *Nyugat*, 1917, and subsequently in *Imago*, Bd. V., 1917 ; reprinted in *Sammlung*, Vierte Folge.
[Translated by Joan Riviere.]

We are left to take the first sounding in our own way. The popular view distinguishes between hunger and love, seeing them as the two representatives of those instincts which aim at self-preservation and at reproduction of the species respectively. We acknowledge this very evident distinction, so that in psycho-analysis also we postulate a similar one between the self-preservative or ego-instincts, on the one hand, and the sexual instincts on the other ; that force by which the sexual instinct is represented in the mind we call ' libido '—sexual hunger—regarding it as analogous to the force of hunger, or the will to power, and other such trends among the ego-tendencies.

With this as a starting-point we then make our first important discovery. We learn that, when we come to try to comprehend neurotic disorders, by far the most significance attaches to the sexual instincts ; in fact neuroses are the specific disorders, so to speak, of the sexual function ; that in general whether or not a person develops a neurosis depends upon the strength of his libido, and upon the possibility of gratifying it and of discharging it through gratification ; that the form taken by the disease is determined by the path which the sexual function of the person in question takes in its development, or, as we put it, by the fixations his libido has undergone in the course of its development ; and, further, that by a special, not very simple technique for influencing the mind we are able to throw light on the nature of many groups of neuroses and at the same time to resolve them. The greatest success of our therapeutic efforts has been with a certain class of neuroses proceeding from a conflict between ego-instincts and sexual instincts. For in human beings it may happen that the demands of the sexual instincts, which of course extend far beyond the individual, seem to the ego to constitute a danger menacing his self-preservation or his self-respect. The ego then takes up the defensive, denies the sexual instincts the satisfaction they claim and forces them into those by-paths of substitutive gratification which become manifest as symptoms of a neurosis.

The psycho-analytic method of treatment is then able to subject this process of repression to revision and to bring about a better solution of the conflict, one compatible with health. Opponents who do not understand the matter accuse us of one-sidedness and of overestimating the sexual instincts : ' Human beings have other interests besides sexual things '. We have not forgotten or denied this for a moment. Our one-sidedness is like that of the chemist who traces all compounds back to the force of chemical attraction. In doing so, he does not deny the force of gravity ; he leaves that to the physicist to reckon with.

During the work of treatment we have to consider the distribution of the patient's libido ; we look for the objects (ideas of them) to which it is attached and free it from them, so as to place it at the disposal of the ego. In the course of this, we have come to form a very curious picture of the direction taken at the outset by the libido in man. We have had to infer that at the beginning of its development the libido (all the erotic tendencies, all capacity for love) in each individual is directed towards the self—as we say, it cathects the self. It is only later that, in association with the satisfaction of the chief natural functions, the libido flows over beyond the ego towards objects outside the self, and not till then are we able to recognize the libidinal trends as such and distinguish them from the ego-instincts. It is possible for the libido to become detached from these objects and withdrawn again into the self.

The condition in which the libido is contained within the ego is called by us ' narcissism ', in reference to the Greek myth of the youth Narcissus who remained faithful to his love for his own reflection.

Thus we look upon the development of the individual as a progress from narcissism to object-love ; but we do not believe that the whole of the libido is ever transferred from the ego to objects outside itself. A certain amount of libido is always retained in the ego ; even when object-love is highly developed, a certain degree of narcissism continues. The ego is a great reservoir from which the libido that is destined for objects flows outward and into which it can flow back from those objects. Object-libido was at first ego-libido and can be again transformed into ego-libido. For complete health it is essential that the libido should not lose this full mobility. As an illustration of this state of things we may think of an amoeba, the proto-plasm of which puts out pseudopodia, elongations into which the substance of the body extends but which can be retracted at any time so that the form of the protoplasmic mass is reinstated.

What I have been trying to describe in this outline is the *libido-theory* of the neuroses, upon which are founded all our conceptions of the nature of these morbid states, together with our therapeutic measures for relieving them. We naturally regard the premises of the libido-theory as valid for normal behaviour as well. We employ the term ' narcissism ' in relation to little children, and it is to the excessive ' narcissism ' of primitive man that we ascribe his belief in the omnipotence of his thoughts and his consequent attempts to influence the course of events in the outer world by magical practices.

After this introduction I shall describe how the general narcissism of man, the self-love of humanity, has up to the present been three times severely wounded by the researches of science.

(*a*) When the first promptings of curiosity about his dwelling-place, the earth, began to arise in him, man believed that it was the stationary centre of the universe, with the sun, moon and planets circling round it. With this he was naïvely following the dictates of his sense-perceptions, for he felt no movement of the earth, and wherever he had an unimpeded view he found himself in the centre of a circle that enclosed the whole world outside him. The central position of the earth was to him a token of its sovereignty in the universe and it appeared to accord very well with his proclivity to regard himself as lord of the world.

The destruction of this narcissistic illusion is associated with the name and work of Copernicus in the sixteenth century. Long before his day the Pythagoreans had already cast doubts upon the privileged position of the earth, and in the third century B.C. Aristarchus of Samos had declared that the earth was much smaller than the sun and moved round that celestial body. Even the great discovery of Copernicus, therefore, had already been made before. But when it achieved general recognition, the self-love of humanity suffered its first blow, the *cosmological* one.

(*b*) In the course of his development towards culture man acquired a dominating position over his fellow-creatures in the animal kingdom. Not content with this supremacy, however, he began to place a gulf between his nature and theirs. He denied the possession of reason to them, and to himself he attributed an immortal soul, and made claims to a divine descent which permitted him to annihilate the bond of community between him and the animal kingdom. It is noteworthy that this piece of arrogance is still as foreign to the child as it is to the savage or to primitive man. It is the result of a later, more pretentious stage of development. At the level of totemism primitive man has no repugnance to tracing his descent from an animal ancestor. In myths, which contain the deposit of this ancient attitude of mind, the gods take animal shapes, and in the art of prehistoric times they are portrayed with animal's heads. A child can see no difference between his own nature and that of animals ; he is not astonished at animals thinking and talking in fairy-tales ; he will transfer to a dog or a horse an emotion of fear which refers to his human father, without thereby intending any derogation of his father. Not until he is grown up does he become so far estranged from the animals as to use their names in vilification of others.

We all know that, little more than half a century ago, the researches of Charles Darwin, his collaborators and predecessors put an end to this presumption on the part of man. Man is not a being different from animals or superior to them ; he himself originates in the animal race and is related more closely to some of its members and more distantly to others. The accretions he has subsequently developed have not served to efface the evidences, both in his physical structure and in his mental dispositions, of his parity with them. This was the second, the *biological* blow to human narcissism.

(c) The third blow, which is psychological in nature, is probably the most wounding.

Although thus humbled in his external relations, man feels himself to be supreme in his own soul. Somewhere in the core of his ego he has developed an organ of observation to keep a watch on his impulses and actions and see that they accord with its demands. If they do not, they are inexorably prohibited and retracted. His inner perception, consciousness, gives the ego news of all the important occurrences in the mind's working, and the will, set in motion by these reports, carries out what the ego directs and modifies all that tends to accomplish itself independently. For this soul is not a simple thing ; on the contrary, it is a hierarchy of superordinated and subordinated agents, a labyrinth of impulses striving independently of one another towards action, corresponding with the multiplicity of instincts and of relations with the outer world, many of which are antagonistic to one another and incompatible. For proper functioning it is necessary that the highest among these agents should have knowledge of all that is going forward and that its will should penetrate throughout to exert its influence. But the ego feels itself secure of the completeness and trustworthiness both of the reports it receives and of the channels by which it can enforce its commands.

In certain diseases, including indeed the very neuroses of which we have made special study, things are different. The ego feels uneasy ; it finds a limit to its power in its own house, the mind. Thoughts suddenly break in without the conscious mind knowing where they come from, nor can it do anything to drive them away. These unwelcome guests seem to be more powerful even than those which are at the ego's command ; they resist all the well-proven measures instituted by the will, remain unmoved by logical rebuttal, and unaffected though reality refutes them. Or else impulses make themselves felt which seem like those of a stranger, so that the ego disowns them ; yet it has to fear them and take precautions against them. The ego says to itself : ' This is an illness, a foreign invasion ' ; it increases its vigilance, but cannot understand why it feels so strangely paralysed.

Psychiatry, it is true, denies that such things mean the intrusion into the mind of evil spirits from without ; beyond this, however, it can only say with a shrug : ' Degeneracy, hereditary disposition, constitutional inferiority ! ' Psycho-analysis sets out to explain these eerie disorders ; it engages in scrupulous and laborious investigations, devises hypotheses and scientific expedients, until at length it can say to the ego : ' Nothing has entered into you from without ; a part of the activity of your own mind has been withdrawn from your knowledge and from the command of your will. That, too, is why you are so weak in your defences ; with one part of your forces you are fighting the other part and you cannot concentrate the whole of your energy as you would against an outer enemy. And it is not even the worst or least effective part of your mental powers that has thus become antagonistic to you and independent of you. The blame, I must tell you, lies with yourself. You overestimated your strength when you thought you could do as you liked with your sexual instincts and could utterly ignore their aims. The result is that they have rebelled and have gone their own way in the dark to rid themselves of this oppression ; they have extorted their rights in a manner you cannot sanction. How they have achieved this and the paths by which they have reached their purpose, you have not learned ; only the result of their work, the symptom which you experience as suffering, has come to your knowledge. Then you do not recognize it as a product of your own rejected impulses and do not know that it is a substitutive gratification of them.

' The whole process, however, only becomes possible through the single circumstance that you are mistaken in another important point as well. You believe that you are informed of all that goes on in your mind if it is of any importance at all, because your consciousness then gives you news of it. And if you have heard nothing of any particular thing in your mind you confidently assume that it does not exist there. Indeed, you go so far as to regard " the mind " as co-extensive with " consciousness ", that is, with what is known to you, in spite of the most obvious evidence that a great deal more is perpetually going on in your mind than can be known to your consciousness. Come, let yourself be taught something on this one point. What is in your mind is not identical with what you are conscious of ; whether something is going on in your mind and whether you hear of it, are two different things. In the ordinary way, I will admit, the intelligence which reaches your consciousness is enough for your needs ; and you may cherish the illusion that you learn of all the more important things. But in some cases, as in that of a conflict between instincts such as I have described, the intelligence department breaks down and your will then extends no further than your knowledge. In all cases, however, the news that reaches your consciousness is incomplete and often not to be relied on ; often enough, too, it happens that you get news of what has taken place only when it is all over and when you can no longer do anything to change it. Even if you are not ill, who can tell all that is stirring in your mind of which you know nothing or are falsely informed ? You conduct yourself like an absolute sovereign who is content with the information supplied him by his highest officials and never goes among the people to hear their voice. Look into the depths of your own soul and learn first to know yourself, then you will understand why this illness was bound to come upon you and perhaps you will thenceforth avoid falling ill.'

It is thus that psycho-analysis wishes to educate the ego. But these two discoveries—that the life of the sexual instincts cannot be totally restrained, and that mental processes are in themselves unconscious and only reach the ego and come under its control through incomplete and untrustworthy perceptions—amount to a statement that *the ego is not master in its own house.* Together they represent the third wound inflicted on man's self-love, that which I call the *psychological* one. No wonder, therefore, that the ego shows no favour to psycho-analysis and persistently refuses to believe in it.

Probably but very few people have realized the momentous significance for science and life of the recognition of unconscious mental processes. It was not psycho-analysis, however, let us hasten to add, which took this first step. There are renowned names among the philosophers who may be cited as its predecessors, above all the great thinker Schopenhauer, whose unconscious ' Will ' is equivalent to the instincts in the mind as seen by psycho-analysis. It was this same thinker, moreover, who in words of unforgettable impressiveness admonished mankind of the importance of their sexual craving, still so depreciated. Psycho-analysis has only this to its credit, that it has not affirmed these two propositions that are so wounding to narcissism on an abstract basis—the importance of sexuality in the mind and the unconsciousness of mental activity—but has demonstrated them in matters that touch every individual personally and force him to take up some attitude towards these problems. It is just for this reason, however, that it brings on itself the aversion and antagonism which still keep at a respectful distance from the name of the great philosopher.

THE MOSES OF MICHELANGELO [1]

(1914)

I MAY say at once that I am no connoisseur in art, but simply a layman. I have often observed that the subject-matter of works of art has a stronger attraction for me than their formal and technical qualities, though to the artist their value lies first and foremost in these latter. I am unable rightly to appreciate many of the methods used and the effects obtained in art. I state this so as to secure the reader's indulgence for the attempt I propose to make here.

Nevertheless, works of art do exercise a powerful effect on me, especially those of literature and sculpture, less often of painting. This has occasioned me, when I have been contemplating such things, to spend a long time before them trying to apprehend them in my own way, *i.e.* to explain to myself what their effect is due to. Wherever I cannot do this, as for instance with music, I am almost incapable of obtaining any pleasure. Some rationalistic, or perhaps analytic, turn of mind in me rebels against being moved by a thing without knowing why I am thus affected and what it is that affects me.

This has brought me to recognize the apparently paradoxical fact that precisely some of the grandest and most overwhelming creations of art are still un-

---

[1] Originally published anonymously in *Imago*, Bd. III., 1914, prefaced by the following editorial note : *Although this paper does not, strictly speaking, conform to the conditions under which contributions are accepted for publication in this Journal, the editors have decided to print it, since the author, who is personally known to them, belongs to psychoanalytical circles, and since his mode of thought has in point of fact a certain resemblance to the methodology of psycho-analysis.* [Translated by Alix Strachey.]

solved riddles to our understanding.   We admire them, we feel overawed by them, but we are unable to say what they represent to us.   I am not sufficiently well-read to know whether this fact has already been remarked upon ; possibly, indeed, some writer on aesthetics has discovered that this state of intellectual bewilderment is a necessary condition when a work of art is to achieve its greatest effects.   It would be only with the greatest reluctance that I could bring myself to believe in any such necessity.

I do not mean that connoisseurs and lovers of art find no words with which to praise such objects to us. They are eloquent enough, it seems to me.   But usually in the presence of a great work of art each says something different from the other ; and none of them says anything that solves the problem for the un-pretending admirer.   In my opinion, it can only be the artist's intention, in so far as he has succeeded in expressing it in his work and in conveying it to us, that grips us so powerfully.   I realize that it cannot be merely a matter of intellectual comprehension ; what he aims at is to awaken in us the same emotional attitude, the same mental constellation as that which in him produced the impetus to create.   But why should the artist's intention not be capable of being communicated and comprehended in words like any other fact of mental life ?   Perhaps where great works of art are concerned this would never be possible without the application of psycho-analysis.   The pro-duct itself after all must admit of such an analysis, if it really is an effective expression of the intentions and emotional activities of the artist.   To discover his intention, though, I must first find out the meaning and content of what is represented in his work ; I must, in other words, be able to *interpret* it.   It is possible, therefore, that a work of art of this kind needs interpretation, and that until I have accomplished that interpretation I cannot come to know why I have been so powerfully affected.   I even venture to hope that

the effect of the work will undergo no diminution after
we have succeeded in thus analysing it.

Let us consider Shakespeare's masterpiece, *Hamlet*,
a play now over three centuries old.[1] I have followed
the literature of psycho-analysis closely, and I accept
its claim that it was not until the material of the
tragedy had been traced back analytically to the
Oedipus theme that the mystery of its effect was at
last explained. But before this was done, what a mass
of differing and contradictory interpretative attempts,
what a variety of opinions about the hero's character
and the dramatist's design ! Does Shakespeare claim
our sympathies on behalf of a sick man, or of an
ineffectual weakling, or of an idealist who is only too
good for the real world ? And how many of these
interpretations leave us cold—so cold that they do
nothing to explain the effect of the play and rather
incline us to the view that its magical appeal rests
solely upon the impressive thoughts in it and the
splendour of its language. And yet, do not those very
endeavours speak for the fact that we feel the need of
discovering in it some source of power beyond these
alone ?

Another of these inscrutable and wonderful works
of art is the marble statue of Moses, by Michelangelo,
in the Church of S. Pietro in Vincoli in Rome. As we
know, it was only a fragment of the gigantic tomb which
the artist was to have erected for the powerful Pope
Julius II.[2] It always delights me to read an apprecia-
tory sentence about this statue, such as that it is ' the
crown of modern sculpture ' (Hermann Grimm). For
no piece of statuary has ever made a stronger impression
on me than this. How often have I mounted the steep
steps of the unlovely Corso Cavour to the lonely place
where the deserted church stands, and have essayed to
support the angry scorn of the hero's glance ! Some-

[1] Probably first performed in 1602.
[2] According to Henry Thode, the statue was made between the
years 1512 and 1516.

times I have crept cautiously out of the half-gloom of
the interior as though I myself belonged to the mob
upon whom his eye is turned—the mob which can hold
fast no conviction, which has neither faith nor patience
and which rejoices when it has regained its illusory
idols.

But why do I call this statue inscrutable ?   There
is not the slightest doubt that it represents Moses, the
Law-giver of the Jews, holding the Tables of the Ten
Commandments.   That much is certain, but that is all.
As recently as 1912 an art critic, Max Sauerlandt, has
said, ' No other work of art in the world has been
judged so diversely as the Moses with the head of Pan.
The mere interpretation of the figure has given rise to
completely opposed views. . . .'   Basing myself on an
essay published only five years ago,[1] I will first set out
what are the doubts associated with this figure of
Moses ; and it will not be difficult to show that behind
them lies concealed all that is most essential and valuable for the comprehension of this work of art.

I

The Moses of Michelangelo is represented as seated ;
his body faces forward, his head with its mighty beard
looks to the left, his right foot rests on the ground and
his left leg is raised so that only the toes touch the
ground.   His right arm links the Tables of the Law
with a portion of his beard ; his left arm lies in his lap.
Were I to give a more detailed description of his attitude, I should have to anticipate what I want to say
later on.   The descriptions of the figure given by
various writers are, by the way, curiously inapt.   What
has not been understood has been inaccurately perceived or reproduced.   Grimm says that the right hand
' under whose arm the Tables rest, grasps his beard '.
So also Lübke : ' Profoundly shaken, he grasps with

[1] Henry Thode, *Michelangelo: kritische Untersuchungen über seine Werke*, Bd. I., 1908.

Courtesy of The Metropolitan Museum of Art, John Taylor Johnston
Memorial Collection, Purchased by subscription, 1891-1895

his right hand his magnificent streaming beard . . .';
and Springer : 'Moses presses one (the left) hand
against his body, and thrusts the other, as though
unconsciously, into the mighty locks of his beard'.
Justi thinks that the fingers of his (right) hand are
playing with his beard, 'as an agitated man nowadays
might play with his watch-chain'. Müntz, too, lays
stress on this playing with the beard. Thode speaks of
the 'calm, firm posture of the right hand upon the
Tables resting against his side'. He does not recognize
any sign of excitement even in the right hand, as Justi
and also Boito do. 'The hand remains grasping his
beard, in the position it was before the Titan turned
his head to one side.' Jakob Burckhardt complains
that 'the celebrated left arm has no other function in
reality than to press his beard to his body'.

If mere descriptions do not agree we shall not be
surprised to find a divergence of view as to the meaning
of various features of the statue. In my opinion we
cannot better characterize the facial expression of
Moses than in the words of Thode, who reads in it 'a
mixture of wrath, pain and contempt ',—' wrath in his
threatening contracted brows, pain in his glance, and
contempt in his protruded under lip and in the down-
drawn corners of his mouth'. But other admirers
must have seen with other eyes. Thus Dupaty says,
'His august brow seems to be but a transparent veil
only half concealing his great mind '.[1] Lübke, on the
other hand, declares that 'one would look in vain in
that head for an expression of higher intelligence ; his
down-drawn brow speaks of nothing but a capacity
for infinite wrath and an all-compelling energy'.
Guillaume (1875) differs still more widely in his interpretation of the expression of the face. He finds no
emotion in it, 'only a proud simplicity, an inspired
dignity, a living faith. The eye of Moses looks into the
future, he foresees the lasting survival of his people,
the immutability of his law.' Similarly, to Müntz, 'the

---

[1] Thode, *loc. cit.* p. 197.

eyes of Moses rove far beyond the race of men. They
are turned towards those mysteries which he alone has
descried.' To Steinmann, indeed, this Moses is ' no
longer the stern Law-giver, no longer the terrible enemy
of sin, armed with the wrath of Jehovah, but the royal
priest, whom age may not approach, beneficent and
prophetic, with the reflection of eternity upon his brow,
taking his last farewell of his people '.

There have even been some for whom the Moses of
Michelangelo had nothing at all to say, and who are
honest enough to admit it. Thus a critic in the
Quarterly Review of 1858 : ' There is an absence of
meaning in the general conception, which precludes
the idea of a self-sufficing whole. . . .' And we are
astonished to learn that there are yet others who find
nothing to admire in the Moses, but who revolt against
it and complain of the brutality of the figure and the
animal cast of the head.

Has then the master-hand indeed traced such a
vague or ambiguous script in the stone, that so many
different readings of it are possible ?

Another question, however, arises, which covers the
first one. Did Michelangelo intend to create a ' timeless study of character and mood ' in this Moses, or did
he portray him at a particular and, if so, at a highly
significant moment of his life ? The majority of judges
have decided in the latter sense and are able to tell us
what episode in his life it is which the artist has
immortalized in stone. It is the descent from Mount
Sinai, where Moses has received the Tables from God,
and it is the moment when he perceives that the
people have meanwhile made themselves a Golden Calf
and are dancing around it and rejoicing. This is the
scene upon which his eyes are turned, this the spectacle
which calls out the feelings depicted in his countenance
—those feelings which in the next instant will launch
his great frame to violent action. Michelangelo has
chosen this last moment of hesitation, of calm before
the storm, for his representation. In the next instant

Moses will spring to his feet—his left foot is already raised from the ground—hurl the Tables to the ground, and let loose his rage upon his faithless people.

Once more many individual differences of opinion exist among those who support this interpretation.

Jacob Burckhardt writes : ' Moses seems to be shown in that moment in which he catches sight of the worship of the Golden Calf, and is springing to his feet. His form is animated by the inception of a mighty movement and the physical strength with which he is endowed causes us to await it with fear and trembling.'

And Lübke says : ' As if at this moment his flashing eye were perceiving the sin of the worship of the Golden Calf and a mighty inward movement were running through his whole frame. Profoundly shaken, he grasps with his right hand his magnificent, streaming beard, as though to master his actions for one instant longer, only for the explosion of his wrath to burst with more annihilation the next.'

Springer agrees with this view, but not without mentioning one misgiving, which will engage our attention later in the course of this paper. He says, ' Burning with energy and zeal, it is with difficulty that the hero subdues his inward emotion. . . . We are thus involuntarily reminded of a dramatic situation and are brought to believe that Moses is represented in that moment when he sees the people of Israel worshipping the Golden Calf and is about to start up in wrath. Such an impression, it is true, is not easy to reconcile with the artist's real intention, since the figure of Moses, like the other five seated figures on the upper part of the Papal tomb, is meant primarily to have a decorative effect. But it testifies very convincingly to the vitality and individuality portrayed in the figure of Moses.'

One or two writers, without actually accepting the Golden Calf theory, do nevertheless agree on its main point, namely, that Moses is just about to spring to his feet and take action.

According to Hermann Grimm, ' The form (of Moses) is filled with a majesty, a consciousness of self, a feeling that all the thunders of heaven are at his command, and that yet he is holding himself in check before loosing them, waiting to see whether his foes whom he means to annihilate will dare to attack him. He sits there as if on the point of starting to his feet, his proud head carried high on his shoulders ; the hand under whose arm the Tables rest grasps his beard which falls in heavy waves over his breast, his nostrils distended and his lips shaped as though words were trembling upon them.'

Heath Wilson declares that Moses' attention has been excited by something, and he is about to leap to his feet, but is still hesitating ; and that his glance of mingled scorn and indignation is still capable of changing into one of compassion.

Wölfflin speaks of ' inhibited movement '. The cause of this inhibition, he says, lies in the will of the man himself ; it is the last moment of self-control before he lets himself go and leaps to his feet.

Justi has gone the furthest of all in his interpretation of the statue as Moses in the act of perceiving the Golden Calf, and he has pointed out details hitherto unobserved in it and worked them into his hypothesis. He directs our attention to the position of the two Tables, and it is indeed an unusual one, for they are about to slip down on to the stone seat. ' He (Moses) might therefore be looking in the direction from which the clamour was coming with an expression of evil foreboding, or it might be the actual sight of the abomination which has dealt him a stunning blow. Quivering with horror and pain he has sunk down.[1] He has sojourned on the mountain forty days and nights and he is weary. A horror, a great turn of

---

[1] It should be remarked that the careful arrangement of the mantle over the knees of the sitting figure invalidates this first part of Justi's view. On the contrary, this would lead us to suppose that Moses is represented as sitting there in calm repose until he is startled by some sudden perception.

fortune, a crime, even happiness itself, can be perceived in a single moment, but not grasped in its essence, its depths or its consequences. For an instant it seems to Moses that his work is destroyed and he despairs of his people. In such moments the inner emotions betray themselves involuntarily in small movements. He lets the Tables slip from his right hand on to the stone seat ; they have been brought up sideways there, pressed by his forearm against the side of his body. His hand, however, comes in contact with his breast and beard and thus, by the turning of the head to the spectator's right, it draws the beard to the left and breaks the symmetry of that masculine ornament. It looks as though his fingers were playing with his beard as an agitated man nowadays might play with his watch-chain. His left hand is buried in his garment over the lower part of his body—in the Old Testament the viscera are the seat of the emotions—but the left leg is already drawn back and the right put forward ; in the next instant he will leap up, his mental energy will be transposed from feeling into action, his right arm will move, the Tables will fall to the ground, and the shameful trespass will be expiated in torrents of blood. . . .' 'Here is not yet the moment of tension of a physical act. The pain of mind still dominates him almost like a paralysis.'

Fritz Knapp takes exactly the same view, except that he does not introduce the doubtful point at the beginning of the description,[1] and carries the idea of the sliding Tables further. ' He who just now was alone with his God is distracted by earthly sounds. He hears a noise ; voices shouting to dance and music wake him from his dream ; he turns his eyes and his head in the direction of the clamour. In one instant fear, rage and unbridled passion traverse his huge frame. The Tables begin to slip down, and will fall to the ground and break when he leaps to his feet and hurls the angry thunder of his words into the midst of

[1] [Cf. previous note.—Trans.]

his back-sliding people. . . . This is the moment of
highest tension which is chosen. . . .' Knapp, therefore, emphasizes the element of preparation for action,
and disagrees with the view that what is being represented is an initial inhibition due to an overmastering
agitation.

It cannot be denied that there is something extraordinarily attractive about attempts at an interpretation of the kind made by Justi and Knapp. This is
because they do not stop short at the general effect of
the figure, but are based on separate features in it ;
these we usually fail to notice, being overcome by the
total impression of the statue and as it were paralysed
by it. The marked turn of the head and eyes to the
left, whereas the body faces forwards, supports the
view that the resting Moses has suddenly seen something on that side to rivet his attention. His lifted
foot can hardly mean anything else but that he is
preparing to spring up ; [1] and the very unusual way in
which the Tables are held (for they are most sacred
objects and are not to be introduced into the composi-
tion like any other belonging) is fully accounted for if
we suppose that they have slipped down as a result of
the agitation of their bearer and will fall to the ground.
According to this view we should believe that the
statue represents a special and important moment in
the life of Moses, and we should be left in no doubt of
what that moment is.

But two remarks of Thode's deprive us of the knowledge we thought to have gained. This critic says that
to his eye the Tables are not slipping down but are
' firmly lodged '. He notes the ' calm, firm pose of the
right hand upon the resting Tables '. If we look for
ourselves we cannot but admit unreservedly that Thode
is right. The Tables are firmly placed and in no danger
of slipping. Moses' right hand supports them or is
supported by them. This does not explain the position

[1] Although the left foot of the reposeful seated figure of Giuliano
in the Medici Chapel is similarly raised from the ground.

in which they are held, it is true, but the interpretation of Justi and others cannot be based upon it.

The second observation is still more final. Thode reminds us that 'this statue was planned as one out of six, and is intended to be seated. Both facts contradict the view that Michelangelo meant to record a particular historical moment. For as to the first consideration, the plan of representing a row of seated figures as types of human beings—as the *vita activa* and the *vita contemplativa*—excluded a representation of particular historic episodes. And as to the second, the representation of a seated posture—a posture necessitated by the artistic conception of the whole monument—contradicts the nature of that episode, namely, the descent of Moses from Mount Sinai into the camp.'

If we accept Thode's objection we shall find that we can add to its weight. The figure of Moses was to have decorated the base of the tomb together with five other statues (in a later sketch, with three). Its immediate complement was to have been a figure of Paul. One other pair, representing the *vita activa* and the *vita contemplativa* in the shape of Leah and Rachel—standing, it is true—has been executed on the tomb as it still exists in its mournfully aborted form. The Moses thus forms part of a whole and we cannot imagine that the figure was meant to arouse an expectation in the spectator that it was on the point of leaping up from its seat and rushing away to create a disturbance on its own account. If the other figures are not also represented as about to take violent action—and this seems very improbable—then it would create a very bad impression for one of them to give us the illusion that it was going to leave its place and its companions, in fact to abandon its rôle in the general scheme. Such an intention would have a chaotic effect and we could not charge a great artist with it unless the facts drove us to it. A figure in the act of instant departure would be utterly at variance with the state of mind which the tomb is meant to induce in us.

The figure of Moses, therefore, cannot be supposed to be springing to his feet ; he must be allowed to remain as he is in sublime repose like the other figures and like the proposed statue of the Pope (which was not, however, executed by Michelangelo himself). But then the statue we see before us cannot be that of a man filled with wrath, of Moses when he came down from Mount Sinai and found his people faithless and threw down the Holy Tables so that they were broken. And, indeed, I can recollect my own disillusionment when, during my first visits to the church, I used to sit down in front of the statue in the expectation that I should now see how it would start up on its raised foot, hurl the Tables of the Law to the ground and let fly its wrath. Nothing of the kind happened. Instead, the stone image became more and more transfixed, an almost oppressively solemn calm emanated from it, and I was obliged to realize that something was represented here that could stay without change ; that this Moses would remain sitting like this in his wrath for ever.

But if we have to abandon our interpretation of the statue as showing Moses just before his outburst of wrath at the sight of the Golden Calf, we have no alternative but to accept one of those hypotheses which regard it as a study of character. Thode's view seems to be the least arbitrary and to have the closest reference to the meaning of its movements. He says, ' Here, as always, he is concerned with representing a certain type of character. He creates the image of a passionate leader of mankind who, conscious of his divine mission as Law-giver, meets the uncomprehending opposition of men. The only means of representing a man of action of this kind was to accentuate the power of his will, and this was done by a rendering of movement pervading the whole of his apparent quiet, as we see in the turn of his head, the tension of his muscles and the position of his left foot. These are the same distinguishing marks that we find again in the *vir activus* of the Medici chapel in Florence. This general character of the figure is further heightened by laying stress on the conflict which is bound to arise between such a reforming genius and the rest of mankind. Emotions of anger, contempt and pain are typified in him. Without them it would not have been possible to portray the nature of a superman of this kind. Michelangelo has created, not an historical figure, but a character-type, embodying an inexhaustible inner force which tames the recalcitrant world ; and he has given a form not only to the Biblical narrative of Moses, but to his own inner experiences, and to his impressions both of the individuality of Julius himself, and also, I believe, of the underlying springs of Savonarola's perpetual conflicts.'

This view may be brought into connection with Knackfuss's remark that the great secret of the effect produced by the Moses lies in the artistic contrast between the inward fire and the outer calm of his bearing.

For myself, I see nothing to object to in Thode's explanation ; but I feel the lack of something in it. Perhaps it is the need to discover a closer parallel between the state of mind of the hero as expressed in his attitude, and the above-mentioned contrast between his ' outward ' calm and ' inward ' emotion.

II

Long before I had any opportunity of hearing about psycho-analysis, I learnt that a Russian art-connoisseur, Ivan Lermolieff,[1] had caused a revolution in the art galleries of Europe by questioning the authorship of many pictures, showing how to distinguish copies from originals with certainty, and constructing hypothetical artists for those works of art whose former supposed authorship had been discredited. He achieved this by insisting that attention should be diverted from the

[1] His first essays were published in German between 1874 and 1876.

general impression and main features of a picture, and
he laid stress on the significance of minor details, of
things like the drawing of the finger-nails, of the lobe
of an ear, of aureoles and such unconsidered trifles
which the copyist neglects to imitate and yet which
every artist executes in his own characteristic way.
I was then greatly interested to learn that the Russian
pseudonym concealed the identity of an Italian
physician called Morelli, who died in 1891 with the rank
of Senator of the Kingdom of Italy.   It seems to me
that his method of inquiry is closely related to the
technique of psycho-analysis.   It, too, is accustomed
to divine secret and concealed things from unconsidered
or unnoticed details, from the rubbish-heap, as it were,
of our observations.

Now in two places in the figure of Moses there are
certain details which have hitherto not only escaped
notice—but, in fact, have not even been properly described.   These are the attitude of his right hand and the
position of the two Tables of the Law.   We may say that
this hand forms a very singular, unnatural link, and one
which calls for explanation, between the Tables and
the wrathful hero's beard.   He has been described as
running his fingers through his beard and playing with
its locks, while the outer edge of his hand rests on the
Tables.   But this is plainly not so.   It is worth while
examining more closely what those fingers of the right
hand are doing, and describing more minutely the
mighty beard with which they are in contact.[1]

We now quite clearly perceive the following things :
the thumb of the hand is concealed and the index
finger alone is in effective contact with the beard.   It
is pressed so deeply against the soft masses of hair that
they bulge out beyond it both above and below, that
is, both towards the head and towards the abdomen.
The other three fingers are propped upon the wall of
his chest and are bent at the upper joints ; they are
barely touched by the extreme right-hand lock of the

[1] Cf. the illustration.

beard which falls past them. They have, as it were, withdrawn themselves from the beard. It is therefore not correct to say that the right hand is playing with the beard or plunged in it ; the simple truth is that the index finger is laid over a part of the beard and makes a deep trough in it. To press one's beard with one finger is assuredly an extraordinary gesture and one not easy to understand.

The much-admired beard of Moses flows from his cheeks, chin and upper lip in a number of waving strands which are kept distinct from one another all the way down. One of the strands on the extreme right, growing from the cheek, flows down to the inward-pressing index finger, where it stops. We may assume that it resumes its course between that finger and the concealed thumb. The corresponding strand on the left side falls practically unimpeded far down over his breast. What has received the most unusual treatment is the thick mass of hair on the inside of this latter strand, the part between it and the middle line. It is not suffered to follow the turn of the head to the left ; it is forced to roll over loosely and form part of a kind of scroll which lies across and over the strands on the inner right side of the beard. This is because it is held fast by the pressure of the right index finger, although it grows from the left side of the face and is, in fact, the main portion of the whole left side of the beard. Thus, the main mass of the beard is thrown to the right of the figure, whereas the head is sharply turned to the left. At the place where the right index finger is pressed in, a kind of whorl of hairs is formed ; strands of hair coming from the left lie over strands coming from the right, both caught in by that despotic finger. It is only beyond this place that the masses of hair, deflected from their course, flow freely once more, and now they fall vertically until their ends are gathered up in Moses' left hand as it lies open on his lap.

I have no illusions as to the clarity of my description, and venture no opinion whether the sculptor

really does invite us to solve the riddle of that knot in
the beard of his statue.   But apart from this, the fact
remains that the pressure of the *right* index-finger
affects mainly the strands of hair from the *left* side ;
and that this oblique hold prevents the beard from
accompanying the turn of the head and eyes to the
left.   Now we may be allowed to ask what this arrangement means and to what motives it owes its existence.
Were they indeed considerations of linear and spatial
design which caused the sculptor to draw the downward-
streaming wealth of hair across to the right of the
figure which is looking to its left, how strangely unsuitable as a means appears the pressure of a single
finger !   And what man who, for some reason or other,
has drawn his beard over to the other side, would take
it into his head to hold down the one half across the
other by the pressure of a single finger ?   Yet may not
these minute particulars mean nothing in reality, and
may we not be racking our brains about things which
were of no moment to their creator ?

Let us proceed on the assumption that even these
details have significance.   There is a solution which
will remove our difficulties and afford a glimpse of a
new meaning.   If the *left* side of Moses' beard lies under
the pressure of his *right* finger, we may perhaps take
this pose as the last stage of some connection between
his right hand and the left half of his beard, a connection which was a much more intimate one at
some moment before that chosen for representation.
Perhaps his hand had seized his beard with far more
energy, had reached across to its left edge, and, in
returning to that position in which the statue shows it,
had been followed by a part of his beard which now
testifies to the movement which has just taken place.
The loop of the beard would thus be an indication of
the path taken by this hand.

Thus we shall have inferred that there had been a
retreating motion of the right hand.   This one assumption necessarily brings others with it.   In imagination

we complete the scene of which this movement, established by the evidence of the beard, is a part ; and we are brought back quite naturally to the hypothesis according to which the resting Moses is startled by the clamour of the people and the spectacle of the Golden Calf. He was sitting there calmly, we will suppose, his head with its flowing beard facing forward, and his hand in all probability not near it at all. Suddenly the clamour strikes his ear ; he turns his head and eyes in the direction from which the disturbance comes, sees the scene and takes it in. Now wrath and indignation seize him ; and he would fain leap up and punish the wrongdoers, annihilate them. His rage, distant as yet from its object, is meanwhile directed in a gesture against his own body. His impatient hand, ready to act, clutches at his beard which has moved with the turn of his head, and shuts it down with his fingers between the thumb and the palm in an iron grasp—it is a gesture whose power and vehemence remind us of other creations of Michelangelo's. But now an alteration takes place, as yet we do not know how or why. The hand that had been put forward and had sunk into his beard is hastily withdrawn and unclasped, and the fingers let go their hold ; but so deeply have they been plunged in that in their withdrawal they drag a great piece of the left side of the beard across to the right, and this piece remains lodged over the hair of the right under the weight of one finger, the longest and uppermost one of the hand. And this new position, which can only be understood with reference to the former one, is now retained.

It is time now to pause and reflect. We have assumed that the right hand was, to begin with, away from the beard ; that then it reached across to the left of the figure in a moment of great emotional tension and seized the beard ; and that it was finally drawn back again, taking a part of the beard with it. We have disposed of this right hand as though we had the free use of it. But may we do this ? Is the hand indeed so free ? Must it not hold or support the Tables ? Are not such mimetic evolutions as these prohibited by its important function ? And further-more, what could have occasioned its withdrawal if such a powerful motive caused its first displacement ?

Here are indeed fresh difficulties. It is undeniable that the right hand is responsible for the Tables ; and also that we have no motive to account for the with-drawal we have ascribed to it. But what if both difficulties could be solved together, then and then only presenting a clear and connected sequence of events ? What if it is precisely something which is happening to the Tables that explains the movements of the hand ?

If we look at the drawing in Fig. D we shall see that the Tables present one or two notable features hitherto not deemed worthy of remark. It has been said that the right hand rests upon the Tables ; or again that it supports them. And we can see at once that the two apposed, rectangular tablets are standing on edge. If we look closer we shall notice that the lower edge is a different shape from the upper one, which is obliquely inclined forward. The top edge is straight, whereas the bottom one has a protuberance like a horn on the part nearest to us, and the Tables touch the stone seat precisely with this protuberance. What can be the meaning of this detail ? [1] It can hardly be doubted that this projection is meant to mark the actual upper side of the Tables, as regards the writing. It is only the upper edge of rectangular tablets of this kind that is curved or notched. Thus we see that the Tables are upside-down. This is a singular way to treat such sacred objects. They are stood on their heads and practically balanced on one corner. What considera-tion of form could have led to such an attitude ? Or was this detail, too, of no importance to the artist Michelangelo ?

[1] Which, by the way, is quite incorrectly reproduced in a large plaster cast in the collection of the Vienna Academy of Plastic Arts.

The view begins to form in us that the Tables also
have arrived at their present position as the result of a
previous movement ; that this movement depended on
the inferred change of place of the right hand and then
in its turn compelled that hand to make its subsequent
retreat. The movements of the hand and of the
Tables can be co-ordinated in this way : at first the
figure of Moses, while it was still sitting quietly, carried

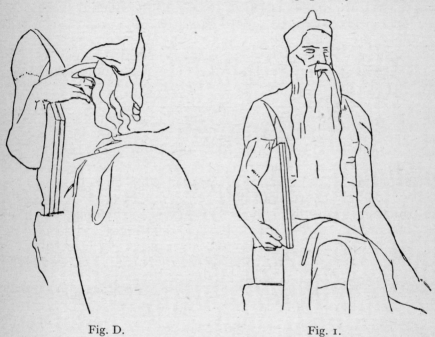

Fig. D.   Fig. I.

the Tables upright under its right arm.   Its right hand
grasped their bottom edge and found a hold in the
projection of their front part.   The greater ease thereby
gained sufficiently accounts for the reversed position
in which the Tables are held.   Then came the moment
when Moses' calm was broken by the disturbance.
He turns his head in its direction, and when he sees the
spectacle he lifts his foot preparatory to starting up,
lets go the Tables with his hand and throws it to the

left and upwards into his beard, as though to turn his vehemence against his own body. The Tables were now consigned to the pressure of his arm, which had to squeeze them against his side. But this support was not sufficient and the Tables began to slip in a forward and downward direction. The upper edge, which had been held horizontally, now began to face forwards

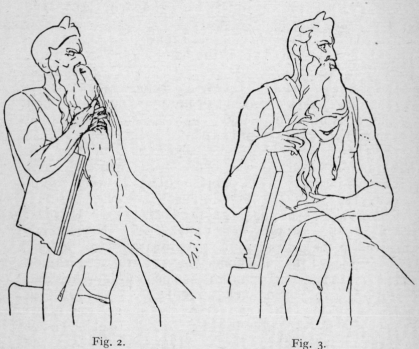

Fig. 2.   Fig. 3.

and downwards; and the lower edge, deprived of its stay, was nearing the stone seat with its front corner. Another instant and the Tables would have pivoted upon this new point of support, have hit the ground with the upper edge foremost, and been shattered to pieces. It is *to prevent this* that the right hand retreats, lets go the beard, a part of which is drawn back with it unintentionally, comes against the top edge of the Tables in time and grips them near the hind corner, which has now come uppermost. Thus the singularly constrained air of the whole—beard, hand and tilted Tables—can be traced to that one passionate movement of the hand and its natural consequences. If we wish to reverse the effects of those stormy movements, we must raise the upper front corner of the Tables and push it back, thus lifting their lower front corner (the one with the protuberance) from the stone seat ; and then lower the right hand and bring it under the now horizontal bottom edge of the Tables.

I have procured from the hand of an artist three drawings to illustrate my meaning. Fig. 3 reproduces the statue as it actually is ; Figs. 1 and 2 represent the preceding stages according to my hypothesis—the first that of calm, the second that of highest tension, in which the figure is preparing to spring up and has abandoned its hold of the Tables, so that these are beginning to slip down. Now it is remarkable how the two postures in the supplementary drawings vindicate the incorrect descriptions of earlier writers. Condivi, a contemporary of Michelangelo's, says : ' Moses, the captain and leader of the Hebrews, is seated in the attitude of a contemplative sage, holding the Tables of the Law under his right arm, and leaning his chin on his left hand (!), as one who is weary and full of care.' No such attitude is to be seen in Michelangelo's statue, but it describes almost exactly the view on which the first drawing is based. Lübke writes, together with other critics : ' Profoundly shaken, he grasps with his right hand his magnificent, streaming beard.' This is incorrect if we look at the reproduction of the actual statue, but it is true of the second sketch (Fig. 2). Justi and Knapp have observed, as we have seen, that the Tables are about to slip down and are in danger of being broken. Thode set them right and showed that the Tables were securely held by the right hand ; yet they would have been correct if they had been describing not the statue itself but the middle stage of our reconstructed action. It almost seems as if they had emancipated themselves from the visual image of the statue and had unconsciously begun an analysis of the motive forces behind it, and that that analysis had led them to make the same claim as we, more consciously and more explicitly, have done.

III

We may now, I believe, permit ourselves to reap the fruits of our endeavours. We have seen how many of those who have felt the influence of this statue have been impelled to interpret it as representing Moses agitated by the spectacle of his people fallen from grace and dancing round an idol. But this interpretation had to be given up, for it made us expect to see him spring up in the next moment, break the Tables and accomplish the work of vengeance. Such a conception, however, would fail to harmonize with the design of making this figure, together with three or five more seated figures, a part of the tomb of Julius II. We may now take up again the abandoned interpretation, for the Moses we have reconstructed will neither leap up nor cast the Tables from him. What we see before us is not the inception of a violent action but the remains of a movement that has already taken place. In his first transport of fury, Moses desired to act, to spring up and take vengeance and forget the Tables ; but he has overcome the temptation, and he will now remain seated and still in his frozen wrath and in his pain mingled with contempt. Nor will he throw away the Tables so that they will break on the stones, for it is on their especial account that he has controlled his anger ; it was to preserve them that he kept his passion in check. In giving way to his rage and indignation, he had to neglect the Tables, and the hand which upheld them was withdrawn. They began to slide down and were in danger of being broken. This brought him to himself. He remembered his mission and renounced for its sake an indulgence of his feelings. His hand returned and saved the unsupported Tables before they had actually fallen to the ground.   In this attitude he remained immobilized, and in this attitude Michelangelo has portrayed him as the guardian of the tomb.

Viewed from above downwards, the figure exhibits three distinct emotional strata.   The lines of the face reflect the feelings which have become predominant ; the middle of the figure shows the traces of suppressed movement ; and the foot still retains the attitude of the projected action.   It is as though the controlling influence had proceeded downwards from above.   No mention has been made so far of the left arm, and it seems to claim a share in our interpretation.   The hand is laid in his lap in a mild gesture and holds as though in a caress the end of his flowing beard.   It seems as if it is meant to counteract the violence with which the other hand had misused the beard a few moments ago.

But here it will be objected that after all this is not the Moses of the Bible.   For that Moses did actually fall into a fit of rage and did throw away the Tables and break them.   This Moses must be a quite different man, a new Moses of the artist's conception ; so that Michelangelo must have had the presumption to emend the sacred text and to falsify the character of that holy man.   Can we think him capable of a boldness which might almost be said to approach an act of blasphemy ?

The passage in the Holy Scriptures which describes Moses' action at the scene of the Golden Calf is as follows : (Exodus xxxii. 7) 'And the Lord said unto Moses, Go, get thee down ; for thy people, which thou broughtest out of the land of Egypt, have corrupted themselves : (8) They have turned aside quickly out of the way which I commanded them : they have made them a molten calf, and have worshipped it, and have sacrificed thereunto, and said, These be thy gods, O Israel, which brought thee up out of the land of

Egypt. (9) And the Lord said unto Moses, I have seen this people, and, behold, it is a stiff-necked people : (10) Now therefore let me alone, that my wrath may wax hot against them, and that I may consume them ; and I will make of thee a great nation. (11) And Moses besought the Lord his God, and said, Lord, why doth thy wrath wax hot against thy people, which thou hast brought forth out of the land of Egypt with great power, and with a mighty hand ? . . .

'(14) And the Lord repented of the evil which he thought to do unto his people. (15) And Moses turned, and went down from the mount, and the two tables of the testimony were in his hand : the tables were written on both their sides ; on the one side and on the other were they written. (16) And the tables were the work of God, and the writing was the writing of God, graven upon the tables. (17) And when Joshua heard the noise of the people as they shouted, he said unto Moses, There is a noise of war in the camp. (18) And he said, It is not the voice of them that shout for mastery, neither is it the voice of them that cry for being overcome ; but the noise of them that sing do I hear. (19) And it came to pass, as soon as he came nigh unto the camp, that he saw the calf, and the dancing : and Moses' anger waxed hot, and he cast the tables out of his hands, and brake them beneath the mount. (20) And he took the calf which they had made, and burnt it in the fire, and ground it to powder, and strawed it upon the water, and made the children of Israel drink of it. . . .

'(30) And it came to pass on the morrow, that Moses said unto the people, Ye have sinned a great sin : and now I will go up unto the Lord ; peradventure I shall make an atonement for your sin. (31) And Moses returned unto the Lord, and said, Oh ! this people have sinned a great sin, and have made them gods of gold ! (32) Yet now, if thou wilt forgive their sin— ; and if not, blot me, I pray thee, out of thy book which thou hast written. (33) And the Lord said unto Moses,

Whosoever hath sinned against me, him will I blot out
of my book. (34) Therefore now go, lead the people
unto the place of which I have spoken unto thee.
Behold, mine Angel shall go before thee : nevertheless,
in the day when I visit, I will visit their sin upon them.
(35) And the Lord plagued the people, because they
made the calf which Aaron made.'

It is impossible to read the above passage in the
light of modern criticism of the Bible without finding
evidence that it has been clumsily put together from
various sources. In verse 8 the Lord Himself tells
Moses that his people have fallen away and made
themselves an idol ; and Moses intercedes for the
wrongdoers. And yet he speaks to Joshua as though
he knew nothing of this (18), and is suddenly aroused
to wrath as he sees the scene of the worshipping of the
Golden Calf (19). In verse 14 he has already gained
a pardon from God for his erring people, yet in verse
31 he returns into the mountains to implore this
forgiveness, tells God about his people's sin and is
assured of the postponement of the punishment.
Verse 35 speaks of a visitation of his people by the
Lord about which nothing more is told us ; whereas
the verses 20-30 describe the punishment which
Moses himself dealt out. It is well known that the
historical parts of the Bible, dealing with the Exodus,
are crowded with still more glaring incongruities and
contradictions.

The age of the Renaissance had naturally no such
critical attitude towards the text of the Bible, but had
to accept it as a consistent whole, with the result that
the passage in question was not a very good subject
for representation. According to the Scriptures Moses
was already instructed about the idolatry of his people
and had ranged himself on the side of mildness and
forgiveness ; nevertheless, when he saw the Golden
Calf and the dancing crowd, he was overcome by a
sudden frenzy of rage. It would therefore not surprise
us to find that the artist, in depicting the reaction of

his hero to that painful surprise, had deviated from the text from inner motives. Moreover, such deviations from the scriptural text on a much slighter pretext were by no means unusual or disallowed to artists. A celebrated picture by Parmigiano possessed by his native town depicts Moses sitting on the top of a mountain and hurling the Tables to the ground, although the Bible expressly says that he broke them ' beneath the mount '. Even the representation of a seated Moses finds no support in the text, and seems rather to bear out those critics who maintain that Michelangelo's statue is not meant to record any particular moment in the prophet's life.

More important than his infidelity to the text of the Scriptures is the alteration which Michelangelo has, in our supposition, made in the character of Moses. The Moses of legend and tradition had a hasty temper and was subject to fits of passion. It was in a transport of divine wrath of this kind that he slew an Egyptian who was maltreating an Israelite, and had to flee out of the land into the wilderness ; and it was in a similar passion that he broke the Tables of the Law, inscribed by God Himself. Tradition, in recording such a characteristic, is unbiased, and preserves the impression of a great personality who once lived. But Michelangelo has placed a different Moses on the tomb of the Pope, one superior to the historical or traditional Moses. He has modified the theme of the broken Tables ; he does not let Moses break them in his wrath, but makes him be influenced by the danger that they will be broken and calm that wrath, or at any rate prevent it from becoming an act. In this way he has added something new and more than human to the figure of Moses ; so that the giant frame with its tremendous physical power becomes only a concrete expression of the highest mental achievement that is possible in a man, that of struggling successfully against an inward passion for the sake of a cause to which he has devoted himself.

We have now completed our interpretation of the statue of Moses. It can still be asked what motives prompted the sculptor to select the figure of Moses, and a so much altered Moses, as an ornament for the tomb of Julius II. In the opinion of many these motives are to be found in the character of the Pope and in Michelangelo's relations with him. Julius II. was akin to Michelangelo in this, that he attempted to realize great and mighty ends, especially designs on a large scale. He was a man of action and he had a definite purpose, which was to unite Italy under the Papal supremacy. He desired to bring about single-handed what was not to happen for several centuries, and then only through the conjunction of many alien forces ; and he worked alone, with impatience, in the short span of sovereignty allowed him, and used violent means. He could appreciate Michelangelo as a man of his own kind, but he often made him smart under his sudden anger and his utter lack of consideration for others. The artist felt the same violent force of will in himself, and, as the more introspective thinker, may have had a premonition of the failure to which they were both doomed. And so he carved his Moses on the Pope's tomb, not without a reproach against the dead pontiff, as a warning to himself, thus rising in self-criticism superior to his own nature.

In 1863 an Englishman, Watkiss Lloyd, devoted a little book to the Moses of Michelangelo.[1] I succeeded in getting hold of this short essay of forty-six pages, and read it with mixed feelings. I once more had occasion to experience in myself what unworthy and puerile motives enter into our thoughts and acts even in a serious cause. My first feeling was one of regret that the author should have anticipated so much of my thought, which seemed precious to me because it was the result of my own efforts ; and it was only in the second instance that I was able to get pleasure from its unexpected confirmation of my opinion.

[1] W. Watkiss Lloyd, *The Moses of Michelangelo*.

Our views, however, diverge on one very important point.

It was Lloyd who first remarked that the usual descriptions of the figure are incorrect, and that Moses is not in the act of rising up [1]—that the right hand is not grasping the beard, but that the index-finger alone is resting upon it.[2] Lloyd has also recognized, and this is much more important, that the attitude portrayed can only be explained by postulating a foregoing one, which is not represented, and that the drawing of the left lock of the beard across to the right signifies that the right hand and the left side of the beard have been in closer and more natural contact before. But he suggests another way of reconstructing that logically inferred earlier contact. According to him, it was not the hand which had been plunged into the beard, but the beard which had been where the hand now is. We must, he says, imagine that the head of the statue was turned far round to its right just before the sudden interruption and rose right over the hand which, then as now, was holding the Tables of the Law. The pressure (of the Tables) against the palm of the hand caused the fingers to open naturally beneath the flowing locks of the beard, and the sudden turn of the head to the other side had the result that a part of the beard was detained for an instant by the motionless hand and formed that loop of hair which is to be looked on as a mark of the course it has taken—its 'wake', to use Lloyd's own word.

In rejecting the other possibility, that of the right hand having previously been in contact with the left side of the beard, Lloyd allows himself to be influenced by a consideration which shows how near he came to

---

[1] ' But he is not rising or preparing to rise ; the bust is fully upright, not thrown forward for the alteration of balance preparatory for such a movement. . . .' (p. 10).

[2] ' Such a description is altogether erroneous ; the fillets of the beard are detained by the right hand but they are not held, nor grasped, enclosed or taken hold of.   They are even detained but momentarily— momentarily engaged, they are on the point of being free for dis-engagement' (p. 11).

our interpretation. He says that it was not possible
for the prophet, even in very great agitation, to have
put out his hand to draw his beard across to the right.
For in that case his fingers would have been in an
entirely different position ; and, moreover, such a
movement would have allowed the Tables to slip down,
since they are only supported by the pressure of the
right arm—unless, in Moses' endeavour to save them
at the last moment, we think of them as being ' clutched
by a gesture so awkward that to imagine it is pro-
fanation '.

It is easy to see what the writer overlooked. He
has correctly interpreted the anomalies of the beard as
indicating a movement that has gone before, but he
has omitted to apply the same explanation to the no
less unnatural details in the position of the Tables. He
examines only the data connected with the beard and
not those connected with the Tables, whose position he
assumes to be the original one. In this way he closes
the door to a conception like ours which, by examining
certain insignificant details, has arrived at an unexpected interpretation of the meaning and aim of the
figure as a whole.

But what if we have both strayed on to a wrong
path ? What if we have taken too serious and profound
a view of details which were nothing to the artist,
details which he had introduced quite arbitrarily or for
some purely formal reasons with no hidden intention
behind ? What if we have shared the fate of so many
interpreters who have thought to see quite clearly
things which the artist did not intend either consciously or unconsciously ? I cannot tell. I cannot
say whether it is reasonable to credit Michelangelo—that
artist in whose works there is so much thought striving
for expression—with such an elementary want of
precision, especially whether this could be assumed in
regard to the striking and singular features of the
statue under discussion. And finally we may be
allowed to point out, in all modesty, that the artist is

no less responsible than his interpreters for the obscurity which surrounds his work. In his creations Michelangelo has often enough gone to the utmost limit of what is expressible in art ; and perhaps in his statue of Moses he has not completely succeeded, if his design was to trace the passage of a violent gust of passion in the signs left by it on the ensuing calm.

A MYTHOLOGICAL PARALLEL TO A VISUAL OBSESSION [1]

(1916)

IN a patient of about twenty-one years of age the unconscious mental activity expressed itself consciously not only in obsessive thoughts but also in obsessive visual images. The two could accompany each other or appear independently of each other. At one particular time, whenever he saw his father coming into the room, there came into his mind in close connection with each other an obsessive word and an obsessive picture. The word was ' father-arse '; the accompanying picture represented the lower part of a trunk, nude and provided with arms and legs, but without the head or chest, and this was the father. The genitals were not shown, and the facial features were represented on the abdomen.

In endeavouring to explain this unusually crazy symptom-formation, it must be noted that the patient, who is a man of highly developed intellect and lofty moral ideals, manifested a very lively anal erotism in the most various ways until after his tenth year. After this was overcome, his sexual life was again forced back to the anal plane by the later struggle against genital erotism. He loved and respected his father greatly, and also feared him not a little ; from the standpoint of his high ideals in regard to asceticism and suppression of the instincts, however, his father seemed to him a debauchee who sought enjoyment in material things.

' Father-arse ' was soon explained as a jocular

[1] First published in Zeitschrift, Bd. IV., 1916; reprinted in *Sammlung*, Vierte Folge. [Translated by C. M. J. Hubback.]

Teutonizing of the honourable title 'patriarch'.[1] The obsessive picture is an obvious caricature. It recalls other representations that derogatorily replace a whole person by one of their organs, e.g. the genitals; it reminds us, too, of unconscious phantasies leading to the identification of the genitals with the whole person, and also of joking expressions, such as 'I am all ears'.

The rendering of the facial features on the abdomen of the caricature struck me at first as most extraordinary. Soon afterwards, however, I remembered having seen the same thing in French caricatures.[2] Chance then brought to my notice an antique instance of it which showed complete correspondence with my patient's obsessive image.

According to Greek legend Demeter came to Eleusis in search of her daughter who had been abducted, and was taken in and housed by Dysaules and his wife Baubo; but in her great sorrow she refused to touch food or drink. By suddenly lifting up her clothes and exposing her body, however, the hostess Baubo made her laugh. A discussion of this anecdote, which is probably to be explained as a no longer intelligible magic ceremonial, is to be found in the fourth volume of Salomon Reinach's work, *Cultes, Mythes, et Religions*, 1912. In the same passage mention is also made of terracottas found in excavations 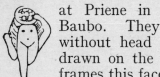 at Priene in Asia Minor, which represent Baubo. They show the body of a woman without head or bosom, and with a face drawn on the abdomen: the lifted clothing frames this face like a crown of hair.[3]

---

[1] [German for 'father' is *Vater*, for 'arse', *arsch*; hence *Vaterarsch*, *Patriarch*.—Trans.]

[2] Cf. 'Das unanständige Albion', a caricature of England in 1901, by Jean Veber, reproduced in E. Fuchs' *Das erotische Element in der Karikatur*, 1904.

[3] S. Reinach, *loc. cit.*, p. 117.

THE RELATION OF THE POET TO DAY-DREAMING [1]

(1908)

WE laymen have always wondered greatly—like the cardinal who put the question to Ariosto— how that strange being, the poet, comes by his material. What makes him able to carry us with him in such a way and to arouse emotions in us of which we thought ourselves perhaps not even capable ? Our interest in the problem is only stimulated by the circumstance that if we ask poets themselves they give us no explanation of the matter, or at least no satisfactory explanation. The knowledge that not even the clearest insight into the factors conditioning the choice of imaginative material, or into the nature of the ability to fashion that material, will ever make writers of us does not in any way detract from our interest.

If we could only find some activity in ourselves, or in people like ourselves, which was in any way akin to the writing of imaginative works ! If we could do so, then examination of it would give us a hope of obtaining some insight into the creative powers of imaginative writers. And indeed, there is some prospect of achieving this—writers themselves always try to lessen the distance between their kind and ordinary human beings ; they so often assure us that every man is at heart a poet, and that the last poet will not die until the last human being does.

We ought surely to look in the child for the first traces of imaginative activity. The child's best loved and most absorbing occupation is play. Perhaps we

[1] First published in *Neue Revue*, I., 1908 ; reprinted in *Sammlung*, Zweite Folge. [Translated by I. F. Grant Duff.]

may say that every child at play behaves like an imaginative writer, in that he creates a world of his own or, more truly, he rearranges the things of his world and orders it in a new way that pleases him better. It would be incorrect to think that he does not take this world seriously ; on the contrary, he takes his play very seriously and expends a great deal of emotion on it. The opposite of play is not serious occupation but—reality. Notwithstanding the large affective cathexis of his play-world, the child distinguishes it perfectly from reality ; only he likes to borrow the objects and circumstances that he imagines from the tangible and visible things of the real world. It is only this linking of it to reality that still distinguishes a child's ' play ' from ' day-dreaming '.

Now the writer does the same as the child at play ; he creates a world of phantasy which he takes very seriously ; that is, he invests it with a great deal of affect, while separating it sharply from reality. Language has preserved this relationship between children's play and poetic creation. It designates certain kinds of imaginative creation, concerned with tangible objects and capable of representation, as ' plays ' ; the people who present them are called ' players '. The unreality of this poetical world of imagination, however, has very important consequences for literary technique ; for many things which if they happened in real life could produce no pleasure can nevertheless give enjoyment in a play—many emotions which are essentially painful may become a source of enjoyment to the spectators and hearers of a poet's work.

There is another consideration relating to the contrast between reality and play on which we will dwell for a moment. Long after a child has grown up and stopped playing, after he has for decades attempted to grasp the realities of life with all seriousness, he may one day come to a state of mind in which the contrast between play and reality is again abrogated. The adult can remember with what intense seriousness he carried on his childish play ; then by comparing his would-be serious occupations with his childhood's play, he manages to throw off the heavy burden of life and obtain the great pleasure of humour.

As they grow up, people cease to play, and appear to give up the pleasure they derived from play. But anyone who knows anything of the mental life of human beings is aware that hardly anything is more difficult to them than to give up a pleasure they have once tasted. Really we never can relinquish anything ; we only exchange one thing for something else. When we appear to give something up, all we really do is to adopt a substitute. So when the human being grows up and ceases to play he only gives up the connection with real objects ; instead of playing he then begins to create phantasy. He builds castles in the air and creates what are called day-dreams. I believe that the greater number of human beings create phantasies at times as long as they live. This is a fact which has been overlooked for a long time, and its importance has therefore not been properly appreciated.

The phantasies of human beings are less easy to observe than the play of children. Children do, it is true, play alone, or form with other children a closed world in their minds for the purposes of play ; but a child does not conceal his play from adults, even though his playing is quite unconcerned with them. The adult, on the other hand, is ashamed of his day-dreams and conceals them from other people ; he cherishes them as his most intimate possessions and as a rule he would rather confess all his misdeeds than tell his day-dreams. For this reason he may believe that he is the only person who makes up such phantasies, without having any idea that everybody else tells themselves stories of the same kind. Day-dreaming is a continuation of play, nevertheless, and the motives which lie behind these two activities contain a very good reason for this different behaviour in the child at play and in the day-dreaming adult.

The play of children is determined by their wishes —really by the child's *one* wish, which is to be grown-up, the wish that helps to ' bring him up '. He always plays at being grown-up ; in play he imitates what is known to him of the lives of adults. Now he has no reason to conceal this wish. With the adult it is otherwise ; on the one hand, he knows that he is expected not to play any longer or to day-dream, but to be making his way in a real world. On the other hand, some of the wishes from which his phantasies spring are such as have to be entirely hidden ; therefore he is ashamed of his phantasies as being childish and as something prohibited.

If they are concealed with so much secretiveness, you will ask, how do we know so much about the human propensity to create phantasies ? Now there is a certain class of human beings upon whom not a god, indeed, but a stern goddess—Necessity—has laid the task of giving an account of what they suffer and what they enjoy. These people are the neurotics ; among other things they have to confess their phantasies to the physician to whom they go in the hope of recovering through mental treatment. This is our best source of knowledge, and we have later found good reason to suppose that our patients tell us about themselves nothing that we could not also hear from healthy people.

Let us try to learn some of the characteristics of day-dreaming. We can begin by saying that happy people never make phantasies, only unsatisfied ones. Unsatisfied wishes are the driving power behind phantasies ; every separate phantasy contains the fulfilment of a wish, and improves on unsatisfactory reality. The impelling wishes vary according to the sex, character and circumstances of the creator ; they may be easily divided, however, into two principal groups. Either they are ambitious wishes, serving to exalt the person creating them, or they are erotic. In young women erotic wishes dominate the phantasies almost exclusively, for their ambition is generally comprised in their erotic longings ; in young men egoistic and ambitious wishes assert themselves plainly enough alongside their erotic desires. But we will not lay stress on the distinction between these two trends ; we prefer to emphasize the fact that they are often united. In many altar-pieces the portrait of the donor is to be found in one corner of the picture ; and in the greater number of ambitious day-dreams, too, we can discover a woman in some corner, for whom the dreamer performs all his heroic deeds and at whose feet all his triumphs are to be laid. Here you see we have strong enough motives for concealment ; a well-brought-up woman is, indeed, credited with only a minimum of erotic desire, while a young man has to learn to suppress the overweening self-regard he acquires in the indulgent atmosphere surrounding his childhood, so that he may find his proper place in a society that is full of other persons making similar claims.

We must not imagine that the various products of this impulse towards phantasy, castles in the air or day-dreams, are stereotyped or unchangeable. On the contrary, they fit themselves into the changing impressions of life, alter with the vicissitudes of life ; every deep new impression gives them what might be called a ' date-stamp '. The relation of phantasies to time is altogether of great importance. One may say that a phantasy at one and the same moment hovers between three periods of time—the three periods of our ideation. The activity of phantasy in the mind is linked up with some current impression, occasioned by some event in the present, which had the power to rouse an intense desire. From there it wanders back to the memory of an early experience, generally belonging to infancy, in which this wish was fulfilled. Then it creates for itself a situation which is to emerge in the future, representing the fulfilment of the wish—this is the day-dream or phantasy, which now carries in it traces both of the occasion which engendered it and of some past memory.

So past, present and future are threaded, as it were, on the string of the wish that runs through them all.

A very ordinary example may serve to make my statement clearer. Take the case of a poor orphan lad, to whom you have given the address of some employer where he may perhaps get work. On the way there he falls into a day-dream suitable to the situation from which it springs. The content of the phantasy will be somewhat as follows : He is taken on and pleases his new employer, makes himself indispensable in the business, is taken into the family of the employer, and marries the charming daughter of the house. Then he comes to conduct the business, first as a partner, and then as successor to his father-in-law. In this way the dreamer regains what he had in his happy childhood, the protecting house, his loving parents and the first objects of his affection. You will see from such an example how the wish employs some event in the present to plan a future on the pattern of the past.

Much more could be said about phantasies, but I will only allude as briefly as possible to certain points. If phantasies become over-luxuriant and over-powerful, the necessary conditions for an outbreak of neurosis or psychosis are constituted ; phantasies are also the first preliminary stage in the mind of the symptoms of illness of which our patients complain. A broad by-path here branches off into pathology.

I cannot pass over the relation of phantasies to dreams. Our nocturnal dreams are nothing but such phantasies, as we can make clear by interpreting them.[1] Language, in its unrivalled wisdom, long ago decided the question of the essential nature of dreams by giving the name of ' day-dreams ' to the airy creations of phantasy. If the meaning of our dreams usually remains obscure in spite of this clue, it is because of the circumstance that at night wishes of which we are ashamed also become active in us, wishes which we

[1] Cf. Freud, *Die Traumdeutung*.

have to hide from ourselves, which were consequently repressed and pushed back into the unconscious. Such repressed wishes and their derivatives can therefore achieve expression only when almost completely disguised. When scientific work had succeeded in elucidating the distortion in dreams, it was no longer difficult to recognize that nocturnal dreams are fulfilments of desires in exactly the same way as daydreams are—those phantasies with which we are all so familiar.

So much for day-dreaming; now for the poet! Shall we dare really to compare an imaginative writer with ' one who dreams in broad daylight ', and his creations with day-dreams? Here, surely, a first distinction is forced upon us; we must distinguish between poets who, like the bygone creators of epics and tragedies, take over their material ready-made, and those who seem to create their material spontaneously. Let us keep to the latter, and let us also not choose for our comparison those writers who are most highly esteemed by critics. We will choose the less pretentious writers of romances, novels and stories, who are read all the same by the widest circles of men and women. There is one very marked characteristic in the productions of these writers which must strike us all: they all have a hero who is the centre of interest, for whom the author tries to win our sympathy by every possible means, and whom he places under the protection of a special providence. If at the end of one chapter the hero is left unconscious and bleeding from severe wounds, I am sure to find him at the beginning of the next being carefully tended and on the way to recovery ; if the first volume ends in the hero being shipwrecked in a storm at sea, I am certain to hear at the beginning of the next of his hairbreadth escape—otherwise, indeed, the story could not continue. The feeling of security with which I follow the hero through his dangerous adventures is the same as that with which a real hero throws himself into the water to save a drowning man, or exposes himself to the fire of the enemy while storming a battery. It is this very feeling of being a hero which one of our best authors has well expressed in the famous phrase, ' *Es kann dir nix g'schehen!* ' [1] It seems to me, however, that this significant mark of invulnerability very clearly betrays—His Majesty the Ego, the hero of all day-dreams and all novels.

The same relationship is hinted at in yet other characteristics of these egocentric stories. When all the women in a novel invariably fall in love with the hero, this can hardly be looked upon as a description of reality, but it is easily understood as an essential constituent of a day-dream. The same thing holds good when the other people in the story are sharply divided into good and bad, with complete disregard of the manifold variety in the traits of real human beings ; the ' good ' ones are those who help the ego in its character of hero, while the ' bad ' are his enemies and rivals.

We do not in any way fail to recognize that many imaginative productions have travelled far from the original naïve day-dream, but I cannot suppress the surmise that even the most extreme variations could be brought into relationship with this model by an uninterrupted series of transitions. It has struck me in many so-called psychological novels, too, that only one person—once again the hero—is described from within ; the author dwells in his soul and looks upon the other people from outside. The psychological novel in general probably owes its peculiarities to the tendency of modern writers to split up their ego by self - observation into many component - egos, and in this way to personify the conflicting trends in their own mental life in many heroes. There are certain novels, which might be called ' excentric ', that seem to stand in marked contradiction to the typical day-

[1] Anzengruber. [The phrase means ' Nothing can happen to *me* ! '—Trans.]

dream; in these the person introduced as the hero plays the least active part of anyone, and seems instead to let the actions and sufferings of other people pass him by like a spectator. Many of the later novels of Zola belong to this class. But I must say that the psychological analysis of people who are not writers, and who deviate in many things from the so-called norm, has shown us analogous variations in their day-dreams in which the ego contents itself with the rôle of spectator.

If our comparison of the imaginative writer with the day-dreamer, and of poetic production with the day-dream, is to be of any value, it must show itself fruitful in some way or other. Let us try, for instance, to examine the works of writers in reference to the idea propounded above, the relation of the phantasy to the wish that runs through it and to the three periods of time; and with its help let us study the connection between the life of the writer and his productions. Hitherto it has not been known what preliminary ideas would constitute an approach to this problem; very often this relation has been regarded as much simpler than it is; but the insight gained from phantasies leads us to expect the following state of things. Some actual experience which made a strong impression on the writer had stirred up a memory of an earlier experience, generally belonging to childhood, which then arouses a wish that finds a fulfilment in the work in question, and in which elements of the recent event and the old memory should be discernible.

Do not be alarmed at the complexity of this formula; I myself expect that in reality it will prove itself to be too schematic, but that possibly it may contain a first means of approach to the true state of affairs. From some attempts I have made I think that this way of approaching works of the imagination might not be unfruitful. You will not forget that the stress laid on the writer's memories of his childhood, which perhaps seems so strange, is ultimately derived from the hypothesis that imaginative creation, like day-dreaming, is a continuation of and substitute for the play of childhood.

We will not neglect to refer also to that class of imaginative work which must be recognized not as spontaneous production, but as a re-fashioning of ready-made material. Here, too, the writer retains a certain amount of independence, which can express itself in the choice of material and in changes in the material chosen, which are often considerable. As far as it goes, this material is derived from the racial treasure-house of myths, legends and fairy-tales. The study of these creations of racial psychology is in no way complete, but it seems extremely probable that myths, for example, are distorted vestiges of the wish-phantasies of whole nations—the age-long dreams of young humanity.

You will say that, although writers came first in the title of this paper, I have told you far less about them than about phantasy. I am aware of that, and will try to excuse myself by pointing to the present state of our knowledge. I could only throw out suggestions and bring up interesting points which arise from the study of phantasies, and which pass beyond them to the problem of the choice of literary material. We have not touched on the other problem at all, *i.e.* what are the means which writers use to achieve those emotional reactions in us that are roused by their productions. But I would at least point out to you the path which leads from our discussion of day-dreams to the problems of the effect produced on us by imaginative works.

You will remember that we said the day-dreamer hid his phantasies carefully from other people because he had reason to be ashamed of them. I may now add that even if he were to communicate them to us, he would give us no pleasure by his disclosures. When we hear such phantasies they repel us, or at least leave us cold. But when a man of literary talent presents his plays, or relates what we take to be his personal day-dreams, we experience great pleasure arising probably from many sources.   How the writer accomplishes this is his innermost secret ; the essential *ars poetica* lies in the technique by which our feeling of repulsion is overcome, and this has certainly to do with those barriers erected between every individual being and all others.   We can guess at two methods used in this technique.   The writer softens the egotistical character of the day-dream by changes and disguises, and he bribes us by the offer of a purely formal, that is, aesthetic, pleasure in the presentation of his phantasies.   The increment of pleasure which is offered us in order to release yet greater pleasure arising from deeper sources in the mind is called an ' incitement premium ' or technically, ' fore-pleasure '.   I am of opinion that all the aesthetic pleasure we gain from the works of imaginative writers is of the same type as this ' fore-pleasure ', and that the true enjoyment of literature proceeds from the release of tensions in our minds.   Perhaps much that brings about this result consists in the writer's putting us into a position in which we can enjoy our own day-dreams without reproach or shame.   Here we reach a path leading into novel, interesting and complicated researches, but we also, at least for the present, arrive at the end of the present discussion.

'THE ANTITHETICAL SENSE OF PRIMAL WORDS'[1]

A Review of a Pamphlet by Karl Abel, *Über den Gegensinn der Urworte*, 1884

(1910)

IN my *Traumdeutung* I made a statement concerning one of the findings of my analytic work which I did not then understand. I will repeat it at the beginning of this review :

'The attitude of dreams towards the category of antithesis and contradiction is most striking. This category is simply ignored; the word "No" does not seem to exist for a dream. Dreams show a special tendency to reduce two opposites to a unity or to represent them as one thing. Dreams even take the liberty, moreover, of representing any element whatever by the opposite wish, so that it is at first impossible to ascertain, in regard to any element capable of an opposite, whether it is to be taken negatively or positively in the dream-thoughts.'[2]

Dream-interpreters of antiquity seem to have made the most extensive use of the supposition that anything in a dream may mean its opposite. This possibility has also been occasionally recognized by modern investigators of dreams, in so far as they have conceded sense and explicability to dreams at all.[3] I do not think I shall meet with any contradiction when I presume that all who have followed me along the path

---

[1] First published in *Jahrbuch*, Bd. II., 1910 ; reprinted in *Sammlung, Dritte Folge*. [Translated by M. N. Searl.]

[2] *Die Traumdeutung*, Section VI.

[3] Cf., for example, B. G. H. v. Schubert, *Die Symbolik des Traumes*, 1862, Kap. II. ' Die Sprache des Traumes '.

of scientific dream-interpretation have found confirmation of the assertion quoted above.

To the chance reading of a work by the philologist
K. Abel I owe my first understanding of the strange
tendency of the dream-work to disregard negation and
to express contraries by identical means of representation ;   this work was published in 1884 as an
independent pamphlet, and in the following year
was included among the author's *Sprachwissenschaft-
liche Abhandlungen*.   The interest of the subject will
justify quotation of the full text of the relevant parts
of Abel's treatise (omitting most of the examples).
For they give us the astonishing information that this
habit of the dream-work to which I refer exactly tallies
with a peculiarity in the oldest languages known to us.

After laying stress on the age of the Egyptian
language, which must have been developed long before
the first hieroglyphic inscriptions, Abel continues
(p. 4) :

' Now in the Egyptian language, this unique relic
of a primitive world, we find a fair number of words
with two meanings, one of which says the exact opposite
of the other.   Imagine, if one can imagine anything so
obviously nonsensical, that the word ' strong ' in
German means ' weak ' as well as ' strong ' ;   that the
noun ' light ' is used in Berlin to denote ' darkness '
as well as ' light ' ;   that one Munich citizen calls beer
' beer ', while another uses the same word when he
speaks of water—the ancient Egyptians habitually
exercised this astonishing practice in their language.
How can one blame anyone for shaking his head
incredulously ? . . . .' (examples) :

(P. 7) :   ' In view of this and many similar cases of
antithetical meaning (*see* Appendix), there can be no
room for doubt that in at least *one* language there
were quite a large number of words which at one and
the same time denoted a thing and the opposite of this
thing.   However astounding it may be, we are faced
with a fact and have to reckon with it.'

The author now rejects the explanation of this state
of affairs through chance similarity of sound, and with
equal decision protests against referring it to the low
state of Egyptian mental development :

(P. 9) : ' But Egypt was anything but a home of
nonsense. It was, on the contrary, one of the earliest
seats of the development of human wisdom. It
recognized a pure and noble morality and had formu-
lated a great part of the Ten Commandments at a time
when those peoples to whom the civilization of to-day
belongs were slaughtering human victims to blood-
thirsty idols. A people which lighted the torch of
rectitude and culture in such dark ages can certainly
not have been positively stupid in everyday speech
and thought. . . . Those who could make glass, and
raise and move huge blocks with machinery, must at
least have had sufficient sense not to regard a thing as
at one and the same time itself and its opposite. How
can we reconcile this with the fact that the Egyptians
permitted themselves such a strangely contradictory
language ? . . . that they used to entrust two most
inimical thoughts to be borne by one and the same
sound, and used to combine in a sort of insoluble
union what was mutually most intensely opposed ? '

Before we make any attempt at explanation,
another still more incomprehensible procedure in the
Egyptian tongue must be mentioned. ' Of all the
eccentricities of the Egyptian lexicon perhaps the most
extraordinary is this : that, in addition to the words
which unite antithetical meanings, it possesses other
compound-words in which two syllables of contrary
meaning are united into a whole, which then has the
meaning of only one of its constituent members. Thus
in this extraordinary language there are not only words
which denote both " strong " and " weak ", or " command " as well as " obey " ; there are also compound-
words like " oldyoung ", " farnear ", " bindloose ",
" outsideinside " . . . ; and of these, in spite of their
conjunction of the extremes of difference, the first

means only " young ", the second only " near ", the
third only " bind ", the fourth only " inside ". . . .
So that in these compound-words contradictory con-
cepts are quite intentionally combined, not in order to
create a third concept, as happens now and then in
Chinese, but only in order to express, by means of the
combination of the two, the meaning of one of its
contradictory members, which alone would have meant
the same. . . .'

However, the riddle is more easily solved than
appears. Our conceptions arise through comparison.
' Were it always light we should not distinguish
between light and dark, and accordingly could not have
either the conception of, nor the word for, light. . . .'
' It is clear that everything on this planet is relative
and has independent existence only in so far as it
is distinguished in its relations to and from other
things. . . .' ' Since every conception is thus the twin
of its opposite, how could it be thought of first, how
could it be communicated to others who tried to think
it, except by being measured against its opposite ? . . .'
(p. 15) : ' Since any conception of strength was impossible except in contrast with weakness, the word which
denoted " strong " contained a simultaneous reminder
of " weak ", as of that by means of which it first came
into existence. In reality this word indicated neither
" strong " nor " weak ", but the relation between the
two, and also the difference between them which
created both in equal proportion'. . . . ' Man has
not been able to acquire even his oldest and simplest
conceptions otherwise than in contrast with their
opposite ; he only gradually learnt to separate the
two sides of the antithesis and think of the one without
conscious comparison with the other.'

Since language serves not only for the expression of
one's own thoughts but essentially for communication
of them to others, one may put the question how the
' primitive Egyptian ' gave his neighbour to understand
' which side of the twin conception he meant on each

occasion '. In writing this was accomplished with the
help of the so-called ' determinative ' pictures, which,
placed against the alphabetical signs, are intended to
give the sense of the latter and not to be spoken
themselves. ' If the Egyptian word *ken* is to mean
" strong " there stands against its alphabetically written
sound the picture of an upright, armed man ; if the
same word has to express " weak " the character is
followed by the picture of a crouching, weary man.
Similarly, most of the other ambiguous words are
accompanied by explanatory pictures.' In speech,
thinks Abel, gesture served to indicate the meaning of
the spoken word which followed.

According to Abel it is in the ' oldest roots ' that the
antithetical double meaning is to be observed. Then
in the further course of its development these double
meanings disappeared from the language and, in Ancient
Egyptian at least, all the transitional stages can be
followed up to the single meaning of the modern
vocabulary. ' The original words with a double meaning separate in the later language into two with single
meanings, while each of the two opposite meanings
takes to itself a slight " reduction " (modification) in the
sound of the original root.' Thus, for example, as
early even as in hieroglyphics, *ken* (' strongweak ')
divides into *ken*, ' strong ' and *kan*, ' weak '. ' In
other words, those conceptions which could be arrived
at only by means of an antithesis become in course of
time sufficiently familiar to the human mind to make
possible an independent existence for each of their two
parts, and therewith creation of a separate phonetic
representative for each part.'

The proof of originally contradictory meanings,
easily made in Egyptian, extends also, according to
Abel, to the Semitic and Indo-European tongues. ' How
far this may happen in other language-groups remains
to be seen ; for although the antithesis of meaning
must originally have been there to the thinking members
of each race, this need not necessarily have become

recognizable or have been retained everywhere in the 'meanings of words.'

Abel further impresses on us that the philosopher Bain, apparently without knowledge of the actual phenomenon, has claimed on purely theoretical grounds as a logical necessity this double meaning of words. The passage in question [1] begins with the sentences :

' The essential relativity of all knowledge, thought, or consciousness cannot but show itself in language. If everything that we can know is viewed as a transition from something else, every experience must have two sides ; and either every name must have a double meaning, or else for every meaning there must be two names.'

From the ' Appendix of Examples of Egyptian, Indo-germanic and Arabian Antithetical Meanings' in Abel's treatise, I select a few cases which may impress even those of us who are not linguistic experts : In Latin, *altus* means high and deep, *sacer* holy and accursed ; thus in both there exists the exactly contrary sense without modification of sound. Phonetic alteration to distinguish the opposites is shown in examples like *clamare,* to cry—*clam,* softly; *siccus,* dry—*succus,* juice. In German *Boden* (garret, ground) still means the attic as well as the ground-floor of the house. To our *bös* (bad) corresponds a *bass* (good) ; in Old Saxon compare *bat* (good) with English *bad* ; in English *to lock* with German *Lücke, Loch* (hole) ; German *kleben* (to stick, to cleave to) English *to cleave* (divide) ; German *stumm* (dumb)—*Stimme* (voice) ; and so on. In this way perhaps the much derided derivation *lucus a non lucendo* would have some real meaning.

In his section on the origin of language,[2] Abel calls attention to yet other traces of the old difficulties of thought. Even to-day the Englishman in order to express ' *ohne* ' says ' without ' (' *mitohne* ' in German) ;

---

[1] *Logic,* vol. i. p. 54.
[2] ' Ursprung der Sprache ', *l.c.* p. 305.

and the East Prussian does the same. 'With' itself, which to-day corresponds with our German '*mit*', originally meant 'without' as well as 'with', as can be recognized from 'withdraw', 'withhold'. The same transformation is to be seen in German '*wider*' (against) and '*wieder*' (together with).

For comparison with the dream-work there is significance in still another very strange characteristic of the Ancient Egyptian tongue. 'In Egyptian, words could—we will at first say, apparently—*reverse their sound as well as their sense*. Let us suppose the word "good" was Egyptian; then it could mean "bad" as well as "good", and be pronounced *doog* as well as *good*. Of such reversals of sound, which are too numerous to be explained as chance-products, plenty of examples can be produced from the Aryan and Semitic languages. If we confine ourselves at first to Germanic, we find: *Topf* (pot)—pot; boat—tub; wait—*täuwen* (wait); hurry—*Ruhe* (rest); care—reck; *Balken* (club)—*Kloben* (club). If we take into consideration the other Indo-Germanic tongues the number of relevant cases grows accordingly; for example: *capere*—*packen*; *ren*—*Niere* (kidney); leaf—*folium*; dum-a, θυμός—(Sanscrit) mêdh, mûdha, *Mut*; *rauchen* (to smoke)—(Russian) *Kur-it*; *kreischen* (to shriek)—shriek; and so on.'

The phenomenon of *reversal of sound* Abel tries to explain as a doubling, reduplication, of the root. Here we should find some difficulty in following the philologist. We remember how fond children are of playing at reversing the sound of words, and how frequently the dream-work makes use for various ends of a reversal of the material to hand for representation. (Here it is no longer letters but visual images of which the order is reversed.) We should therefore rather be inclined to derive the reversal of sound from a factor of deeper origin.[1]

---

[1] On the phenomenon of reversal of sound (metathesis), which has perhaps a still more intimate relation to the dream-work than contra-

In the agreement between that peculiarity of the dream-work mentioned at the beginning of this paper and this which philologists have discovered to be habitual in the oldest languages, we may see a confirmation of our supposition in regard to the regressive, archaic character of thought-expression in dreams. And we cannot dismiss the conjecture, which forces itself on us psychiatrists, that we should understand the language of dreams better and translate it more easily if we knew more about the development of language.[1]

---

diction (antithesis), compare further W. Meyer-Rinteln in *Kölnische Zeitung*, March 7, 1909.

[1] We may easily suppose, too, that the original antithetical meaning of words is the prototype of that frequent mechanism by which slips of the tongue make use of contraries in the service of various tendencies.

THE THEME OF THE THREE CASKETS [1]

(1913)

I

Two scenes from Shakespeare, one from a comedy and the other from a tragedy, have lately given me occasion for setting and solving a little problem.

The former scene is the suitors' choice between the three caskets in *The Merchant of Venice*. The fair and wise Portia, at her father's bidding, is bound to take for her husband only that one among her suitors who chooses the right casket from among the three before him. The three caskets are of gold, silver and lead : the right one is that containing her portrait. Two suitors have already withdrawn, unsuccessful : they have chosen gold and silver. Bassanio, the third, elects for the lead ; he thereby wins the bride, whose affection was already his before the trial of fortune. Each of the suitors had given reasons for his choice in a speech in which he praised the metal he preferred, while depreciating the other two. The most difficult task thus fell to the share of the third fortunate suitor ; what he finds to say in glorification of lead as against gold and silver is but little and has a forced ring about it. If in psycho-analytic practice we were confronted with such a speech, we should suspect concealed motives behind the unsatisfying argument.

Shakespeare did not invent this oracle of choosing a casket ; he took it from a tale in the *Gesta Romanorum*, in which a girl undertakes the same choice to

[1] First published in *Imago*, Bd. II., 1913 ; reprinted in *Sammlung*, Vierte Folge. [Translated by C. J. M. Hubback.]

win the son of the Emperor.[1]   Here too the third metal,
the lead, is the bringer of fortune.   It is not hard to
guess that we have here an ancient theme, which
requires to be interpreted and traced back to its origin.
A preliminary conjecture about the meaning of this
choice between gold, silver and lead is soon confirmed
by a statement from E. Stucken,[2] who has made a
study of the same material in far-reaching connections.
He says, ' The identity of the three suitors of Portia
is clear from their choice : the Prince of Morocco
chooses the gold casket : he is the sun ; the Prince of
Arragon chooses the silver casket : he is the moon ;
Bassanio chooses the leaden casket : he is the star
youth '.   In support of this explanation he cites an
episode from the Esthonian folk-epic ' Kalewipoeg ', in
which the three suitors appear undisguisedly as the sun,
moon and star youths (' the eldest son of the Pole
star ') and the bride again falls to the lot of the third.

Thus our little problem leads to an astral myth.
The only pity is that with this explanation we have
not got to the end of the matter. The question goes
further, for we do not share the belief of many investigators that myths were read off direct from the
heavens ; we are more inclined to judge with Otto
Rank [3] that they were projected on to the heavens after
having arisen quite otherwise under purely human
conditions. Now our interest is in this human content.

Let us glance once more at our material. In the
Esthonian epic, as in the tale from the *Gesta Romanorum,* the subject is the choice of a maiden among three
suitors ; in the scene from *The Merchant of Venice*
apparently the subject is the same, but at the same
time in this last something in the nature of an inversion
of the idea makes its appearance : a man chooses
between three—caskets. If we had to do with a
dream, it would at once occur to us that caskets are

[1] G. Brandes, *William Shakespeare.*
[2] *Astralmythen,* p. 655.
[3] O. Rank, *Der Mythus von der Geburt des Helden,* p. 8 *et seq.*

also women, symbols of the essential thing in woman, and therefore of a woman herself, like boxes, large or small, baskets, and so on. If we let ourselves assume the same symbolic substitution in the story, then the casket scene in *The Merchant of Venice* really becomes the inversion we suspected. With one wave of the hand, such as usually only happens in fairy-tales, we have stripped the astral garment from our theme ; and now we see that the subject is an idea from human life, a man's choice between three women.

This same content, however, is to be found in another scene of Shakespeare's, in one of his most powerfully moving dramas ; this time not the choice of a bride, yet linked by many mysterious resemblances to the casket-choice in *The Merchant of Venice*. The old King Lear resolves to divide his kingdom while he yet lives among his three daughters, according to the love they each in turn express for him. The two elder ones, Goneril and Regan, exhaust themselves in asseverations and glorifications of their love for him, the third, Cordelia, refuses to join in these. He should have recognized the unassuming, speechless love of the third and rewarded it, but he misinterprets it, banishes Cordelia, and divides the kingdom between the other two, to his own and the general ruin. Is not this once more a scene of choosing between three women, of whom the youngest is the best, the supreme one ?

There immediately occur to us other scenes from myth, folk-tale and literature, with the same situation as their content : the shepherd Paris has to choose between three goddesses, of whom he declares the third to be the fairest. Cinderella is another such youngest, and is preferred by the prince to the two elder sisters ; Psyche in the tale of Apuleius is the youngest and fairest of three sisters ; on the one hand, she becomes human and is revered as Aphrodite, on the other, she is treated by the goddess as Cinderella was treated by her stepmother and has to sort a heap of mixed seeds, which she accomplishes with the help of little creatures (doves for Cinderella, ants for Psyche).[1] Anyone who cared to look more closely into the material could undoubtedly discover other versions of the same idea in which the same essential features had been retained.

Let us content ourselves with Cordelia, Aphrodite, Cinderella and Psyche ! The three women, of whom the third surpasses the other two, must surely be regarded as in some way alike if they are represented as sisters. It must not lead us astray if in *Lear* the three are the daughters of him who makes the choice ; this means probably nothing more than that Lear has to be represented as an old man. An old man cannot very well choose between three women in any other way : thus they become his daughters.

But who are these three sisters and why must the choice fall on the third ? If we could answer this question, we should be in possession of the solution we are seeking. We have once already availed ourselves of an application of psycho-analytic technique, in explaining the three caskets as symbolic of three women. If we have the courage to continue the process, we shall be setting foot on a path which leads us first to something unexpected and incomprehensible, but perhaps by a devious route to a goal.

It may strike us that this surpassing third one has in several instances certain peculiar qualities besides her beauty. They are qualities that seem to be tending towards some kind of unity ; we certainly may not expect to find them equally well marked in every example. Cordelia masks her true self, becomes as unassuming as lead, she remains dumb, she ' loves and is silent '. Cinderella hides herself, so that she is not to be found. We may perhaps equate concealment and dumbness. These would of course be only two instances out of the five we have picked out. But there is an intimation of the same thing to be found, curiously enough, in two other cases. We have decided

---

[1] I have to thank Dr. Otto Rank for calling my attention to these similarities.

to compare Cordelia, with her obstinate refusal, to lead.
In Bassanio's short speech during the choice of the
caskets these are his words of the lead—properly
speaking, without any connection :

> Thy paleness moves me more than eloquence
> ('plainness', according to another reading)

Thus : Thy plainness moves me more than the blatant
nature of the other two.   Gold and silver are ' loud ' ;
lead is dumb, in effect like Cordelia, who ' loves and is
silent '.[1]

In the ancient Greek tales of the Judgement of
Paris, nothing is said of such a withholding of herself
on the part of Aphrodite.   Each of the three goddesses
speaks to the youth and tries to win him by promises.
But, curiously enough, in a quite modern handling of
the same scene this characteristic of the third that has
struck us makes its appearance again.   In the libretto
of Offenbach's *La Belle Hélène*, Paris, after telling of the
solicitations of the other two goddesses, relates how
Aphrodite bore herself in this contest for the prize of
beauty :

> La troisième, ah ! la troisième !
> La troisième ne dit rien,
> Elle eut le prix tout de même. . . .

If we decide to regard the peculiarities of our
' third one ' as concentrated in the ' dumbness ', then
psycho-analysis has to say that dumbness is in dreams
a familiar representation of death.[2]

More than ten years ago a highly intelligent man
told me a dream which he wanted to look upon as
proof of the telepathic nature of dreams.   He saw an
absent friend from whom he had received no news for
a very long time, and reproached him warmly for his

---

[1] In Schlegel's translation this allusion is quite lost ; indeed,
changed into the opposite meaning :   *Dein schlichtes Wesen spricht
beredt mich an*.   (Thy plainness speaks to me with eloquence.)
[2] In Stekel's *Sprache des Traumes*, dumbness is also mentioned
among the ' death ' symbols (p. 351).

silence. The friend made no reply. It then proved
that he had met his death by suicide about the time of
the dream. Let us leave the problem of telepathy on
one side : there seems to be no doubt that here the
dumbness in the dream represents death. Concealment, disappearance from view, too, which the prince
in the fairy-tale of Cinderella has to experience three
times, is in dreams an unmistakable symbol of death ;
and no less so is a striking pallor, of which the paleness
of the lead in one reading of Shakespeare's text reminds
us.[1] The difficulty of translating these significations
from the language of dreams into the mode of expression
in the myth now occupying our attention is much
lightened if we can show with any probability that
dumbness must be interpreted as a sign of death in
other productions that are not dreams.

I will single out at this point the ninth of Grimm's
Fairy Tales, the one with the title ' The Twelve
Brothers '. A king and a queen have twelve children,
all boys. Thereupon the king says, ' If the thirteenth
child is a girl, the boys must die '. In expectation of
this birth he has twelve coffins made. The twelve sons
flee with their mother's help into a secret wood, and
swear death to every maiden they shall meet.

A girl-child is born, grows up, and learns one day
from her mother that she had twelve brothers. She
decides to seek them out, and finds the youngest in
the wood ; he recognizes her but wants to hide her on
account of the brothers' oath. The sister says : ' I will
gladly die, if thereby I can save my twelve brothers '.
The brothers welcome her gladly, however, and she
stays with them and looks after their house for them.

In a little garden near the house grow twelve lilies :
the maiden plucks these to give one to each brother.
At that moment the brothers are changed into ravens,
and disappear, together with the house and garden.
Ravens are spirit-birds, the killing of the twelve brothers
by their sister is thus again represented by the plucking

[1] Stekel, *loc. cit.*

of the flowers, as at the beginning of the story by the coffins and the disappearance of the brothers. The maiden, who is once more ready to save her brothers from death, is now told that as a condition she is to be dumb for seven years, and not speak one single word. She submits to this test, by which she herself goes into danger, *i.e.* she herself dies for her brothers, as she promised before meeting with them. By remaining dumb she succeeds at last in delivering the ravens.

In the story of ' The Six Swans ' the brothers who are changed into birds are released in exactly the same way, *i.e.* restored to life by the dumbness of the sister. The maiden has taken the firm resolve to release her brothers, ' an if it cost her life ' ; as the king's wife she again risks her own life because she will not relinquish her dumbness to defend herself against evil accusations.

Further proofs could undoubtedly be gathered from fairy-tales that dumbness is to be understood as representing death. If we follow these indications, then the third one of the sisters between whom the choice lies would be a dead woman. She may, however, be something else, namely, Death itself, the Goddess of Death. By virtue of a displacement that is not infrequent, the qualities that a deity imparts to men are ascribed to the deity himself. Such a displacement will astonish us least of all in relation to the Goddess of Death, since in modern thought and artistic representation, which would thus be anticipated in these stories, death itself is nothing but a dead man.

But if the third of the sisters is the Goddess of Death, we know the sisters. They are the Fates, the Moerae, the Parcae or the Norns, the third of whom is called Atropos, the inexorable.

II

Let us leave on one side for a while the task of inserting this new-found meaning into our myth, and let us hear what the mythologists have to say about the origin of and the part played by the Fates.[1]

The earliest Greek mythology only knows one Μοῖρα, personifying the inevitable doom (in Homer). The further development of this one Moera into a group of three sisters—goddesses—, less often two, probably came about in connection with other divine figures to which the Moerae are clearly related : the Graces and the Horae, the Hours.

The Hours are originally goddesses of the waters of the sky, dispensing rain and dew, and of the clouds from which rain falls ; and since these clouds are conceived of as a kind of web it comes about that these goddesses are looked on as spinners, a character that then became attached to the Moerae. In the sun-favoured Mediterranean lands it is the rain on which the fertility of the soil depends, and thus the Hours become the goddesses of vegetation. The beauty of flowers and the abundance of fruit is their doing, and man endows them plentifully with charming and graceful traits. They become the divine representatives of the Seasons, and possibly in this connection acquire their triple number, if the sacred nature of the number three is not sufficient explanation of this. For these ancient peoples at first distinguished only three seasons : winter, spring, summer. Autumn was only added in late Graeco-Roman times, after which four Hours were often represented in art.

The relation to time remained attached to the Hours : later they presided over the time of day, as at first over the periods of the year : at last their name came to be merely a designation for the period of sixty minutes (hour, *heure*, *ora*). The Norns of German mythology are akin to the Hours and the Moerae and exhibit this time-signification in their names. The nature of these deities could not fail, however, to be apprehended more profoundly in time, so that the

---

[1] What follows is taken from Roscher's *Lexikon der griechischen und römischen Mythologie*, under the relevant headings.

essential thing about them was shifted until it came to consist of the abiding law at work in the passage of time : the Hours thus became guardians of the law of Nature, and of the divine order of things whereby the constant recurrence of the same things in unalterable succession in the natural world takes place.

This knowledge of nature reacted on the conception of human life. The nature-myth changed into a myth of human life : the weather-goddesses became goddesses of destiny. But this aspect of the Hours only found expression in the Moerae, who watch over the needful ordering of human life as inexorably as do the Hours over the regular order of nature. The implacable severity of this law, the affinity of it with death and ruin, avoided in the winsome figures of the Hours, was now stamped upon the Moerae, as though mankind had only perceived the full solemnity of natural law when he had to submit his own personality to its working.

The names of the three spinners have been interpreted significantly by mythologists. Lachesis, the name of the second, seems to mean ' the accidental within the decrees of destiny ' [1]—we might say ' that which is experienced '—while Atropos means ' the inevitable '—Death—, and then for Clotho there remains ' the fateful tendencies each one of us brings into the world '.

And now it is time to return to the idea contained in the choice between the three sisters, which we are endeavouring to interpret. It is with deep dissatisfaction that we find how unintelligible insertion of the new interpretation makes the situations we are considering and what contradictions of the apparent content then result. The third of the sisters should be the Goddess of Death, nay, Death itself ; in the Judgement of Paris she is the Goddess of Love, in the tale of Apuleius one comparable to the goddess for her beauty, in *The Merchant of Venice* the fairest and wisest of women, in *Lear* the one faithful daughter. Can a contradiction be more complete ? Yet perhaps close

[1] Roscher, after Preller-Robert's *Grieschische Mythologie*.

at hand there lies even this, improbable as it is—the acme of contradiction. It is certainly forthcoming if every time in this theme of ours there occurs a free choice between the women, and if the choice is thereupon to fall on death—that which no man chooses, to which by destiny alone man falls a victim.

However, contradictions of a certain kind, replacements by the exact opposite, offer no serious difficulty to analytic interpretation. We shall not this time take our stand on the fact that contraries are constantly represented by one and the same element in the modes of expression used by the unconscious, such as dreams. But we shall remember that there are forces in mental life tending to bring about replacement by the opposite, such as the so-called reaction-formation, and it is just in the discovery of such hidden forces that we look for the reward of our labours. The Moerae were created as a result of a recognition which warns man that he too is a part of nature and therefore subject to the immutable law of death. Against this subjection something in man was bound to struggle, for it is only with extreme unwillingness that he gives up his claim to an exceptional position. We know that man makes use of his imaginative faculty (phantasy) to satisfy those wishes that reality does not satisfy. So his imagination rebelled against the recognition of the truth embodied in the myth of the Moerae, and constructed instead the myth derived from it, in which the Goddess of Death was replaced by the Goddess of Love and by that which most resembles her in human shape. The third of the sisters is no longer Death, she is the fairest, best, most desirable and the most lovable among women. Nor was this substitution in any way difficult : it was prepared for by an ancient ambivalence, it fulfilled itself along the lines of an ancient context which could at that time not long have been forgotten. The Goddess of Love herself, who now took the place of the Goddess of Death, had once been identical with her. Even the Greek Aphrodite had not wholly relinquished her connection with the underworld, although she had long surrendered her rôle of goddess of that region to other divine shapes, to Persephone, or to the tri-form Artemis-Hecate. The great Mother-goddesses of the oriental peoples, however, all seem to have been both founts of being and destroyers ; goddesses of life and of fertility, and death-goddesses. Thus the replacement by the wish-opposite of which we have spoken in our theme is built upon an ancient identity.

The same consideration answers the question how the episode of a choice came into the myth of the three sisters. A wished-for reversal is again found here. Choice stands in the place of necessity, of destiny. Thus man overcomes death, which in thought he has acknowledged. No greater triumph of wish-fulfilment is conceivable. Just where in reality he obeys compulsion, he exercises choice ; and that which he chooses is not a thing of horror, but the fairest and most desirable thing in life.

On a closer inspection we observe, to be sure, that the original myth is not so much disguised that traces of it do not show through and betray its presence. The free choice between the three sisters is, properly speaking, no free choice, for it must necessarily fall on the third if every kind of evil is not to come about, as in *Lear*. The fairest and the best, she who has stepped into the place of the Death-goddess, has kept certain characteristics that border on the uncanny, so that from them we might guess at what lay beneath.[1]

---

[1] The Psyche of Apuleius' story has kept many traits that remind us of her kinship with death. Her wedding is celebrated like a funeral, she has to descend into the underworld, and afterwards sinks into a death-like sleep (Otto Rank).

On the significance of Psyche as goddess of the spring and as ' Bride of Death ', cf. A. Zinzow, *Psyche und Eros*.

In another of Grimm's Tales (' The Goose-girl at the Fountain ') there is, as in ' Cinderella ', an alternation between the ugly and the beautiful aspect of the third sister, in which may be seen an indication of her double nature—before and after the substitution. This third one is repudiated by her father, after a test which nearly corresponds with that in *King Lear*. Like the other sisters, she has to say how dear she holds their father, and finds no expression for her love except the comparison of it with salt. (Kindly communicated by Dr. Hanns Sachs.)

So far we have followed out the myth and its transformation, and trust that we have rightly indicated the
hidden causes of this transformation. Now we may
well be interested in the way in which the poet has
made use of the idea. We gain the impression that in
his mind a reduction to the original idea of the myth is
going on, so that we once more perceive the original
meaning containing all the power to move us that had
been weakened by the distortion of the myth. It is
by means of this undoing of the distortion and partial
return to the original that the poet achieves his profound effect upon us.

To avoid misunderstandings, I wish to say that I
have no intention of denying that the drama of *King
Lear* inculcates the two prudent maxims : that one
should not forgo one's possessions and privileges in
one's lifetime and that one must guard against accepting flattery as genuine. These and similar warnings
do undoubtedly arise from the play ; but it seems to
me quite impossible to explain the overpowering effect
of *Lear* from the impression that such a train of
thought would produce, or to assume that the poet's
own creative instincts would not carry him further
than the impulse to illustrate these maxims. Moreover, even though we are told that the poet's intention
was to present the tragedy of ingratitude, the sting of
which he probably felt in his own heart, and that the
effect of the play depends on the purely formal element,
its artistic trappings, it seems to me that this information cannot compete with the comprehension that
dawns upon us after our study of the theme of a choice
between the three sisters.

Lear is an old man. We said before that this is
why the three sisters appear as his daughters. The
paternal relationship, out of which so many fruitful
dramatic situations might arise, is not turned to further
account in the drama. But Lear is not only an old
man ; he is a dying man. The extraordinary project
of dividing the inheritance thus loses its strangeness.

The doomed man is nevertheless not willing to renounce the love of women ; he insists on hearing how much he is loved. Let us now recall that most moving last scene, one of the culminating points reached in modern tragic drama : ' Enter Lear with Cordelia dead in his arms '. Cordelia is Death. Reverse the situation and it becomes intelligible and familiar to us—the Death-goddess bearing away the dead hero from the place of battle, like the Valkyr in German mythology. Eternal wisdom, in the garb of the primitive myth, bids the old man renounce love, choose death and make friends with the necessity of dying.

The poet brings us very near to the ancient idea by making the man who accomplishes the choice between the three sisters aged and dying. The regressive treatment he has thus undertaken with the myth, which was disguised by the reversal of the wish, allows its original meaning so far to appear that perhaps a superficial allegorical interpretation of the three female figures in the theme becomes possible as well. One might say that the three inevitable relations man has with woman are here represented : that with the mother who bears him, with the companion of his bed and board, and with the destroyer. Or it is the three forms taken on by the figure of the mother as life proceeds : the mother herself, the beloved who is chosen after her pattern, and finally the Mother Earth who receives him again. But it is in vain that the old man yearns after the love of woman as once he had it from his mother ; the third of the Fates alone, the silent goddess of Death, will take him into her arms.

THE OCCURRENCE IN DREAMS
OF MATERIAL FROM FAIRY-TALES [1]

(1913)

IT is not surprising to find that psycho - analysis confirms us in our recognition of how great an influence folk fairy-tales have upon the mental life of our children. In some people a recollection of their favourite fairy-tales takes the place of memories of their own childhood : they have made the fairy-tales into screen-memories.

Elements and situations derived from fairy-tales are also frequently to be found in dreams. In interpreting those portions of the dreams the patient will produce the significant fairy-tale as an association. In the present paper I shall give two instances of this very common occurrence. But it will not be possible to do more than hint at the relation of the fairy-tales to the history of the dreamer's childhood and to his neurosis, though this limitation will involve the risk of snapping threads which were of the utmost importance in the analysis.

I

Here is a dream of a young married woman (who had had a visit from her husband a few days before) : *She was in a room that was entirely brown. A little door led to the top of a steep staircase, and up this staircase there came into the room a curious manikin—small, with white hair, a bald top to his head and a red nose. He danced round the room in front of her, carried on in the*

[1] First published in *Zeitschrift*, Bd. I., 1913 ; reprinted in *Sammlung*, Vierte Folge. [Translated by James Strachey.]

funniest way, and then went down the staircase again.
He was dressed in a grey garment, through which his
whole figure was visible. (A correction was made subsequently : *He was wearing a long black coat and grey*
trousers.)

The analysis was as follows. The description of the
manikin's personal appearance fitted the dreamer's
father-in-law without any alteration being necessary.[1]
Immediately afterwards, however, the story of ' Rumpelstiltskin ' occurred to her ; for he danced around
in the same funny way as the man in the dream and in
so doing betrayed his name to the queen. But by that
he also lost his claim upon the queen's first child, and
in his fury he tore himself in two.

On the day before she had the dream she herself
had been furious with her husband and had exclaimed :
' I could tear him in two '.

The brown room at first gave rise to difficulties.
All that occurred to her was her parents' dining-room,
which was panelled in that colour—in brown wood.
She then told some stories of beds which were so uncomfortable for two people to sleep in. A few days
before, when the subject of conversation had been beds
in other countries, she had said something very *mal
à propos*—quite innocently, as she maintained—and
everyone in the room had roared with laughter.

The dream was now already intelligible. The brown
wood room[2] was in the first place a bed, and through
the connection with the dining-room it was a double
bed.[3] She was therefore in her double bed. Her
visitor should have been her young husband, who, after
an absence of several months, had visited her to play
his part in the double bed. But to begin with it was
her husband's father, her father-in-law.

[1] Except for the detail that the manikin had his hair cut short,
whereas her father-in-law wore his long.
[2] Wood, as is well known, is frequently a female or maternal
symbol : *e.g. materia, Madeira*, etc.
[3] Literally, ' marriage-bed '. For table and bed stand for marriage.
[Cf. the legal phrase : *a mensa et toro*.—Ed.]

Behind this interpretation we have a glimpse of a deeper and purely sexual content. The room, at this level, was the vagina. (The room was in her—this was reversed in the dream.) The little man who made grimaces and behaved so funnily was the penis. The narrow door and the steep stairs confirmed the view that the situation was a representation of coitus. As a rule we are accustomed to find the penis symbolized by a child ; but we shall find that there was good reason for a father being introduced to represent the penis in this instance.

The solution of the remaining portion of the dream will entirely confirm us in this interpretation. The dreamer herself explained the transparent grey garment as a condom. We may gather that considerations of preventing conception and worries whether this visit of her husband's might not have sown the seed of a second child were among the instigating causes of the dream.

The black coat. Coats of that kind suited her husband admirably. She was eager to influence him always to wear them, instead of his usual clothes. Dressed in the black coat, therefore, her husband was as she would like to see him. *The black coat and the grey trousers.* At two different levels, one above the other, this had the same meaning : ' I should like you to be dressed like that. I like you like that.'

Rumpelstiltskin was connected with the contemporary thoughts underlying the dream—the day's residues—by a neat antithetic relation. He comes in the fairy-tale in order to take away the queen's first child. The little man in the dream comes in the shape of a father, because he has presumably brought a second child. But Rumpelstiltskin also gave access to the deeper, infantile stratum of the dream-thoughts. The droll little fellow, whose very name is unknown, whose secret is so eagerly canvassed, who can perform such extraordinary tricks—in the fairy-tale he turns straw into gold—the fury against him, or rather against his possessor, who is envied for possessing him (the penis-envy felt by girls)—all of these are elements whose relation to the foundations of the patient's neurosis can, as I have said, barely be touched upon in this paper. The short-cut hair of the manikin in the dream was no doubt also connected with the subject of castration.

If we carefully observe from clear instances the way in which the dreamer uses the fairy-tale and the point at which he brings it in, we may perhaps also succeed in picking up some hints which will help in interpreting any remaining obscurities in the fairy-tale itself.

II

A young man [1] told me the following dream. He had a chronological basis for his early memories in the circumstance that his parents moved from one country estate to another just before the end of his fifth year ; the dream, which he said was his earliest one, occurred while he was still upon the first estate.

' *I dreamt that it was night and that I was lying in my bed. (My bed stood with its foot towards the window ; in front of the window there was a row of old walnut trees. I know it was winter when I had the dream, and night-time.) Suddenly the window opened of its own accord, and I was terrified to see that some white wolves were sitting on the big walnut tree in front of the window. There were six or seven of them. The wolves were quite white, and looked more like foxes or sheep-dogs, for they had big tails like foxes and they had their ears pricked like dogs when they are attending to something. In great terror, evidently of being eaten up by the wolves, I screamed* and woke up. My nurse hurried to my bed, to see what had happened to me. It took quite a long while before

---

[1] [A detailed analysis of this patient's case will be found in ' From the History of an Infantile Neurosis ', COLLECTED PAPERS, vol. iii.— Trans.]

I was convinced that it had only been a dream ; I had had such a clear and life-like picture of the window opening and the wolves sitting on the tree. At last I grew quieter, felt as though I had escaped from some danger, and went to sleep again.

' The only piece of action in the dream was the opening of the window ; for the wolves sat quite still and without any movement on the branches of the tree, to the right and left of the trunk, and looked at me. It seemed as though they had riveted their whole attention upon me.—I think this was my first anxiety-dream. I was three, four, or at most five years old at the time. From then until my eleventh or twelfth year I was always afraid of seeing something terrible in my dreams.'

He added a drawing of the tree with the wolves, which confirmed his description. The analysis of the dream brought the following material to light.

He had always connected this dream with the recollection that during these years of his childhood he was most tremendously afraid of the picture of a wolf in a book of fairy-tales. His elder sister, who was very much his superior, used to tease him by holding up this particular picture in front of him on some excuse or other, so that he was terrified and began to scream. In this picture the wolf was standing upright, striding out with one foot, with its claws stretched out and its ears pricked. He thought this picture must have been an illustration to the story of ' Little Red Riding Hood '.

Why were the wolves white ? This made him think of the sheep, large flocks of which were kept in the neighbourhood of the estate. His father occasionally took him with him to visit these flocks, and every time this happened he felt very proud and blissful. Later on—according to inquiries that were made it may easily have been shortly before the time of the dream—an epidemic broke out among the sheep. His father sent for a follower of Pasteur's, who inoculated the animals, but after the inoculation even more of them died than before.

How did the wolves come to be on the tree ? This reminded him of a story that he had heard his grandfather tell. He could not remember whether it was before or after the dream, but its subject is a decisive argument in favour of the former view. The story ran as follows. A tailor was sitting at work in his room, when the window opened and a wolf leapt in. The tailor hit after him with his yard—no (he corrected himself), caught him by his tail and pulled it off, so that the wolf ran away in terror. Some time later the tailor went into the forest, and suddenly saw a pack of wolves coming towards him ; so he climbed up a tree to escape from them. At first the wolves were in perplexity ; but the maimed one, which was among them and wanted to revenge himself upon the tailor, proposed that they should climb one upon another till the last one could reach him. He himself—he was a vigorous old fellow—would be the base of the pyramid. The wolves did as he suggested, but the tailor had recognized the visitor whom he had punished, and suddenly called out as he had before : ' Catch the grey one by his tail ! ' The tailless wolf, terrified by the recollection, ran away, and all the others tumbled down.

In this story the tree appears, upon which the wolves were sitting in the dream. But it also contains an unmistakable allusion to the castration-complex. The *old* wolf was docked of his tail by the tailor. The fox-tails of the wolves in the dream were probably compensations for this taillessness.

Why were there six or seven wolves ? There seemed to be no answer to this question, until I raised a doubt whether the picture that had frightened him could be connected with the story of ' Little Red Riding Hood '. This fairy-tale only offers an opportunity for two illustrations—Little Red Riding Hood's meeting with the wolf in the wood, and the scene in which the wolf lies in bed in the grandmother's night-cap. There must therefore be some other fairy-tale behind his recollection of the picture. He soon discovered that it could only be the story of ' The Wolf and the Seven Little Goats '. Here the number seven occurs, and also the number six, for the wolf only ate up six of the little goats, while the seventh hid itself in the clock-case. The white, too, comes into this story, for the wolf had his paw made white at the baker's after the little goats had recognized him on his first visit by his grey paw. Moreover, the two fairy-tales have much in common. In both there is the eating up, the cutting open of the belly, the taking out of the people who have been eaten and their replacement by heavy stones, and finally in both of them the wicked wolf perishes. Besides all this, in the story of the little goats the tree appears. The wolf lay down under a tree after his meal and snored.

I shall have, for a special reason, to deal with this dream again elsewhere, and interpret it and consider its significance in greater detail. For it is the earliest anxiety-dream that the dreamer remembered from his childhood, and its content, taken in connection with other dreams that followed it soon afterwards and with certain events in his earliest years, is of quite peculiar interest. We must confine ourselves here to the relation of the dream to the two fairy-tales which have so much in common with each other, ' Little Red Riding Hood ' and ' The Wolf and the Seven Little Goats '. The effect produced by these stories was shown in the little dreamer by a regular animal-phobia. This phobia was only distinguished from other similar cases by the fact that the anxiety-animal was not an object easily accessible to observation (such as a horse or a dog), but was known to him only from stories and picture-books.

I shall discuss on another occasion the explanation of these animal-phobias and the significance attaching to them. I will only remark in anticipation that this explanation is in complete harmony with the principal characteristic shown by the neurosis from which the present dreamer suffered in the later part of his life. His fear of his father was the strongest motive for his falling ill, and his ambivalent attitude towards every father-surrogate was the dominating feature of his life as well as of his behaviour during the treatment.

If in my patient's case the wolf was merely a first father-surrogate, the question arises whether the hidden content in the fairy-tales of the wolf that ate up the little goats and of ' Little Red Riding Hood ' may not simply be infantile fear of the father.[1] Moreover, my patient's father had the characteristic, shown by so many people in relation to their children, of indulging in ' *affectionate abuse* ' ; and it is possible that during the patient's earlier years his father (though he grew severe later on) may more than once, as he caressed the little boy or played with him, have threatened in fun to ' gobble him up '. One of my patients told me that her two children could never get to be fond of their grandfather, because in the course of his affectionate romping with them he used to frighten them by saying he would cut open their tummies.

[1] Compare the similarity between these two fairy-tales and the myth of Cronos, which was pointed out by Rank in his paper, ' Völker-psychologische Parallelen zu den infantilen Sexualtheorien ' (1912).

SOME CHARACTER-TYPES MET WITH IN PSYCHO-ANALYTIC WORK [1]

(1915)

WHEN the physician is carrying out psycho-analytic treatment of a neurotic, his interest is by no means primarily directed to the patient's character. He is far more desirous to know what the symptoms signify, what instinctual impulses lurk behind them and are satisfied by them, and by what transitions the mysterious path has led from those impulses to these symptoms. But the technique which he is obliged to follow soon constrains him to direct his immediate curiosity towards other objectives. He observes that his investigation is threatened by resistances set up against him by the patient, and these resistances he may justly attribute to the latter's character, which now acquires the first claim on his interest.

What opposes itself to the physician's labours is not always those traits of character which the patient recognizes in himself and which are attributed to him by those around him. Peculiarities in the patient which he had seemed to possess only in a modest degree are often displayed in surprising intensity, or attitudes reveal themselves in him which in other relations of life would not have been betrayed. The following pages will be devoted to describing and tracing back to their origin some of these astonishing traits of character.

[1] First published in *Imago*, Bd. IV., 1915-16 ; reprinted in *Sammlung*, Vierte Folge. [Translated by E. Colburn Mayne.]

I

THE ' EXCEPTIONS '

The psycho-analytic worker is continually con-fronted with the task of inducing the patient to renounce an immediate and directly attainable source of pleasure. He need not renounce all pleasure ; that one could probably expect of no human being, and even religion is obliged to support its ordinance that earthly pleasure shall be set aside by the promise of an incomparably greater degree of more inestimable bliss in another world. No, the patient need merely renounce such gratifications as will inevitably be detrimental to him ; he need only temporarily abjure, only learn to exchange an immediate source of pleasure for one better assured though longer delayed. Or, in other words, under the physician's guidance he must make that advance from the pleasure-principle to the reality-principle by which the mature human being is distinguished from the child. In this educative process, the clearer insight of the physician plays but an insignificant part ; as a rule, he can say to his patient only what the latter's own reason can say to him. But it is not the same thing to know a thing in oneself and to hear it from someone outside oneself ; the physician takes the part of this significant outsider ; he makes use of the influence which one human being can exercise over another. Or—remembering that the practice of psycho-analysis is to replace etiolated derivatives by the original and fundamental—let us say that the physician in his educative work makes use of one of the com-ponents of love. In this work of after-education, he probably does no more than repeat the process which first of all made training of any kind possible. By the side of the necessities of existence, love is the great teacher ; and it is by his love for those nearest him that the incomplete human being is induced to respect the decrees of necessity and to spare himself the punishment attendant on any infringement of it.

Thus, when one exacts from the patient a provisional renunciation of any source of pleasure, a sacrifice, a readiness to accept some temporary suffering in view of a better end, or even only the resolve to submit to a necessity which applies to all human beings, one will come upon individuals who resist such an appeal on special grounds. They say that they have renounced enough and suffered enough, and have a claim to be spared any further exactions ; they will submit no longer to disagreeable necessity, for they are *exceptions* and intend to remain so too. In one patient of the kind this claim had grown into the conviction that a special providence watched over him, which would protect him from any painful sacrifices of the sort. Against an inner confidence expressing itself thus strongly the arguments of the physician will achieve nothing ; even his influence, indeed, is powerless at first, and it becomes clear to him that he must find out the sources which are feeding the injurious prepossession.

Now it is surely indubitable that everyone would fain consider himself an ' exception ' and claim privileges over others. But precisely because of this there must be a particular reason, and one not universally available, if any individual actually proclaims himself an exception and behaves as such. This reason may be of more than one kind ; in the cases I investigated I succeeded in tracing it to a common peculiarity in the earlier experiences of these patients' lives. Their neuroses were connected with an event or painful experience from which they had suffered in their earliest childhood, one in respect of which they knew themselves to be guiltless, and which they could look upon as an unjust injury inflicted upon them. The privileges that they claimed as a result of this injustice, and the rebellious-ness it engendered, had contributed not a little to intensifying the conflicts leading to the outbreak of neurosis. In one of these patients, a woman, the attitude in question developed when she learnt that a painful organic trouble, which had hindered her from

attaining the aim of her life, was of congenital origin.
So long as she looked upon this trouble as an accidental
acquisition during later life, she bore it patiently ;
as soon as she knew it was part of her congenital
inheritance, she became rebellious. The young man
who believed himself watched over by a special
providence had been in infancy the victim of an
accidental infection from his wet-nurse, and had lived
his whole later life on the ' insurance-dole ', as it were,
of his claims to compensation, without having any idea
on what he based those claims. In his case the analysis,
which reconstructed this event out of obscure glimmer-
ings of memory and interpretations of the symptoms, was
confirmed objectively by information from the family.

For reasons which will be easily understood I
cannot communicate very much about these and other
case-histories. Nor do I propose to go into the obvious
analogy between deformities of character resulting from
protracted sickliness in childhood and the behaviour of
whole nations whose past history has been full of
suffering. Instead, however, I will take the opportunity
of pointing to that figure in the creative work of the
greatest of poets in whose character the claim to be an
exception is closely bound up with and motivated by
the circumstance of congenital injury.

In the opening soliloquy to Shakespeare's *Richard
III.*, Gloucester, who subsequently becomes King, says :

> But I, that am not shaped for sportive tricks,
> Nor made to court an amorous looking-glass ;
> I, that am rudely stamp'd, and want love's majesty
> To strut before a wanton ambling nymph ;
> I, that am curtail'd of this fair proportion,
> Cheated of feature by dissembling Nature,
> Deform'd, unfinish'd, sent before my time
> Into this breathing world, scarce half made up,
> And that so lamely and unfashionable,
> That dogs bark at me as I halt by them ;
>   *   *   *   *   *
> And therefore, since I cannot prove a lover,
> To entertain these fair well-spoken days,
> I am determined to prove a villain,
> And hate the idle pleasures of these days.

At a first glance this tirade will possibly seem unrelated to our present theme. Richard seems to say nothing more than ' I find this idle way of life tedious, and I want to enjoy myself. As I cannot play the lover on account of my deformity, I will play the villain ; I will intrigue, murder, do anything I please.' So wanton a cause of action could not but stifle any stirring of sympathy in the audience, if it were not a screen for something much more serious. And besides, the play would be psychologically impossible, for the writer must know how to furnish us with a secret background of sympathy for his hero, if we are to admire his boldness and adroitness without some inward protest ; and such sympathy can only be based on understanding or on a sense of a possible inner fellowship with him.

I think, therefore, that Richard's soliloquy does not say everything ; it merely gives a hint, and leaves us to fill up the indications. When we complete it, however, the appearance of wantonness vanishes, the bitterness and minuteness with which Richard has depicted his deformity make their full effect, and we clearly perceive the bond of fellowship which constrains us to sympathy with the miscreant. The soliloquy then signifies : ' Nature has done me a grievous wrong in denying me that beauty of form which wins human love. Life owes me reparation for this, and I will see that I get it. I have a right to be an exception, to overstep those bounds by which others let themselves be circumscribed. I may do wrong myself, since wrong has been done to me '—and now we feel that we ourselves could be like Richard, nay, that we are already a little like him. Richard is an enormously magnified representation of something we can all discover in ourselves. We all think we have reason to reproach nature and our destiny for congenital and infantile disadvantages ; we all demand reparation for early wounds to our narcissism, our self-love. Why did not nature give us the golden curls of Balder or the strength of Siegfried or the lofty brow of genius or the noble profile of aristocracy ? Why were we born in a middle-class dwelling instead of in a royal palace ? We could as well carry off beauty and distinction as any of those whom now we cannot but envy.

It is, however, a subtle economy of art in the poet not to permit his hero to give complete expression to all his secret springs of action. By this means he obliges us to supplement, he engages our·intellectual activity, diverts it from critical reflections, and keeps us closely identified with his hero. A bungler in his place would deliberately express all that he wishes to reveal to us, and would then find himself confronted by our cool, untrammelled intelligence, which would preclude any great degree of illusion.

We will not, however, dismiss the ' exceptions ' without pointing out that the claim of women to privileges and to exemption from so many of the importunities of existence rests upon the same foundation. As we learn from psycho-analytic work, women regard themselves as wronged from infancy, as undeservedly cut short and set back ; and the embitterment of so many daughters against their mothers derives, in the last analysis, from the reproach against her of having brought them into the world as women instead of as men.

II

THOSE WRECKED BY SUCCESS

Psycho-analytic work has furnished us with the rule that people fall ill of a neurosis as a result of *frustration*. The frustration meant is that of satisfaction for their libidinal desires and a long circumlocution is necessary before the law becomes comprehensible. That is to say, for a neurosis to break out there must be a conflict between the libidinal desires of a person and that part of his being which we call his ego, the expression of his instinct of self-preservation, which also contains his ideals of his own character. A pathogenic conflict of this kind takes place only when the libido is desirous of pursuing paths and aims which the ego has long overcome and despised, and has therefore henceforth proscribed ; and this the libido never does until it is deprived of the possibility of an ideal satisfaction consistent with the ego. Hence privation, frustration of a real satisfaction, is the first condition for the outbreak of a neurosis, although, indeed, it is far from being the only one.

So much the more surprising, indeed bewildering, must it appear when as a physician one makes the discovery that people occasionally fall ill precisely because a deeply-rooted and long-cherished wish has come to fulfilment. It seems then as though they could not endure their bliss, for of the causative connection between this fulfilment and the falling-ill there can be no question. I had an opportunity in this way of obtaining insight into a woman's story, which I propose to describe as typical of these tragic occurrences.

Well-born and well-brought-up, as a quite young girl she could not restrain her zest for life ; she ran away from home and roved adventurously till she made the acquaintance of an artist who could appreciate her feminine charms but could also divine, despite her degradation, the finer qualities she possessed. He took her to live with him, and she proved a faithful and devoted companion, apparently needing only social rehabilitation for complete happiness. After many years of life together, he succeeded in getting his family to recognize her, and was then prepared to make her his legal wife. At this critical moment she began to go to pieces. She neglected the house whose rightful mistress she was now about to become, imagined herself persecuted by his relatives, who wanted to take her into the family, debarred her lover, through senseless jealousy, from all social intercourse, hindered him in his artistic work, and soon fell into incurable mental illness.

On another occasion I observed a most respectable man who, himself professor at a university, had for many years cherished the natural wish to succeed the master who had initiated him into the life of learning. When this elder man retired, and the other's colleagues intimated that it was he whom they desired as successor, he began to hesitate, depreciated his own merits, declared himself unworthy to fill the position designed for him, and fell into a state of melancholy which unfitted him for all activity for some years after.

Different as these two cases are, they yet coincide on this one point—that illness followed close upon the wish-fulfilment, and annihilated all enjoyment of it.

The contradiction between such experiences and the rule that frustration induces illness is not insoluble. The distinction between an *internal* and an *external* frustration dispels it. When in actuality the object in which the libido can find its satisfaction is withheld, this is an external frustration. In itself it is inoperative, not pathogenic, until an internal frustration has joined hands with it. This must proceed from the ego, and must dispute the right of the libido to the other objects that it then desires to possess. Only then does a conflict arise, and the possibility of neurotic illness, *i.e.* of a substitutive gratification proceeding circuitously by way of the repressed unconscious. The internal frustration is present, therefore, in every case, only it does not come into operation until the external, actual frustration has prepared the ground for it. In those exceptional cases where illness ensues on success, the internal frustration has operated alone—has indeed only made its appearance when an external frustration has been replaced by fulfilment of the wish. At first sight there remains something astonishing about this ; but on closer consideration we shall reflect that it is not so very unusual for the ego to tolerate a wish as harmless so long as this exists in phantasy alone and seems remote from fulfilment, while it will defend itself hotly against such a wish as soon as it approaches fulfilment and threatens to become an actuality. The distinction between this and familiar situations in neurosis-formation is merely that usually it is internal intensifications of the libidinal cathexis which turn the phantasy, that has hitherto been thought little of and tolerated, into a dreaded opponent ; while in these cases of ours the signal for the outbreak of conflict is given by an actual external alteration in circumstances.

Analytic work soon shows us that it is forces of conscience which forbid the person to gain the long-hoped-for enjoyment from the fortunate change in reality. It is a difficult task, however, to discover the essence and origin of these censuring and punishing tendencies, which so often surprise us by their presence where we do not expect to find them. What we know or conjecture on the point I shall discuss, for the usual reasons, in relation not to cases of clinical observation, but 'to figures which great writers have created from the wealth of their knowledge of the soul.

A person who collapses on attaining her aim, after striving for it with single-minded energy, is Shakespeare's Lady Macbeth. In the beginning there is no hesitation, no sign of any inner conflict in her, no endeavour but that of overcoming the scruples of her ambitious and yet gentle-hearted husband. She is ready to sacrifice even her womanliness to her murderous intention, without reflecting on the decisive part which this womanliness must play when the question arises of preserving the aim of her ambition, which has been attained through a crime.

> Come, you spirits
> That tend on mortal thoughts, unsex me here
> . . . Come to my woman's breasts,
> And take my milk for gall, you murdering ministers !
> (Act I. Sc. 5.)

> . . . I have given suck, and know
> How tender 'tis to love the babe that milks me :

> I would, while it was smiling in my face,
> Have pluck'd my nipple from his boneless gums,
> And dashed the brains out, had I so sworn as you
> Have done to this.
>
> (Act I. Sc. 7.)

One solitary stirring of unwillingness comes over her before the deed :

> . . . Had he not resembled
> My father as he slept, I had done it. . . .

Then, when she has become Queen by the murder of Duncan, she betrays for a moment something like disillusion, like satiety.   We know not why.

> . . . Nought's had, all's spent,
> Where our desire is got without content :
> 'Tis safer to be that which we destroy,
> Than by destruction dwell in doubtful joy.
>
> (Act III. Sc. 2.)

Nevertheless, she holds out.   In the banquet-scene which follows on these words, she alone keeps her head, cloaks her husband's distraction, and finds a pretext for dismissing the guests.   And then we see her no more ; until (in the first scene of the fifth act) we again behold her as a sleep-walker, with the impressions of that night of murder fixed on her mind.   Again, as then, she seeks to put heart into her husband :

' Fie, my lord, fie ! a soldier, and afeard ?   What need we fear who knows it, when none can call our power to account ? '

She hears the knocking at the door, which terrified her husband after the deed.   Next, she strives to ' undo the deed which cannot be undone '.   She washes her hands, which are blood-stained and smell of blood, and is conscious of the futility of the attempt.   Remorse seems to have borne her down—she who had seemed so remorseless.   When she dies, Macbeth, who meanwhile has become as inexorable as she had been in the beginning, can find only a brief epitaph for her :

> She should have died hereafter ;
> There would have been a time for such a word.
>
> (Act V. Sc. 5.)

And now we ask ourselves what it was that broke this character which had seemed forged from the most perdurable metal ? Is it only disillusion, the different aspect shown by the accomplished deed, and are we to infer that even in Lady Macbeth an originally gentle and womanly nature had been worked up to a concentration and high tension which could not long endure, or ought we to seek for such signs of a deeper motivation as will make this collapse more humanly intelligible to us ?

It seems to me impossible to come to any decision. Shakespeare's *Macbeth* is a *pièce d'occasion*, written for the accession of James, who had hitherto been King of Scotland. The plot was ready-made, and had been handled by other contemporary writers, whose work Shakespeare probably made use of in his customary manner. It offered remarkable analogies to the actual situation. The ' virginal ' Elizabeth, of whom it was rumoured that she had never been capable of child-bearing and who had once described herself as ' a barren stock ',[1] in an anguished outcry at the news of James's birth, was obliged by this very childlessness of hers to let the Scottish king become her successor. And he was the son of that Mary Stuart whose execution she, though reluctantly, had decreed, and who, despite the clouding of their relations by political concerns, was yet of her blood and might be called her guest.

The accession of James I. was like a demonstration of the curse of unfruitfulness and the blessings reserved for those who carry on the race. And Shakespeare's *Macbeth* develops on the theme of this same contrast.

---

[1] Cf. *Macbeth*, Act III. Sc. 1 :

> Upon my head they placed a fruitless crown,
> And put a barren sceptre in my gripe,
> Thence to be wrenched with an unlineal hand,
> No son of mine succeeding. . . .

The three Fates, the 'weird sisters', have assured him that he shall indeed be king, but to Banquo they promise that *his* children shall obtain possession of the crown.   Macbeth is incensed by this decree of destiny ; he is not content with the satisfaction of his own ambition, he desires to found a dynasty and not to have murdered for the benefit of strangers.   This point is overlooked when Shakespeare's play is regarded only as a tragedy of ambition.   It is clear that Macbeth cannot live for ever, and thus there is but one way for him to disprove that part of the prophecy which opposes his wishes—namely, to have children himself, children who can succeed him.   And he seems to expect them from his vigorous wife :

> Bring forth men-children only !
> For thy undaunted mettle should compose
> Nothing but males. . . .
> (Act I. Sc. 7.)

And equally it is clear that if he is deceived in this expectation he must submit to destiny ; otherwise his actions lose all purpose and are transformed into the blind fury of one doomed to destruction, who is resolved to destroy beforehand all that he can reach.   We watch Macbeth undergo this development, and at the height of the tragedy we hear that shattering cry from Macduff, which has often ere now been recognized to have many meanings and possibly to contain the key to the change in Macbeth :

> He has no children !
> (Act IV. Sc. 3.)

Undoubtedly that signifies ' Only because he is himself childless could he murder my children ' ; but more may be implied in it, and above all it might be said to lay bare the essential motive which not only forces Macbeth to go far beyond his own true nature, but also assails the hard character of his wife at its only weak place.   If one looks back upon *Macbeth* from the culmination reached in these words of Macduff's, one sees that the whole play is sown with references to the father-and-children relation. The murder of the kindly Duncan is little else than parricide ; in Banquo's case, Macbeth kills the father while the son escapes him ; and he kills Macduff's children because the father has fled from him. A bloody child, and then a crowned one, are shown him by the witches in the conjuration-scene ; the armed head seen previously is doubtless Macbeth's own. But in the background arises the sinister form of the avenger, Macduff, who is himself an exception to the laws of generation, since he was not born of his mother but ripp'd from her womb.

It would be a perfect example of poetic justice in the manner of the talion if the childlessness of Macbeth and the barrenness of his Lady were the punishment for their crimes against the sanctity of geniture—if Macbeth could not become a father because he had robbed children of their father and a father of his children, and if Lady Macbeth had suffered the un-sexing she had demanded of the spirits of murder. I believe one could without more ado explain the illness of Lady Macbeth, the transformation of her callousness into penitence, as a reaction to her childlessness, by which she is convinced of her impotence against the decrees of nature, and at the same time admonished that she has only herself to blame if her crime has been barren of the better part of its desired results.

In the *Chronicle* of Holinshed (1577), whence Shake-speare took the plot of *Macbeth*, Lady Macbeth is only once mentioned as the ambitious wife who instigates her husband to murder that she may herself be queen. Of her subsequent fate and of the development of her character there is no word at all. On the other hand, it would seem that there the change in Macbeth to a sanguinary tyrant is motivated just in the way we have suggested. For in Holinshed ten years pass between the murder of Duncan, whereby Macbeth becomes king, and his further misdeeds ; and in these ten years he is shown as a stern but righteous ruler.

It is not until after this period that the change begins
in him, under the influence of the tormenting apprehension that the prophecy to Banquo will be fulfilled
as was that of his own destiny. Then only does he
contrive the murder of Banquo, and, as in Shakespeare,
is driven from one crime to another. Holinshed does
not expressly say that it was his childlessness which
urged him to these courses, but there is warrant
enough—both time and occasion—for this probable
motivation. Not so in Shakespeare. Events crowd
breathlessly on one another in the tragedy, so that to
judge by the statements made by the persons in the
play about one week represents the duration of time
assigned to it.[1] This acceleration takes the ground
from under our attempts at reconstructing the motives
for the change in the characters of Macbeth and his
wife. There is no time for a long-drawn disappointment
of their hopes of offspring to enervate the woman and
drive the man to an insane defiance ; and it remains
impossible to resolve the contradiction that so many
subtle inter-relations in the plot, and between it and
its occasion, point to a common origin of them in the
motive of childlessness, and that yet the period of time
in the tragedy expressly precludes a development of
character from any but a motive contained in the play.

What, however, these motives can have been which
in so short a space of time could turn the hesitating,
ambitious man into an unbridled tyrant, and his steely-
hearted instigator into a sick woman gnawed by
remorse, it is, in my view, impossible to divine. I
think we must renounce the hope of penetrating the
triple obscurity of the bad preservation of the text,
the unknown intention of the dramatist, and the
hidden purport of the legend. But I should not admit
that such investigations are idle in view of the powerful effect which the tragedy has upon the spectator.
The dramatist can indeed, during the representation,
overwhelm us by his art and paralyse our powers of

[1] J. Darmstetter, *Macbeth*, Édition classique, p. lxxv., Paris, 1887.

reflection ; but he cannot prevent us from subsequently attempting to grasp the psychological mechanism of that effect.   And the contention that the dramatist is at liberty to shorten at will the natural time and duration of the events he brings before us, if by the sacrifice of common probability he can enhance the dramatic effect, seems to me irrelevant in this instance. For such a sacrifice is justified only when it merely affronts probability,[1] and not when it breaks the causal connection ; besides, the dramatic effect would hardly have suffered if the time-duration had been left in uncertainty, instead of being expressly limited to some few days.

One is so unwilling to dismiss a problem like that of *Macbeth* as insoluble that I will still make another attempt, by introducing another comment which points towards a new issue. Ludwig Jekels, in a recent Shakespearean study, thinks he has divined a technical trick of the poet, which might have to be reckoned with in *Macbeth*, too. He is of opinion that Shakespeare frequently splits up a character into two personages, each of whom then appears not altogether comprehensible until once more conjoined with the other. It might be thus with Macbeth and the Lady ; and then it would of course be futile to regard her as an independent personage and seek to discover her motivation without considering the Macbeth who completes her.   I shall not follow this hint any further, but I would add, nevertheless, a remark which strikingly confirms the idea—namely, that the stirrings of fear which arise in Macbeth on the night of the murder, do not develop further in him, but in the Lady.[2] It is he who has the hallucination of the dagger before the deed, but it is she who later succumbs to mental disorder ; he, after the murder, hears the cry from the house : ' Sleep no more ! Macbeth does

---

[1] As in Richard III.'s wooing of Anne beside the bier of the King whom he has murdered.
[2] Cf. Darmstetter, *loc. cit.*

murder sleep . . .', and so ' Macbeth shall sleep no more ', but we never hear that King Macbeth could not sleep, while we see that the Queen rises from her bed and betrays her guilt in somnambulistic wanderings. He stands helpless with bloody hands, lamenting that not great Neptune's ocean can wash them clean again, while she comforts him : ' A little water clears us of this deed ' ; but later it is she who washes her hands for a quarter of an hour and cannot get rid of the blood-stains. ' All the perfumes of Arabia will not sweeten this little hand.' Thus is fulfilled in her what his pangs of conscience had apprehended ; she is incarnate remorse after the deed, he incarnate defiance—together they exhaust the possibilities of reaction to the crime, like two disunited parts of the mind of a single individuality, and perhaps they are the divided images of a single prototype.

If we have been unable to give any answer to the question why Lady Macbeth should collapse after her success, we may perhaps have a better chance with the creation of another great dramatist, who loves to pursue with unrelenting rigour the task of the psychological reckoning.

Rebecca Gamvik, the daughter of a midwife, has become, under the influence of her adoptive father, Dr. West, a freethinker and a contemner of all those restrictions upon desires in life which are imposed by morality founded on religious belief. After the doctor's death she obtains a footing at Rosmersholm, the ancestral seat of an old family whose members are unacquainted with laughter and have sacrificed joy to stern fulfilment of duty. At Rosmersholm dwell Pastor Johannes Rosmer and his invalid wife, the childless Beata. Overcome by ' a wild, uncontrollable passion ' for the love of the aristocratic Rosmer, Rebecca resolves to remove the wife who stands in her way, and to this end is served by her ' fearless, free-born ' will, which is restrained by no ethical considerations. She contrives that Beata shall read a medical book in which the begetting of offspring is represented as the sole aim of marriage, so that the poor woman begins to doubt whether her own union is an honourable one. Rebecca then hints that Rosmer, whose studies and ideas she shares, is about to abandon the old faith and join the party of enlightenment ; and after she has thus shaken the wife's confidence in the moral uprightness of her husband, gives her finally to understand that she, Rebecca, must soon leave the house in order to conceal the consequences of illicit intercourse with Rosmer. The criminal scheme succeeds. The poor wife, who has passed for melancholic and crazy, throws herself from the path beside the mill into the mill-race, possessed by the sense of her own worthlessness and desirous of standing no longer between her beloved husband and his bliss.

For more than a year Rebecca and Rosmer have been living alone at Rosmersholm in a relationship which he wishes to regard as a purely intellectual and ideal friendship. But when from outside the first shadow of evil gossip falls upon this relationship, and at the same time there arise tormenting doubts in Rosmer in regard to the motives for which his wife had put an end to herself, he begs Rebecca to become his second wife, so that they may oppose to the unhappy past a new living reality (Act II.). For one instant she cries out with joy at this proposal, but immediately afterwards declares that it can never be, and that if he urges her further she will ' go the way Beata went '. Rosmer cannot at all understand this rejection ; and still less can we, who know more of Rebecca's actions and designs. All we can be certain of is that her ' No ' is meant in good earnest.

How has it come about that the adventuress with the fearless, freeborn will, which forged its way relentlessly to its desired goal, should now refuse to pluck the fruit which is offered her ? She herself gives us the explanation in the fourth Act : ' *This* is the terrible part of it : that now, when all life's happiness

CHARACTER-TYPES IN PSYCHO-ANALYTIC WORK

is within my grasp—my heart is changed, and my own past bars my way to happiness'. That is, she has become a different being, her conscience has awakened, she has a conviction of guilt which denies her happiness.

And how has her conscience been awakened ? Let us listen to her, and consider whether we can accord her our full credence : ' It is the Rosmer view of life— or your view, at any rate—that has infected my will. . . . And made it sick. Enslaved it to laws that had no power over me before. You—life with you—has ennobled my mind.'

This influence, we are further to understand, has only become effective since she has been living alone with Rosmer : ' In quiet—in solitude—when you showed me all your thoughts without reserve—every tender and delicate feeling, just as it came to you—then the great change came over me '.

Shortly before this she has lamented the other aspect of the change : ' Because Rosmersholm has sapped my strength, my old fearless will has had its wings clipped here. It is paralysed ! The time is past when I had courage for anything in the world. I have lost the power of action, Rosmer.'

Rebecca makes this declaration after she has revealed herself a wrong-doer in a voluntary confession to Rosmer and Rector Kroll, the brother of the dead wife. Ibsen has made it clear by many little touches, worked in with masterly subtlety, that this Rebecca does not actually lie, but is never entirely straight-forward. Just as, in spite of all her freedom from prejudice, she understated her age by a year, so is her confession to the two men not entirely complete, and through the persistence of Kroll it is supplemented on some important points. Hence it is open to us, too, to conjecture that the explanation of her refusal only exposes one motive in order to conceal another.

Assuredly we have no reason to disbelieve her when she declares that the atmosphere of Rosmersholm and her intercourse with the high-souled Rosmer have

ennobled and—paralysed her. She expresses there
what she knows and has felt. But this is not necessarily
all that has happened to her, nor is she necessarily competent to explain to herself that all. The influence of
Rosmer might even only be a cloak which conceals
another influence that was operative, and a notable
indication points in this new direction.

Even after her confession, in their last interview
which brings the play to an end, Rosmer again be-
seeches her to be his wife. He forgives her the crime
committed for love of him. And now she does not
answer, as she might, that no forgiveness can rid her
of the consciousness of guilt incurred by her malignant
deception of poor Beata ; but charges herself with
another reproach which affects us as coming strangely
from this freethinking woman, and in no wise corresponds to the importance which Rebecca attaches to
it : ' Dear—never speak of this again ! It is impossible—. For you must know, Rosmer, I have—a
past behind me.' She means, of course, that she has
had sexual relations with another man ; and we do
not fail to observe that these relations, which occurred
at a time when she was free and accountable to nobody,
seem to her a greater hindrance to the union with
Rosmer than her truly criminal action against his wife.

Rosmer refuses to hear anything about this past.
We can divine what it was, though everything that
refers to it in the play is, so to speak, subterranean
and has to be pieced together from hints. But it is
true they are hints inserted with such art that it is
impossible to misunderstand them.

Between Rebecca's first refusal and her confession
something occurs which has a decisive influence on her
future destiny. Rector Kroll arrives one day at the
house on purpose to humiliate Rebecca by telling her
that he knows she is an illegitimate child, the daughter
of that very Dr. West who had adopted her after her
mother's death. Hate has sharpened his perceptions,
yet he does not suppose that this is any news to her.

' I really did not suppose you were ignorant of this, otherwise it would have been very odd that you should have let Dr. West adopt you——' ' And then he takes you into his house—as soon as your mother dies. He treats you harshly. And yet you stay with him. You know that he won't leave you a halfpenny—as a matter of fact you got only a case of books—and yet you stay on ; you bear with him ; you nurse him to the last.' ' I attribute your care for him to the natural filial instinct of a daughter. Indeed, I believe your whole conduct is a natural result of your origin.'

But Kroll was mistaken. Rebecca had no idea at all that she could be West's daughter. When Kroll began with dark hints at her past, she could not but think he was referring to something else. After she knew what he did mean, she could still retain her composure awhile, for she was able to suppose that her enemy was basing his calculations on her age, which she had given falsely on an earlier visit of his. But when Kroll demolished this objection by saying : ' Well, so be it, but my calculation may be right, none the less ; for Dr. West was up there on a short visit the year before he got the appointment ' . . . after this new information, she loses all control. ' It is not true ! ' She walks about wringing her hands. ' It is impossible. You want to cheat me into believing it. This can never, never be true. It cannot be true. Never in this world !——' Her agitation is so extreme that Kroll cannot attribute it to his information alone.

KROLL : But, my dear Miss West—why in Heaven's name are you so terribly excited ? You quite frighten me. What am I to think—to believe——?

REBECCA : Nothing ! You are not to think anything or believe anything.

KROLL : Then you must really tell me how you can take this affair—this possibility—so terribly to heart.

REBECCA (*controlling herself*). It is perfectly simple, Rector Kroll. I have no wish to be taken for an illegitimate child.

The enigma of Rebecca's behaviour is susceptible of only one solution. The news that Dr. West was her father is the heaviest blow that can befall her, for she was not only the adopted daughter, but she had been the mistress of this man. When Kroll began to speak, she thought that he was hinting at these relations, the truth about which she would probably have admitted and justified by her emancipated ideas. But this was far from the Rector's intention ; he knew nothing of the love-affair with Dr. West, as she knew nothing of West being her father. She *cannot* have had anything else in her mind when she accounted for her final rejection of Rosmer on the ground that she had a past which made her unworthy to be his wife. Probably, if Rosmer had consented to hear of this past, she would have made only a half-confession and have kept silence on the more serious part of it.

But now we do indeed understand that this past must seem to her the more serious obstacle to their union—the more serious . . . crime.

After she has learnt that she has been the mistress of her own father, she surrenders herself wholly to her now overmastering sense of guilt. She confesses to Rosmer and Kroll that she was a murderess ; she rejects for ever the happiness to which she has paved the way by crime ; and prepares for departure. But the true origin of her sense of guilt, which wrecks her at the moment of attainment, remains a secret. We have seen that it is something quite other than the atmosphere of Rosmersholm and the refining influence of Rosmer.

No one who has followed us so far will neglect to bring forward an objection which may justify some doubts. The first refusal of Rosmer by Rebecca occurs before the second visit of Kroll, and therefore before his exposure of her illicit origin and at a time when she as yet knows nothing of her incest—if we have rightly understood the dramatist. Yet her first refusal is given in very serious earnest. The sense of guilt which bids her renounce the fruit of her actions is thus effective before she knows anything of her cardinal crime ; and if we grant so much it is perhaps incumbent on us to ignore the incest as the source of that sense of guilt.

Hitherto, we have treated Rebecca West as if she were a living person and not a creation of Ibsen's phantasy, one which is always subject to the most critical tests of reason. We shall attempt to meet the objection aforesaid on this same ground. It is a just objection that, before the knowledge of her incest, conscience was in some sort awakened in Rebecca. There is nothing to prevent our making the influence which is acknowledged and accused by Rebecca herself responsible for this change. But we shall not thus escape recognition of the second motive. The behaviour of Rebecca on hearing what Kroll has to tell her, the confession which is her immediate reaction, leave no doubt that now only does the stronger and more decisive motive for renunciation begin to take effect. It is in fact a case of manifold motivation, in which a deeper motive comes to the surface from beneath the superficial one. Laws of poetical economy necessitate this way of presenting the situation, for this deeper motive could not be explicitly set forth, it had to be dissimulated, kept from the direct perception of the spectator or the reader ; otherwise such serious resistances, based on most painful emotions, would have arisen that the effect of the tragedy might have been imperilled.

We have, however, a right to demand that the ostensible motive shall not be without an inherent relation to the dissimulated one, but shall appear as a mitigation of, and a derivation from, the latter. And relying on the dramatist to have arranged his conscious dramatic combination in logical accordance with unconscious possibilities, we can now try to show that he has fulfilled this demand. Rebecca's feeling of guilt finds its source in the shame of incest, even before Kroll with his analytic insight has made her aware of it. When we fully reconstruct and supplement the past indicated by the author, we shall feel sure that she cannot have been without an inkling of the intimate relation between her mother and Dr. West. It must have made a strong impression on her when she became her mother's successor with this man ; and she thus stood under the domination of the Oedipus-complex, even though she did not know that this universal phantasy had been a reality in her case. When she came to Rosmersholm, the inward force of this first experience drove her to bring about, by definite action, the same situation which had been realized in the original instance, though not by her doing—to get rid of the wife and mother, that she might take her place with the husband and father. She describes with a convincing insistence how against her will she was obliged to proceed, step by step, to the removal of Beata.

' You think then that I was cool and calculating and self-possessed all the time ! I was not the same woman then that I am now, as I stand here telling it all. Besides, there are two sorts of will in us, I believe. I wanted Beata away by one means or another, but I never really believed that it would come to pass. As I felt my way forward, at each step I ventured, I seemed to hear something within me cry out : No farther ! Not a step farther !—And yet I could not stop. I *had* to venture the least little bit farther. And only one hair's-breadth more. And then one more—and always one more. . . . And so it happened. That is the way such things come about.'

That is no plea for extenuation, but an authentic description. Everything that befell her at Rosmersholm, the passion for Rosmer and the enmity towards his wife, was from the first a consequence of the Oedipus-complex—a compulsive replica of her relations with her mother and Dr. West.

And so the sense of guilt which first causes her to reject Rosmer's proposal is at bottom indistinguishable from the deeper one which drives her to confession after Kroll has opened her eyes. But just as under the influence of Dr. West she had become a freethinker and contemner of religious morality, so she is transformed by her love for Rosmer into a being with a conscience and an ideal. This much of the mental processes within her she does herself understand, and so she is justified in describing Rosmer's influence as the motive of the change in her—the only one of which she could be aware.

The practising psycho-analytic physician knows how frequently, or how invariably, the girl who enters a household as servant, companion or governess, will consciously or unconsciously weave a day-dream, which derives from the Oedipus-complex, about the disappearance of the mistress of the house and the master taking the newcomer to wife in her stead. *Rosmersholm* is the greatest work of art among those which treat of this common girlish phantasy. What makes it a tragedy is the circumstance that the early history of the heroine in actual fact had completely anticipated her day-dream.[1]

After long lingering in the sphere of literature, we now return to clinical experience. But only to establish in a few words the complete agreement between them. Psycho-analytic work teaches that the forces of conscience which induce illness on attainment of success, as in other cases on a frustration, are closely connected with the Oedipus-complex, the relation to father and mother, as perhaps, indeed, is all our sense of guilt in general.

[1] An exposition of the incest-theme in *Rosmersholm* has already been made, by similar methods to my own, in the extremely comprehensive work by Otto Rank, *Das Inzest-Motiv in Dichtung und Sage*.

III

CRIMINALITY FROM A SENSE OF GUILT

In their narrations about their early years, particularly before puberty, people who have afterwards become very upright have told me of forbidden actions which they had formerly committed—such as thefts, frauds, and even arson. I was wont to dismiss these statements with the comment that we know the weakness of moral inhibiting influences at that time of life, and I made no attempt to give them an important place in the connected story. But eventually I was constrained to make a more fundamental study of such incidents, by reason of some glaring and more accessible cases in which the transgressions took place while the patients were under my treatment, and were people of riper age. The analytic work then afforded the surprising conclusion that such deeds are done precisely *because* they are forbidden, and because by carrying them out the doer enjoys a sense of mental relief. He suffered from an oppressive feeling of guilt, of which he did not know the origin, and after he had committed a misdeed the oppression was mitigated. The sense of guilt was at least in some way accounted for.

Paradoxical as it may sound, I must maintain that the sense of guilt was present prior to the transgression, that it did not arise from this, but contrariwise—the transgression from the sense of guilt. These persons we might justifiably describe as criminals from a sense of guilt. The pre-existence of the guilty feeling had of course to be demonstrated by a whole succession of other manifestations and effects.

But scientific work is not satisfied with establishing a departure from the norm. There are two further questions to answer : whence derives the obscure sense of guilt before the deed, and whether it is probable that this kind of causation plays a considerable part in the transgressions of mankind.

Prosecution of the former inquiry would hold out hope of some explanation regarding the source of mankind's sense of guilt in general. The invariable result of analytic work is that this obscure sense of guilt derives from the Oedipus-complex and is a reaction to the two great criminal intentions of killing the father and having sexual relations with the mother. In comparison with these two, to be sure, the crimes committed in order to account for the sense of guilt were comparatively light ones for the sufferer to bear. We must remember in this connection that parricide and incest with the mother are the two greatest crimes man can commit, the only ones which in primitive communities are avenged and abhorred as such. And we must remember, too, that other investigations have caused us to entertain the hypothesis that the conscience of mankind, which now appears as an inherited power in the mind, was originally acquired from the Oedipus-complex.

The answer to the second question lies outside the scope of psycho-analytic work. With children, it is easy to perceive that they are often ' naughty ' on purpose to provoke punishment, and are quiet and contented after the chastisement. Later analytic investigation can often find a trace of the guilty feeling which bid them seek for punishment. Among adult criminals one must probably except those who transgress without any sense of guilt, who either have developed no moral inhibitions or consider themselves justified in their deed by their conflict with society. But in the majority of other criminals, those for whom punitive measures are really designed, such a motivation towards crime might very well be present, casting light on many obscure points in the psychology of the criminal, and furnishing punishment with a new psychological basis.

A friend has recently called my attention to the fact that the ' criminal from a sense of guilt ' was recognized by Nietzsche. The pre-existence of the guilty consciousness, and the efficacy of the deed in rationalizing this feeling, gleam forth from the dark discourse of Zarathustra ' On the Pale Criminal '. Let us leave to future research the decision how many criminals are to be reckoned among these ' pale ' ones.

A CHILDHOOD RECOLLECTION FROM
'*DICHTUNG UND WAHRHEIT*'[1]

(1917)

'IF we try to recollect what happened to us in the earliest years of childhood, it often occurs that we confound what we have heard from others with what is really our own possession from actual visual experience.' This remark is found on one of the first pages of Goethe's account of his life, which he began to write at the age of sixty. It is preceded only by some information about his own birth which ' took place on August 28, 1749, at midday on the stroke of twelve '. The stars were in a favourable conjunction and may well have been the cause of his preservation, for at his entry into the world he was ' taken for dead ', and it was only after great efforts that he was brought round to life. There follows on this a short description of the house and of the place in it where the children—he and his younger sister—best liked to play. After this, however, Goethe relates in fact only one single event that one could place in the ' earliest years of child-hood ' (? the years up to four) and of which he seems to have preserved a real recollection.

The account of it runs as follows : ' And three brothers (von Ochsenstein by name) who lived opposite became very fond of me ; they were orphan sons of the late magistrate, and they took an interest in me and used to tease me in all sorts of ways.

' My people used to like to tell of all kinds of tricks in which these men, otherwise of a serious and retiring disposition, used to encourage me. I will quote only

[1] First published in *Imago*, Bd. V., 1917 ; reprinted in *Sammlung*, Vierte Folge. [Translated by C. M. J. Hubback.]

one of these exploits. The crockery-fair was just over and not only had the kitchen been fitted up with these goods for the next season, but miniature things of the same ware had been bought for us children to play with. One fine afternoon, when all was quiet in the house, I betook myself with my dishes and pots to the garden-room (the play-place already mentioned, which looked on to the street) and, since nothing seemed to be doing, I threw a plate into the street, and was overjoyed to see it go to bits so merrily. The von Ochsensteins, who saw how delighted I was and how joyfully I clapped my hands, called out "Do it again!" I did not hesi-tate to sling a pot on to the paving-stones, and then, as they kept crying "Another!", one after another all my dishes, saucepans and pans. My neighbours continued to signify their approval and I was delighted to have amused them. But my stock was all used up and still they cried "Another!". So I ran off straight into the kitchen and fetched the earthenware plates, which made an even finer show as they smashed to bits : and thus I ran backwards and forwards, bringing one plate after another, as I could reach them in turn from the rack, and, as they were not content at that, I hurled everything I could find of the same sort to the same ruin. Only later did someone appear to interfere and put a stop to it all. The damage was done, and instead of so much broken earthenware there was at least an amusing story, which the rascals who had been the instigators enjoyed to the end of their lives.'

In pre-analytic days one could read this without finding occasion to stop and without surprise, but later on the analytic conscience became active. Definite opinions and expectations had been formed about recollections from early childhood and one would have been glad to claim universal application for them. It should not be a matter of indifference or entirely with-out meaning which detail of a child's life had escaped the general oblivion. It might rather be conjectured that what had remained in memory was the most significant element in that whole period of life, equally so whether it had possessed such an importance at the time, or whether it had gained subsequent importance from the influence of later events.

The high value of such childish recollections was, it is true, obvious only in a few cases. Generally they seemed indifferent, worthless even, and it remained at first incomprehensible why just these memories should have resisted amnesia : nor could the person who had preserved them for long years as his own store of memory see more in them than any stranger to whom he might relate them. Before their significance could be appreciated, a certain work of interpretation was necessary, which would either show how their content must be replaced by some other, or would reveal their connection with some other unmistakably important experiences, for which they were appearing as so-called ' screen-memories '.

In every analytic work on a life-history it is always possible to explain the meaning of the earliest memories along these lines. Indeed, it usually happens that the very recollection to which the patient gives precedence, that he relates first, with which he introduces his confession, proves to be the most important, the very one that holds the key to his mental life. But in the case of this little childish episode related in *Dichtung und Wahrheit* there is too little awaiting our expectations. The ways that with our patients lead to interpretation are of course not open to us here ; the episode does not seem in itself to admit of any traceable connection with important impressions at a later date. A mischievous trick with bad results for the household economy, carried out under the spur of encouragement by strangers, is certainly not a fitting vignette for all that Goethe has to tell us of his full life. An impression of utter harmlessness and irrelevancy persists in regard to this childish memory, and we might let it be a warning not to stretch the claims of psycho-analysis too far nor to apply it in unsuitable places.

For a long time, therefore, the little problem had slipped out of my mind, when one day chance brought me a patient in whom a similar childhood-memory appeared in a clearer connection. He was a man of seven-and-twenty, highly educated and gifted, whose life at the time consisted entirely in a conflict with his mother that affected all his interests, and from the effects of which his capacity for love and his independent career had suffered greatly. This conflict went far back into childhood : certainly to his fourth year. Before that he had been a very weakly child, always ailing, and yet that time was glorified into a very paradise in his memory ; for then he had had exclusive, uninterrupted possession of his mother's affection. When he was not yet four, a brother, who was still living, was born, and in his reaction to this disturbing event he became transformed into an obstinate, unmanageable boy, who perpetually provoked his mother's severity. Moreover, he never regained the right path.

When he came to me for treatment—by no means the least reason for his coming was that his bigoted mother had a horror of psycho-analysis—his jealousy of the younger brother (which had once taken the form of an attack on the infant in its cradle) had long been forgotten. He now treated his brother with great consideration ; but certain curious fortuitous actions of his, such as suddenly inflicting injuries on favourite animals, like his sporting dog or birds he had carefully fostered, were probably to be understood as echoes of that hostile impulse against the little brother.

Now this patient related that, at about the time of the attack on the child he so hated, he had thrown all the crockery he could lay hands on out of the window of the villa into the road—the very same thing that Goethe relates of his childhood in *Dichtung und Wahrheit* ! I may remark that my patient was of foreign nationality and was not acquainted with German literature : he had never read Goethe's autobiography.

This communication naturally suggested to me that an attempt might be made to explain Goethe's childish memory on the lines that were impossible to ignore in my patient's story. But could the necessary conditions for this explanation be shown to exist in the poet's childhood? Goethe himself, indeed, makes the eagerness of the von Ochsenstein brothers responsible for his childish trick. But from his own narrative it can be seen that the grown-up neighbours only encouraged him to go on with what he was doing. The beginning was on his own initiative, and the reason he gives for this beginning—' since nothing seemed to be doing '—is surely, without any forcing of its meaning, a confession that at the time of writing it down and probably for many years previously he was not aware of the real motive of his behaviour.

It is well known that Johann Wolfgang and his sister Cornelia were the eldest survivors of a family of very weakly children. Dr. Hanns Sachs has been so kind as to supply me with the following details referring to these brothers and sisters of Goethe, who died in childhood :

(a) Hermann Jakob, baptized Monday, November 27, 1752 ; reached the age of six years and six weeks ; buried January 13, 1759.

(b) Katharina Elisabetha, baptized Monday, September 9, 1754 ; buried Thursday, December 22, 1755 (one year, four months old).

(c) Johanna Maria, baptized Tuesday, March 29, 1757, and buried Saturday, August 11, 1759 (two years, four months old). (This was doubtless the very pretty and attractive little girl mentioned by her brother.)

(d) Georg Adolph, baptized Sunday, June 15, 1760 ; buried, eight months old, Wednesday, February 18, 1761.

Goethe's next sister, Cornelia Friederica Christiana, was born on December 7, 1750, when he was fifteen months old. This slight difference in age almost excludes the possibility of her having been an object

of jealousy. It is known that, when their passions
awake, children never develop such violent reactions
against the brothers and sisters they find in existence,
but direct their hostility against newcomers. Nor is
the scene we are endeavouring to interpret reconcilable
with Goethe's tender age at the time of, or shortly
after, Cornelia's birth.

At the time of the birth of the first little brother,
Hermann Jakob, Johann Wolfgang was three-and-a-
quarter years old. Nearly two years later, when he
was about five years old, the second sister was born.
Both ages come under consideration in dating the
episode of the crockery-smashing: the first perhaps
is to be preferred. It also would best correspond with
the case of my patient, who was about three-and-three-
quarter years old at the birth of his brother.

The brother Hermann Jakob, to whom we are thus
led in our attempt at interpretation, did not, by the
way, have so brief a sojourn in the nursery of the
Goethe family as the children born afterwards. One
might feel some surprise that the autobiography
does not contain a word of remembrance of him.[1] He
was over six, and Johann Wolfgang was nearly ten,
when he died. Dr. Hitschmann, who was kind enough
to place his notes on this subject at my disposal,
says:

'Goethe, too, as a little boy saw a younger brother
die without regret. At least, according to Bettina
Brentano's narrative, his mother gave the following
account: "It struck her as very extraordinary that
he shed no tears at the death of his younger brother
Jakob who was his playfellow; he seemed instead to
feel annoyance at the grief of his parents and sisters;

[1] *Additional Note*, 1924.—I take this opportunity of withdrawing an
incorrect statement which ought not to have been made. In a later
passage in this first volume the younger brother is mentioned and
described. It occurs together with recollections about the troublesome
ailments of childhood, from which this brother also suffered ' not a
little '. ' He was a delicate child, quiet and self-willed, and we never
had much to do with each other. Besides, he hardly survived the years
of infancy.'

he stood out against it, and when his mother asked him later if he had not been fond of his brother, he ran into his room, brought out from under the bed a heap of papers on which lessons and little stories were written, saying that he had done all this to teach his brother ''. The elder brother would therefore have been glad enough all the same to play the father to the younger and show him his superiority.'

We might thus form the opinion that throwing crockery out of the window is a symbolic action, or, let us say more correctly, a magical action, by which a child (both Goethe as well as my patient) violently expresses his wish to get rid of a disturbing intruder. We do not need to dispute a child's enjoyment of smashing things ; if an action is pleasurable in itself, that is not a hindrance but rather an inducement to repeat it for other ends. We do not believe, how- ever, that the pleasure in the crash of the breakages could have ensured the recollection a lasting place in the memory of the adult. Nor have we any objection to complicating the motivation of the action by a further consideration. A child who breaks crockery knows quite well that he is doing something naughty for which grown-ups will scold him, and, if he is not restrained by this knowledge, he probably has a grudge against his parents that he wants to satisfy ; he wants to show that he is naughty.

The pleasure in smashing and in broken things would be satisfied, too, if the child simply threw the breakable object on the ground. The hurling them out of the window into the street would still remain unexplained. This ' Out with it ! ' seems to be an essential part of the magic action and to arise directly from its hidden meaning. The new baby must be *thrown out*, through the window, perhaps because he came through the window. The whole action would thus be equivalent to the familiar things said by children who are told that the stork has brought a little brother or sister. ' Then the stork is to take it away again ' is the verdict.

All the same, however, we are not blind to the objections that exist—apart from any internal un-certainties—against basing the explanation of a childish act on a single analogy. For this reason I had for years kept back my theory about the little scene in *Dichtung und Wahrheit*. Then one day I had a patient who began his analysis with the following remarks, which I set down word for word : ' I am the eldest of a family of eight or nine children.[1] One of my earliest recollections is of my father sitting on the bed in his night-shirt, and telling me laughingly that I had a brother. I was then three years and three-quarters old ; and that is the difference in age between me and my next brother. Then I know that a short time after (or was it a year before ?)[2] I threw a lot of things, brushes—or was it only one brush ?—shoes and other things, out of the window into the street. I have a still earlier recollection. When I was two years old, I spent a night with my parents in a hotel bedroom at Linz on the way to the Salzkammergut. I was so restless in the night and made such a noise that my father had to beat me.'

After this avowal I threw all doubts to the winds. When in analysis two things are brought out one immediately after the other, as though in one breath, we have to interpret this proximity as a connection. It was, therefore, as if the patient had said, ' *Because* I found that I had got a brother, I shortly after threw these things into the street '. The act of flinging the brushes, shoes, and so on, out of the window must be recognized as a reaction to the birth of the brother. It is quite satisfactory, too, that the things thrown out in this instance were not crockery but other things, probably anything the child could reach at the moment.

[1] A careless mistake of a striking character, which was undoubtedly induced by the influence of the intention, already active, to get rid of a brother. (Cf. Ferenczi, ' Transitory Symptom-Formations during Analysis '.)

[2] This doubt, attaching to the essential point of the communication for purposes of resistance, was spontaneously withdrawn shortly after by the patient.

Hurling them out (through the window into the street) thus proves to be the essential thing in the act, while the pleasure in the smashing, and the noise, and the kind of things on which 'execution is done', are variable and unessential points.

Naturally, if we are concerned with tracing connections, the patient's third childish recollection cannot be left out either ; it is the earliest, though it was put at the end of the little series. It is easy to account for it. We gather that the two-year-old child was so restless because it did not like the parents being together in bed. On the journey it was probably not possible to avoid the child being a witness of this. Among the feelings which were then aroused in the jealous little one there was an embitterment against women, which persisted and permanently interfered with the development of his capacity for love.

After these two observations I expressed the opinion at a meeting of the Vienna Psycho-Analytical Society that occurrences of the same kind might be not infrequent among young children, whereupon Frau Dr. von Hug-Hellmuth placed two further observations at my disposal, which I append here :

I

At the age of about three-and-a-half, little Eric quite suddenly acquired the habit of throwing everything he did not like out of the window. He did it, moreover, with things that were not in his way and did not concern him. On his father's birthday—he was three years and four-and-a-half months old—he threw a heavy rolling-pin, which he had dragged out of the kitchen into the dining-room, out of the window of a third-floor flat into the street. Some days later he sent after it the mortar-pestle, and then a pair of heavy mountaineering shoes of his father's, which he first had to take out of the cupboard.[1]

[1] He always chose heavy objects.

At that time his mother had a miscarriage, in the seventh or eighth month of pregnancy, and after that the child was ' sweet and quiet and so good that he seemed quite changed '. In the fifth or sixth month he repeatedly said to his mother, ' Mother, I am jumping on your tummy '—or, ' Mother, I am pushing in your tummy ! '. And shortly before the miscarriage, in October, he said, ' If I must have a brother, at least I don't want it till after Christmas '.

II

A young lady of nineteen gave her earliest recollection spontaneously as follows : ' I can see myself frightfully naughty, sitting under the table in the dining-room, ready to creep out. On the table is my mug of coffee—I can still see the pattern of the crockery quite plainly—which I was just going to throw out of the window when grandmamma came into the room.

' In fact, no one had been bothering about me, and in the meantime a skin had formed on the coffee, which was always perfectly dreadful to me and still is.

' On that day my brother, who is two-and-a-half years younger than I, was born, and so no one had had any time for me.

' They always tell me that I was insupportable on that day : at dinner I threw my father's favourite glass on the floor, I smeared and stained my frock many times, and was in the worst temper from dawn to evening. In my rage I broke a bath-doll to bits.'

These two cases scarcely need any commentary. They establish without further analytic effort that the bitterness children feel about the expected or actual appearance of a rival finds expression in throwing objects out of the window and in other acts of naughtiness and destructiveness. In the first case the ' heavy objects ' probably symbolize the mother herself, against whom the child's anger is directed so long as the new child is not yet there. The three-and-a-half-year-old boy knows about the pregnancy of the mother and has no doubt that she is harbouring the child in her body. ' Little Hans ' [1] and his special dread of heavily loaded carts may be recalled here.[2] In the second case the very young age of the child, two-and-a-half years, is noteworthy.

If we now return to Goethe's childhood-memory and put in the place it occupies in *Dichtung und Wahrheit* what we believe we have obtained through observations of other children, a flawless connection appears which we should not otherwise have discovered. It would run thus : ' I was a child of fortune : destiny had preserved me for life, although I came into the world for dead. Even more, destiny removed my brother, so that I did not have to share my mother's love with him.' And then the train of thought goes on to someone else who died in those early days, the grandmother who lived like a quiet friendly spirit in another part of the house.

I have, however, already declared elsewhere that he who has been the undisputed darling of his mother retains throughout life that victorious feeling, that confidence in ultimate success, which not seldom brings actual success with it. And a saying such as 'My strength has its roots in my relation to my mother ' might well have been put at the head of Goethe's autobiography.

[1] Cf. ' Analysis of a Phobia in a Five-Year-Old Boy ', COLLECTED PAPERS, vol. iii.

[2] Further confirmation of this pregnancy-symbolism was given me some time ago by a lady of over fifty. She had often been told that as a little child, when she could hardly talk, she used to drag her father to the window in great agitation whenever a heavy lorry was passing along the street. In view of other recollections of the houses they had inhabited, it became possible to establish that she was then younger than two-and-three-quarter years. At about that time the brother next to her was born, and in consequence of this addition to the family a move was made. At about the same time, she often had before going to sleep an alarming feeling of something monstrously large, that came up to her, and ' her hands became so thick '.

THE 'UNCANNY' [1]

(1919)

I

IT is only rarely that a psycho-analyst feels impelled to investigate the subject of aesthetics even when aesthetics is understood to mean not merely the theory of beauty, but the theory of feeling. He works in other planes of mental life and has little to do with those subdued emotional activities which, inhibited in their aims and dependent upon a multitude of concurrent factors, usually furnish the material for the study of aesthetics. But it does occasionally happen that he has to interest himself in some particular province of that subject ; and then it usually proves to be a rather remote region of it and one that has been neglected in standard works.

The subject of the ' uncanny ' is a province of this kind. It undoubtedly belongs to all that is terrible— to all that arouses dread and creeping horror ; it is equally certain, too, that the word is not always used in a clearly definable sense, so that it tends to coincide with whatever excites dread. Yet we may expect that it implies some intrinsic quality which justifies the use of a special name. One is curious to know what this peculiar quality is which allows us to distinguish as ' uncanny ' certain things within the boundaries of what is ' fearful '.

As good as nothing is to be found upon this subject in elaborate treatises on aesthetics, which in general prefer to concern themselves with what is beautiful, attractive and sublime, that is with feelings of a positive

---

[1] First published in *Imago*, Bd. V., 1919 ; reprinted in *Sammlung*, Fünfte Folge. [Translated by Alix Strachey.]

nature, with the circumstances and the objects that call them forth, rather than with the opposite feelings of unpleasantness and repulsion. I know of only one attempt in medico-psychological literature, a fertile but not exhaustive paper by E. Jentsch.[1] But I must confess that I have not made a very thorough examination of the bibliography, especially the foreign literature, relating to this present modest contribution of mine, for reasons which must be obvious at this time ;[2] so that my paper is presented to the reader without any claim to priority.

In his study of the ' uncanny ', Jentsch quite rightly lays stress on the obstacle presented by the fact that people vary so very greatly in their sensitivity to this quality of feeling. The writer of the present contribution, indeed, must himself plead guilty to a special obtuseness in the matter, where extreme delicacy of perception would be more in place. It is long since he has experienced or heard of anything which has given him an uncanny impression, and he will be obliged to translate himself into that state of feeling, and to awaken in himself the possibility of it before he begins. Still, difficulties of this kind make themselves felt powerfully in many other branches of aesthetics; we need not on this account despair of finding instances in which the quality in question will be recognized without hesitation by most people.

Two courses are open to us at the start. Either we can find out what meaning has come to be attached to the word ' uncanny ' in the course of its history ; or we can collect all those properties of persons, things, sensations, experiences and situations which arouse in us the feeling of uncanniness, and then infer the unknown nature of the uncanny from what they all have in common. I will say at once that both courses lead to the same result : the ' uncanny ' is that class of the terrifying which leads back to something long known

---

[1] ' Zur Psychologie des Unheimlichen.'
[2] [An allusion to the European War only just concluded.—Trans.]

to us, once very familiar. How this is possible, in what circumstances the familiar can become uncanny and frightening, I shall show in what follows. Let me also add that my investigation was actually begun by collecting a number of individual cases, and only later received confirmation after I had examined what language could tell us. In this discussion, however, I shall follow the opposite course.

The German word *unheimlich* [1] is obviously the opposite of *heimlich, heimisch*, meaning ' familiar ' ; ' native ', ' belonging to the home ' ; and we are tempted to conclude that what is,' uncanny ' is frightening precisely because it is *not* known and familiar. Naturally not everything which is new and unfamiliar is frightening, however ; the relation cannot be inverted. We can only say that what is novel can easily become frightening and uncanny ; some new things are frightening but not by any means all. Something has to be added to what is novel and unfamiliar to make it uncanny.

On the whole, Jentsch did not get beyond this relation of the uncanny to the novel and unfamiliar. He ascribes the essential factor in the production of the feeling of uncanniness to intellectual uncertainty ; so that the uncanny would always be that in which one does not know where one is, as it were. The better orientated in his environment a person is, the less readily will he get the impression of something uncanny in regard to the objects and events in it.

It is not difficult to see that this definition is incomplete, and we will therefore try to proceed beyond the equation of *unheimlich* with unfamiliar. We will first turn to other languages. But foreign dictionaries tell us nothing new, perhaps only because we speak a different language. Indeed, we get the impression that many languages are without a word for this particular variety of what is fearful.

[1] [Throughout this paper ' uncanny ' is used as the English translation of ' *unheimlich* ', literally ' unhomely '.—Trans.]

I wish to express my indebtedness to Dr. Th. Reik for the following excerpts :

LATIN : (K. E. Georges, *Deutschlateinisches Wörterbuch*, 1898). Ein *unheimlicher* Ort [an uncanny place] —locus suspectus ; in *unheimlicher* Nachtzeit [in the dismal night hours]—intempesta nocte.

GREEK : (Rost's and Schenkl's Lexikons). ξένος— strange, foreign.

ENGLISH : (from dictionaries by Lucas, Bellow, Flügel, Muret - Sanders). Uncomfortable, uneasy, gloomy, dismal, uncanny, ghastly ; (of a house) haunted ; (of a man) a repulsive fellow.

FRENCH : (Sachs - Villatte). Inquiétant, sinistre, lugubre, mal à son aise.

SPANISH : (Tollhausen, 1889). Sospechoso, de mal agüero, lugubre, siniestro.

The Italian and the Portuguese seem to content themselves with words which we should describe as circumlocutions. In Arabic and Hebrew ' uncanny ' means the same as ' daemonic ', ' gruesome '.

Let us therefore return to the German language. In Daniel Sanders' *Wörterbuch der deutschen Sprache* (1860), the following remarks[1] [abstracted in translation] are found upon the word *heimlich* ; I have laid stress on certain passages by italicizing them.

Heimlich, adj. : I. Also *heimelich, heimelig*, belonging to the house, not strange, familiar, tame, intimate, comfortable, homely, etc.

(a) (Obsolete) belonging to the house or the family, or regarded as so belonging (cf. Latin *familiaris*) : *Die Heimlichen*, the members of the household ; *Der heimliche Rat* [him to whom secrets are revealed] Gen. xli. 45 ; 2 Sam. xxiii. 23 ; now more usually *Geheimer Rat* [Privy Councillor], cf. *Heimlicher*.

(b) Of animals : tame, companionable to man. As opposed

---

[1] Vol. i. p. 729. Heimlich, a. (-keit, f. -en) : 1. auch Heimelich, heimelig, zum Hause gehörig, nicht fremd, vertraut, zahm, traut und traulich, anheimelnd etc. (a) (veralt.) zum Haus, zur Familie gehörig, oder : wie dazu gehörig betrachtet, vgl. lat. familiaris, vertraut : Die Heimlichen, die Hausgenossen ; Der heimliche Rat. 1. Mos. 41, 45 ; 2. Sam. 23, 23. 1 Chr. 12, 25. Weish. 8, 4., wofür jetzt : Geheimer (s. d 1.) Rat üblich ist, s. Heimlicher—(b) von Tieren zahm, sich den Menschen traulich anschließend. Ggstz. wild, z. B. Tier, die weder wild

to wild, *e.g.* ' Wild animals . . . that are trained to be *heimlich*
and accustomed to men '. ' If these young creatures are
brought up from early days among men they become quite
heimlich, friendly ', etc.

(*c*) Friendly, intimate, homelike ; the enjoyment of quiet
content, etc., arousing a sense of peaceful pleasure and
security as in one within the four walls of his house.
' Is it still *heimlich* to you in your country where strangers
are felling your woods ? ' ' She did not feel all too *heimlich*
with him.' ' To destroy the *Heimlichkeit* of the home.'
' I could not readily find another spot so intimate and *heimlich*
as this.' ' In quiet *Heimlichkeit*, surrounded by close walls.'
' A careful housewife, who knows how to make a pleasing
Heimlichkeit (*Häuslichkeit*) [1] out of the smallest means.' ' The
protestant rulers do not feel . . . *heimlich* among their
catholic subjects.' ' When it grows *heimlich* and still, and the
evening quiet alone watches over your cell.' ' Quiet, lovely
and *heimlich*, no place more fitted for her rest.' ' The in and
outflowing waves of the current, dreamy and *heimlich* as a
cradle-song.' Cf. in especial *Unheimlich*. Among Swabian

---

noch heimlich sind, etc. Eppendorf. 88 ; Wilde Thier . . . so man sie
h. und gewohnsam um die Leute aufzeucht. 92. So diese Thierle von
Jugend bei den Menschen erzogen, werden sie ganz h., freundlich etc.,
Stumpf 608a etc. — So noch : So h. ist's (das Lamm) und frißt aus
meiner Hand. Hölty ; Ein schöner, heimelicher (s. *c*) Vogel bleibt der
Storch immerhin. Linck, Schl. 146. s. Häuslich. 1 etc.—(*c*) traut,
traulich anheimelnd ; das Wohlgefühl stiller Befriedigung etc.,
behaglicher Ruhe u. sichern Schutzes, wie das umschlossne wohnliche
Haus erregend (vgl. Geheuer) : Ist dir's h. noch im Lande, wo die
Fremden deine Wälder roden ? Alexis H. 1, 1, 289 ; Es war ihr nicht
allzu h. bei ihm. Brentano Wehm. 92 ; Auf einem hohen h—en
Schattenpfade . . ., längs dem rieselnden rauschenden und plätschern-
den Waldbach. Forster B. 1, 417. Die H—keit der Heimath zerstören.
Gervinus Lit. 5, 375. So vertraulich und heimlich habe ich nicht
leicht ein Plätzchen gefunden. G. 14, 14 ; Wir dachten es uns so
bequem, so artig, so gemütlich und h. 15, 9 ; In stiller H—keit, umzielt
von engen Schranken. Haller : Einer sorglichen Hausfrau, die mit
dem Wenigsten eine vergnügliche H—keit (Häuslichkeit) zu schaffen
versteht. Hartmann Unst. 1, 188 ; Desto h—er kam ihm jetzt der
ihm erst kurz noch so fremde Mann vor. Kerner 540 ; Die protestan-
tischen Besitzer fühlen sich . . . nicht h. unter ihren katholischen
Unterthanen. Kohl. Irl. 1, 172 ; Wenns h. wird und leise / die Abend-
stille nur an deiner Zelle lauscht. Tiedge 2, 39 ; Still und lieb und h.,
als sie sich / zum Ruhen einen Platz nur wünschen möchten. W. 11,
144 ; Es war ihm garnicht h. dabei 27. 170, etc.—Auch : Der Platz
war so still, so einsam, so schatten-h. Scherr Pilg. 1, 170 ; Die ab- und
zuströmenden Fluthwellen, träumend und wiegenlied-h. Körner, Sch.
3, 320, etc.—Vgl. namentl. Un-h.—Namentl. bei schwäb., schwzr.

---

[1] [From *Haus* = house ; *Häuslichkeit* = domestic life.—Trans.]

and Swiss authors in especial, often as a trisyllable : ' How *heimelich* it seemed again of an evening, back at home '. ' The warm room and the *heimelig* afternoon.' ' Little by little they grew at ease and *heimelig* among themselves.' ' That which comes from afar . . . assuredly does not live quite *heimelig* (*heimatlich* [at home], *freundnachbarlich* [in a neighbourly way]) among the people.' ' The sentinel's horn sounds so *heimelig* from the tower, and his voice invites so hospitably.' *This form of the word ought to become general in order to protect the word from becoming obsolete in its good sense through an easy confusion with II.* [see below]. ' " *The Zecks* [a family name] *are all ' heimlich '.*" " ' *Heimlich* ' *? What do you understand by ' heimlich '?*" " *Well,* . . . *they are like a buried spring or a dried-up pond. One cannot walk over it without always having the feeling that water might come up there again.*" " *Oh, we call it ' unheimlich '; you call it ' heimlich '. Well, what makes you think that there is something secret and untrustworthy about this family?*" ' Gutzkow.

II. Concealed, kept from sight, so that others do not get to know about it, withheld from others, cf. *geheim* [secret] ;

Schriftst. oft dreisilbig : Wie ' heimelich ' war es dann Ivo Abends wieder, als er zu Hause lag. Auerbach, D. 1, 249 ; In dem Haus ist mir's so heimelig gewesen. 4. 307 ; Die warme Stube, der heimelige Nachmittag. Gotthelf, Sch. 127, 148 ; Das ist das wahre Heimelig, wenn der Mensch so von Herzen fühlt, wie wenig er ist, wie groß der Herr ist. 147 ; Wurde man nach und nach recht gemütlich und heimelig mit einander. U. 1, 297 ; Die trauliche Heimeligkeit. 380, 2, 86 ; Heimelicher wird es mir wohl nirgends werden als hier. 327 ; Pestalozzi 4, 240 ; Was von ferne herkommt . . . lebt gw. nicht ganz heimelig (heimatlich, freundnachbarlich) mit den Leuten. 325 ; Die Hütte, wo / er sonst so heimelig, so froh / . . . im Kreis der Seinen oft gesessen. Reithard 20 ; Da klingt das Horn des Wächters so heimelig vom Thurm / da ladet seine Stimme so gastlich. 49 ; Es schläft sich da so lind und warm/so wunderheim'lig ein. 23, etc.—Diese Weise verdiente allgemein zu werden, um das gute Wort vor dem Veralten wegen nahe liegender Verwechslung mit 2 zu bewahren. vgl. : ' Die Zecks sind alle h. (2) ' H . . . ? Was verstehen sie unter h . . .?—' Nun . . . es kommt mir mit ihnen vor, wie mit einem zugegrabenen Brunnen oder einem ausgetrockneten Teich. Man kann nicht darüber gehen, ohne daß es Einem immer ist, als könnte da wieder einmal Wasser zum Vorschein kommen.' Wir nennen das un—h. , Sie nennen's h. Worin finden Sie denn, daß diese Familie etwas Verstecktes und Unzuverlässiges hat ? etc. Gutzkow R. 2, 61*).—(*d*) (s. *c*) namentl. schles. : fröhlich, heiter, auch vom Wetter, s. Adelung und Weinhold.—2. versteckt, verborgen gehalten, so daß man Andre nicht davon oder darum wissen lassen, es ihnen verbergen will, vgl. Geheim (2), von welchem erst nhd. Ew. es doch zumal in der älteren Sprache, z. B. in der Bibel, wie Hiob 11, 6 ; 15, 8, Weish. 2, 22 ; 1. Kor.

* Sperrdruck (auch im folgenden) vom Referenten.

so also *Heimlichkeit* for *Geheimnis* [secret]. To do something *heimlich, i.e.* behind someone's back ; to steal away *heimlich* ; *heimlich* meetings and appointments ; to look on with *heimlich* pleasure at someone's discomfiture ; to sigh or weep *heimlich* ; to behave *heimlich*, as though there was something to conceal ; *heimlich* love, love-affair, sin ; *heimlich* places (which good manners oblige us to conceal). 1 Sam. v. 6 ; ' The *heimlich* chamber ' [privy]. 2 Kings x. 27 etc. ; ' To throw into pits or *Heimlichkeit* '. Led the steeds *heimlich* before Laomedon.' ' As secretive, *heimlich*, deceitful and malicious towards cruel masters . . . as frank, open, sympathetic and helpful towards a friend in misfortune.' ' The *heimlich* art ' (magic). ' Where public ventilation has to stop, there *heimlich* machinations begin.' ' Freedom is the whispered watchword of *heimlich* conspirators and the loud battle-cry of professed revolution- aries.' ' A holy, *heimlich* effect.' ' I have roots that are most *heimlich*, I am grown in the deep earth.' ' My *heimlich* pranks.' (Cf. *Heimtücke* [mischief]).   To discover, disclose, betray

---

2, 7 etc., und so auch H—keit statt Geheimnis.   Math. 13, 35 etc., nicht immer genau geschieden wird : H. (hinter Jemandes Rücken) etwas thun, treiben ; Sich h. davon schleichen ; H—e Zusammen- künfte, Verabredungen ; Mit h—er Schadenfreude zusehen ; H. seufzen, weinen ; H. thun, als ob man etwas zu verbergen hätte ; H—e Liebe, Liebschaft, Sünde ; H—e Orte (die der Wohlstand zu verhüllen gebietet), 1. Sam. 5, 6 ; Das h—e Gemach (Abtritt) 2. Kön. 10, 27 ; W. 5, 256 etc., auch : Der h—e Stuhl. Zinkgräf 1, 249 ; In Graben, in H—keiten werfen. 3, 75 ; Rollenhagen Fr. 83 etc.—Führte h. vor Laomedon / die Stuten vor. B. 161 b etc.—Ebenso versteckt, h., hinterlistig und boshaft gegen grausame Herren . . . wie offen, frei, theilnehmend und dienstwillig gegen den leidenden Freund.   Burmeister g B 2, 157 ; Du sollst mein h. Heiligstes noch wissen.   Chamisso 4, 56 ; Die h—e Kunst (der Zauberei). 3, 224 ; Wo die öffentliche Ventilation aufhören muß, fängt die h—e Machination an.   Forster, Br. 2, 135 ; Freiheit ist die leise Parole h. Verschworener, das laute Feldgeschrei der öffentlich Umwälzenden. G. 4, 222 ; Ein heilig, h. Wirken. 15 ; Ich habe Wurzeln / die sind gar h., / im tiefen Boden / bin ich gegründet. 2, 109 ; Meine h—e Tücke (vgl. Heimtücke). 30, 344 ; Empfängt er es nicht offenbar und gewissenhaft, so mag er es h. und gewissenlos ergreifen. 39, 22 ; Ließ h. und geheimnisvoll achromatische Fernröhre zusam- mensetzen. 375 ; Von nun an, will ich, sei nichts H—es mehr unter uns. Sch. 369 b.—Jemandes H—keiten entdecken, offenbaren, verra- then ; H—keiten hinter meinem Rücken zu brauen.   Alexis. H. 2, 3, 168 ; Zu meiner Zeit / befliß man sich der H—keit. Hagedorn 3, 92 ; Die H—keit und das Gepuschele unter der Hand.   Immermann, M. 3, 289 ; Der H—keit (des verborgnen Golds) unmächtigen Bann / kann nur die Hand der Einsicht lösen. Novalis. 1, 69 ; / Sag an, wo du sie verbirgst . . . in welches Ortes verschwiegener H. Schr. 495 b ; Ihr Bienen, die ihr knetet / der H—keiten Schloß (Wachs zum Siegeln). Tieck, Cymb. 3, 2 ; Erfahren in seltnen H—keiten (Zauberkünsten). Schlegel Sh. 6, 102 etc. vgl. Geheimnis L. 10 : 291 ff.

someone's *Heimlichkeiten*; 'to concoct *Heimlichkeiten* behind my back '. Cf. *Geheimnis*.

Compounds and especially also the opposite follow meaning I. (above): *Unheimlich*, uneasy, eerie, blood-curdling; 'Seeming almost *unheimlich* and ghostly to him '. ' I had already long since felt an *unheimlich*, even gruesome feeling.' ' Feels an *unheimlich* horror.' ' *Unheimlich* and motionless like a stone-image.' ' The *unheimlich* mist called hill-fog.' ' These pale youths are *unheimlich* and are brewing heaven knows what mischief.' ' " *Unheimlich* " is the name for everything that ought to have remained . . . hidden and secret and has become visible ', Schelling. ' To veil the divine, to surround it with a certain *Unheimlichkeit*.'—*Unheimlich* is not often used as opposite to meaning II. (above).

What interests us most in this long extract is to find that among its different shades of meaning the word *heimlich* exhibits one which is identical with its opposite, *unheimlich*. What is *heimlich* thus comes to be *unheimlich*. (Cf. the quotation from Gutzkow : ' We call it *unheimlich*; you call it *heimlich* '.) In general we are reminded that the word *heimlich* is not unambiguous, but belongs to two sets of ideas, which without being contradictory are yet very different : on the one hand, it means that which is familiar and congenial, and on the other, that which is concealed and kept out of sight. The word *unheimlich* is only used customarily, we are told, as the contrary of the first signification, and not of the second. Sanders tells us nothing concerning a possible genetic connection between these two sets of meanings. On the other hand, we notice that Schelling says something which throws quite a new light on the

---

Zsstzg. s. 1 *c*, so auch nam. der Ggstz. : Un- : unbehagliches, banges Grauen erregend: Der schier ihm un-h., gespenstisch erschien. Chamisso 3, 238 ; Der Nacht un-h. bange Stunden. 4, 148 ; Mir war schon lang' un-h., ja graulich zu Mute. 242 ; Nun fängts mir an, un-h. zu werden. Gutzkow R. 2, 82 ; Empfindet ein u—es Grauen. Verm. 1, 51 ; Un-h. und starr wie ein Steinbild. Reis, 1, 10 ; Den u—en Nebel, Haarrauch geheißen. Immermann M., 3, 299 ; Diese blassen Jungen sind un-h. und brauen Gott weiß was Schlimmes. Laube, Band 1, 119 ; Un-h. nennt man Alles, was im Geheimnis, im Verborgnen . . . bleiben sollte und hervorgetreten ist. Schelling, 2, 2, 649 etc.— Das Göttliche zu verhüllen, mit einer gewissen U—keit zu umgeben 658, etc.—Unüblich als Ggstz. von (2), wie es Campe ohne Beleg anführt.

concept of the ' uncanny ', one which we had certainly
not awaited.   According to him everything is uncanny
that ought to have remained hidden and secret, and
yet comes to light.

Some of the doubts that have thus arisen are
removed if we consult Grimm's dictionary.[1]

We read :

Heimlich ; adj. and adv. *vernaculus, occultus* ; MHG.
heimelîch, heîmlich.

P. 874. In a slightly different sense : ' I feel *heimlich*,
well, free from fear. . . .'

(*b*) *Heimlich*, also in the sense of a place free from ghostly
influences . . . familiar, friendly, intimate.

4. *From the idea of ' homelike ', ' belonging to the house ',
the further idea is developed of something withdrawn from the
eyes of others, something concealed, secret, and this idea is ex-
panded in many ways.* . . .

P. 876. ' On the left bank of the lake there lies a meadow
heimlich in the wood.'   Schiller, *Tell.* . . . Poetic licence,
rarely so used in modern speech . . . In conjunction with a verb
expressing the act of concealing : ' In the secret of his tabernacle
he shall hide me (*heimlich*).' Ps. xxvii. 5 . . . *Heimlich* places
in the human body, pudenda . . . ' the men that died not
were smitten ' (on their *heimlich* parts). I Samuel v. 12. . . .

(*c*) Officials who give important advice which has to be

---

[1] Grimm, Jakob und Wilhelm, *Deutsches Wörterbuch*, Leipzig, 1877,
IV./2, p. 874 *et seq.*
  ' Heimlich ; adj. und adv. vernaculus, occultus ; mhd. heimelîch,
heîmlich.
  S. 874 : In etwas anderem sinne : es ist mir heimlich, wohl, frei
von furcht. . . .
  (*b*) heimlich ist auch der von gespensterhaften freie ort . . .
  S. 875 : (ß) vertraut ; freundlich, zutraulich.
  4. aus dem heimatlichen, häuslichen entwickelt sich weiter
der begriff des fremden augen entzogenen, verborgenen,
geheimen, eben auch in mehrfacher beziehung ausgebildet . . .
  S. 876 :   ' links am see
            liegt eine matte heimlich im gehölz '.
                                  Schiller, Tell I., 4.
. . . frei und für den modernen Sprachgebrauch ungewöhnlich . . .
heimlich ist zu einem verbum des verbergens gestellt : er verbirgt mich
heimlich in seinem gezelt. ps. 27, 5. (. . . heimliche orte am mensch-
lichen Körper, pudenda . . . welche leute nicht stürben, die wurden
geschlagen an heimlichen örten. I Samuel 5, 12 . . .
  (*c*) Beamtete, die wichtige und geheim zu haltende ratschläge in

kept secret in matters of state are called *heimlich* councillors ;
the adjective, according to modern usage, having been replaced
by *geheim* [secret]. . . . ' Pharaoh called Joseph's name " him
to whom secrets are revealed " ' (*heimlich* councillor).   Gen.
xli. 45.

P. 878. 6. *Heimlich*, as used of knowledge, mystic,
allegorical : a *heimlich* meaning, *mysticus, divinus, occultus,
figuratus.*

P. 878. *Heimlich* in a different sense, as withdrawn from
knowledge, unconscious : . . . *Heimlich* also has the meaning
of that which is obscure, inaccessible to knowledge. . . . ' Do
you not see ? They do not trust me ; they fear the *heimlich*
face of the Duke of Friedland.' *Wallensteins Lager*, Act 2.

9. *The notion of something hidden and dangerous, which is
expressed in the last paragraph, is still further developed, so
that ' heimlich ' comes to have the meaning usually ascribed to
' unheimlich '.* Thus : ' At times I feel like a man who walks
in the night and believes in ghosts ; every corner is *heimlich*
and full of terrors for him '. Klinger.

Thus *heimlich* is a word the meaning of which
develops towards an ambivalence, until it finally
coincides with its opposite, *unheimlich. Unheimlich*
is in some way or other a sub-species of *heimlich.*
Let us retain this discovery, which we do not yet
properly understand, alongside of Schelling's definition
of the ' uncanny '. Then if we examine individual
instances of uncanniness, these indications will become
comprehensible to us.

---

staatssachen ertheilen, heißen heimliche räthe, das adjektiv nach
heutigem sprachgebrauch durch geheim (s.d.) ersetzt : . . . (Pharao)
nennet ihn (Joseph) den heimlichen rath. 1. Mos. 41, 45 ;
  S. 878. 6. Heimlich für die erkenntnis, mystisch, allegorisch :
heimliche bedeutung, mysticus, divinus, occultus, figuratus.
  S. 878. Anders ist heimlich im folgenden, der erkenntnis ent-
zogen, unbewuszt : . . .
  Dann aber ist heimlich auch verschlossen, undurchdringlich in
bezug auf erforschung : . . .
        ' Merkst du wohl ? sie trauen mir nicht,
        fürchten des Friedländers heimlich gesicht.'
                          Wallensteins lager, 2. aufz.
  9. die bedeutung des versteckten, gefährlichen, die in
der vorigen nummer hervortritt, entwickelt sich noch weiter,
so daß heimlich den sinn empfängt, den sonst unheimlich
(gebildet nach heimlich, 3*b* sp. 874) hat : ' mir ist zu zeiten wie dem
menschen der in nacht wandelt und an gespenster glaubt, jeder winkel
ist ihm heimlich und schauerhaft '. Klinger, theater, 3, 298.

II

In proceeding to review those things, persons, impressions, events and situations which are able to arouse in us a feeling of the uncanny in a very forcible and definite form, the first requirement is obviously to select a suitable example to start upon. Jentsch has taken as a very good instance ' doubts whether an apparently animate being is really alive ; or conversely, whether a lifeless object might not be in fact animate ' ; and he refers in this connection to the impression made by wax-work figures, artificial dolls and automatons. He adds to this class the uncanny effect of epileptic seizures and the manifestations of insanity, because these excite in the spectator the feeling that automatic, mechanical processes are at work, concealed beneath the ordinary appearance of animation. Without entirely accepting the author's view, we will take it as a starting-point for our investigation because it leads us on to consider a writer who has succeeded better than anyone else in producing uncanny effects.

Jentsch says : ' In telling a story, one of the most successful devices for easily creating uncanny effects is to leave the reader in uncertainty whether a particular figure in the story is a human being or an automaton ; and to do it in such a way that his attention is not directly focussed upon his uncertainty, so that he may not be urged to go into the matter and clear it up immediately, since that, as we have said, would quickly dissipate the peculiar emotional effect of the thing. Hoffmann has repeatedly employed this psychological artifice with success in his fantastic narratives.'

This observation, undoubtedly a correct one, refers primarily to the story of ' The Sand-Man ' in Hoffmann's *Nachtstücken*,[1] which contains the original of Olympia,

---

[1] Hoffmann's *Sämtliche Werke*, Grisebach Edition, vol. iii.

the doll in the first act of Offenbach's opera, *Tales of Hoffmann*. But I cannot think—and I hope that most readers of the story will agree with me—that the theme of the doll, Olympia, who is to all appearances a living being, is by any means the only element to be held responsible for the quite unparalleled atmosphere of uncanniness which the story evokes ; or, indeed, that it is the most important among them. Nor is this effect of the story heightened by the fact that the author himself treats the episode of Olympia with a faint touch of satire and uses it to make fun of the young man's idealization of his mistress. The main theme of the story is, on the contrary, something different, something which gives its name to the story, and which is always re-introduced at the critical moment : it is the theme of the ' Sand-Man ' who tears out children's eyes.

This fantastic tale begins with the childhood-recollections of the student Nathaniel : in spite of his present happiness, he cannot banish the memories associated with the mysterious and terrifying death of the father he loved. On certain evenings his mother used to send the children to bed early, warning them that ' the Sand-Man was coming ' ; and sure enough Nathaniel would not fail to hear the heavy tread of a visitor with whom his father would then be occupied that evening. When questioned about the Sand-Man, his mother, it is true, denied that such a person existed except as a form of speech ; but his nurse could give him more definite information : ' He is a wicked man who comes when children won't go to bed, and throws handfuls of sand in their eyes so that they jump out of their heads all bleeding. Then he puts the eyes in a sack and carries them off to the moon to feed his children. They sit up there in their nest, and their beaks are hooked like owls' beaks, and they use them to peck up naughty boys' and girls' eyes with.'

Although little Nathaniel was sensible and old enough not to believe in such gruesome attributes to the figure of the Sand-Man, yet the dread of him became fixed in his breast. He determined to find out what the Sand-Man looked like ; and one evening, when the Sand-Man was again expected, he hid himself in his father's study. He recognized the visitor as the lawyer Coppelius, a repulsive person of whom the children were frightened when he occasionally came to a meal ; and he now identified this Coppelius with the dreaded Sand-Man. Concerning the rest of the scene, Hoffmann already leaves us in doubt whether we are witnessing the first delirium of the panic-stricken boy, or a succession of events which are to be regarded in the story as being real. His father and the guest begin to busy themselves at a hearth with glowing flames. The little eavesdropper hears Coppelius call out, ' Here with your eyes ! ' and betrays himself by screaming aloud ; Coppelius seizes him and is about to drop grains of red-hot coal out of the fire into his eyes, so as to cast them out on to the hearth. His father begs him off and saves his eyes. After this the boy falls into a deep swoon ; and a long illness followed upon his experience. Those who lean towards a rationalistic interpretation of the Sand-Man will not fail to recognize in the child's phantasy the continued influence of his nurse's story. The grains of sand that are to be thrown into the child's eyes turn into red-hot grains of coal out of the flames ; and in both cases they are meant to make his eyes jump out. In the course of another visit of the Sand-Man's, a year later, his father was killed in his study by an explosion. The lawyer Coppelius vanished from the place without leaving a trace behind.

Nathaniel, now a student, believes that he has recognized this childhood's phantom of horror in an itinerant optician, an Italian called Giuseppe Coppola. This man had offered him barometers for sale in his university town, and when Nathaniel refused had added : ' Eh, not barometers, not barometers—also got fine eyes, beautiful eyes '. The student's terror was allayed on finding that the proffered eyes were only harmless spectacles, and he bought a pocket-telescope from Coppola. With its aid he looks across into Professor Spalanzani's house opposite and there spies Spalanzani's beautiful, but strangely silent and motionless daughter, Olympia. He soon falls in love with her so violently that he quite forgets his clever and sensible betrothed on her account. But Olympia was an automaton whose works Spalanzani had made, and whose eyes Coppola, the Sand-Man, had put in. The student surprises the two men quarrelling over their handiwork. The optician carries off the wooden, eyeless doll ; and the mechanician, Spalanzani, takes up Olympia's bleeding eye-balls from the ground and throws them at Nathaniel's breast, saying that Coppola had stolen them from him (Nathaniel). Nathaniel succumbs to a fresh attack of madness, and in his delirium his recollection of his father's death is mingled with this new experience. He cries, ' Faster—faster—faster—rings of fire—rings of fire ! Whirl about, rings of fire—round and round ! Wooden doll, ho ! lovely wooden doll, whirl about——', then falls upon the professor, Olympia's so - called father, and tries to strangle him.

Rallying from a long and serious illness, Nathaniel seemed at last to have recovered. He was going to marry his betrothed with whom he was reconciled. One day he was walking through the town and market-place, where the high tower of the Town-Hall threw its huge shadow. On the girl's suggestion they mounted the tower, leaving her brother, who was walking with them, down below. Up there, Clara's attention is drawn to a curious object coming along the street. Nathaniel looks at this thing through Coppola's spy-glass, which he finds in his pocket, and falls into a new fit of madness. Shouting out, ' Whirl about, my wooden doll ! ' he tries to fling the girl into the depths below. Her brother, brought to her side by her cries, rescues her and hastens down to safety with her. Up

above, the raving man rushes round, shrieking ' Rings
of fire, whirl about ! '—words whose origin we know.
Among the people who begin to gather below there
comes forward the figure of the lawyer Coppelius,
suddenly returned. We may suppose it was his
approach, seen through the telescope, that threw
Nathaniel into his madness. People want to go up
and overpower the madman, but Coppelius [1] laughs
and says, ' Wait a bit ; he'll come down of himself '.
Nathaniel suddenly stands still, catches sight of
Coppelius, and with a wild shriek ' Yes ! " Fine eyes—
beautiful eyes " ', flings himself down over the parapet.
No sooner does he lie on the paving-stones with a
shattered skull than the Sand-Man vanishes in the
throng.

This short summary leaves, I think, no doubt that
the feeling of something uncanny is directly attached
to the figure of the Sand-Man, that is, to the idea of
being robbed of one's eyes ; and that Jentsch's point
of an intellectual uncertainty has nothing to do with
this effect. Uncertainty whether an object is living
or inanimate, which we must admit in regard to the
doll Olympia, is quite irrelevant in connection with
this other, more striking instance of uncanniness. It
is true that the writer creates a kind of uncertainty in
us in the beginning by not letting us know, no doubt
purposely, whether he is taking us into the real world
or into a purely fantastic one of his own creation. He
has admittedly the right to do either ; and if he chooses
to stage his action in a world peopled with spirits,
demons and ghosts, as Shakespeare does in *Hamlet,* in
Macbeth and, in a different sense, in *The Tempest* and
A Midsummer - Night's Dream, we must bow to his
decision and treat his setting as though it were real
for as long as we put ourselves into his hands. But this
uncertainty disappears in the course of Hoffmann's

---

[1] Frau Dr. Rank has pointed out the association of the name with
' Coppella ' = crucible, connecting it with the chemical operations that
caused the father's death ; and also with ' coppo ' = eye-socket.

story, and we perceive that he means to make us, too, look through the fell Coppola's glasses—perhaps, indeed, that he himself once gazed through such an instrument. For the conclusion of the story makes it quite clear that Coppola the optician really is the lawyer Coppelius and thus also the Sand-Man.

There is no question, therefore, of any ' intellectual uncertainty ' ; we know now that we are not supposed to be looking on at the products of a madman's imagination behind which we, with the superiority of rational minds, are able to detect the sober truth ; and yet this knowledge does not lessen the impression of uncanniness in the least degree. The theory of ' intellectual uncertainty ' is thus incapable of explaining that impression.

We know from psycho-analytic experience, however, that this fear of damaging or losing one's eyes is a terrible fear of childhood. Many adults still retain their apprehensiveness in this respect, and no bodily injury is so much dreaded by them as an injury to the eye. We are accustomed to say, too, that we will treasure a thing as the apple of our eye. A study of dreams, phantasies and myths has taught us that a morbid anxiety connected with the eyes and with going blind is often enough a substitute for the dread of castration. In blinding himself, Oedipus, that mythical law-breaker, was simply carrying out a mitigated form of the punishment of castration—the only punishment that according to the *lex talionis* was fitted for him. We may try to reject the derivation of fears about the eye from the fear of castration on rationalistic grounds, and say that it is very natural that so precious an organ as the eye should be guarded by a proportionate dread ; indeed, we might go further and say that the fear of castration itself contains no other significance and no deeper secret than a justifiable dread of this kind. But this view does not account adequately for the substitutive relation between the eye and the male member which is seen to exist in

dreams and myths and phantasies; nor can it dispel
the impression one gains that it is the threat of being
castrated in especial which excites a peculiarly violent
and obscure emotion, and that this emotion is what
first gives the idea of losing other organs its intense
colouring. All further doubts are removed when we
get the details of their ' castration-complex ' from the
analyses of neurotic patients, and realize its immense
importance in their mental life.

Moreover, I would not recommend any opponent
of the psycho-analytic view to select precisely the
story of the Sand-Man upon which to build his case
that morbid anxiety about the eyes has nothing to do
with the castration-complex. For why does Hoffmann
bring the anxiety about eyes into such intimate
connection with the father's death? And why does
the Sand-Man appear each time in order to interfere
with love? He divides the unfortunate Nathaniel
from his betrothed and from her brother, his best
friend; he destroys his second object of love, Olympia,
the lovely doll; and he drives him into suicide at the
moment when he has won back his Clara and is about
to be happily united to her. Things like these and
many more seem arbitrary and meaningless in the
story so long as we deny all connection between fears
about the eye and castration; but they become
intelligible as soon as we replace the Sand-Man by the
dreaded father at whose hands castration is awaited.[1]

---

[1] In fact, Hoffmann's imaginative treatment of his material has
not played such havoc with its elements that we cannot reconstruct
their original arrangement. In the story from Nathaniel's childhood,
the figures of his father and Coppelius represent the two opposites
into which the father-imago is split by the ambivalence of the child's
feeling; whereas the one threatens to blind him, that is, to castrate
him, the other, the loving father, intercedes for his sight. That part
of the complex which is most strongly repressed, the death-wish against
the father, finds expression in the death of the good father, and
Coppelius is made answerable for it. Later, in his student days,
Professor Spalanzani and Coppola the optician reproduce this double
representation of the father-imago, the Professor is a member of the
father-series, Coppola openly identified with the lawyer Coppelius.
Just as before they used to work together over the fire, so now they
have jointly created the doll Olympia; the Professor is even called

We shall venture, therefore, to refer the uncanny effect of the Sand-Man to the child's dread in relation to its castration-complex. But having gained the idea that we can take this infantile factor to account for feelings of uncanniness, we are drawn to examine whether we can apply it to other instances of uncanny things. We find in the story of the Sand-Man the other theme upon which Jentsch lays stress, of a doll that appears to be alive. Jentsch believes that a particularly favourable condition for awakening uncanny sensations is created when there is intellectual uncertainty whether an object is alive or not, and when an inanimate object becomes too much like an animate one. Now, dolls happen to be rather closely connected with infantile life. We remember that in their early

---

the father of Olympia. This second occurrence of work in common shows that the optician and the mechanician are also components of the father-imago, that is, both are Nathaniel's father as well as Olympia's. I ought to have added that in the terrifying scene in childhood, Coppelius, after sparing Nathaniel's eyes, had screwed off his arms and legs as an experiment ; that is, he had experimented on him as a mechanician would on a doll. This singular feature, which seems quite out of perspective in the picture of the Sand-Man, introduces a new castration-equivalent ; but it also emphasizes the identity of Coppelius and his later counterpart, Spalanzani the mechanician, and helps us to understand who Olympia is. She, the automatic doll, can be nothing else than a personification of Nathaniel's feminine attitude towards his father in his infancy. The father of both, Spalanzani and Coppola, are, as we know, new editions, reincarnations of Nathaniel's ' two ' fathers. Now Spalanzani's otherwise incomprehensible statement that the optician has stolen Nathaniel's eyes so as to set them in the doll becomes significant and supplies fresh evidence for the identity of Olympia and Nathaniel. Olympia is, as it were, a dissociated complex of Nathaniel's which confronts him as a person, and Nathaniel's enslavement to this complex is expressed in his senseless obsessive love for Olympia. We may with justice call such love narcissistic, and can understand why he who has fallen victim to it should relinquish his real, external object of love. The psychological truth of the situation in which the young man, fixated upon his father by his castration-complex, is incapable of loving a woman, is amply proved by numerous analyses of patients whose story, though less fantastic, is hardly less tragic than that of the student Nathaniel.

Hoffmann was the child of an unhappy marriage. When he was three years old, his father left his small family, never to be united to them again. According to Grisebach, in his biographical introduction to Hoffmann's works, the writer's relation to his father was always a most sensitive subject with him.

games children do not distinguish at all sharply between living and lifeless objects, and that they are especially fond of treating their dolls like live people. In fact, I have occasionally heard a woman patient declare that even at the age of eight she had still been convinced that her dolls would be certain to come to life if she were to look at them in a particular way, with as concentrated a gaze as possible. So that here, too, it is not difficult to discover a factor from childhood ; but curiously enough, while the Sand-Man story deals with the excitation of an early childhood fear, the idea of a ' living doll ' excites no fear at all ; the child had no fear of its doll coming to life, it may even have desired it. The source of the feeling of an uncanny thing would not, therefore, be an infantile fear in this case, but rather an infantile wish or even only an infantile belief. There seems to be a contradiction here ; but perhaps it is only a complication, which may be helpful to us later on.

Hoffmann is in literature the unrivalled master of conjuring up the uncanny. His *Elixire des Teufels* [The Devil's Elixir] contains a mass of themes to which one is tempted to ascribe the uncanny effect of the narrative ; but it is too obscure and intricate a story to venture to summarize. Towards the end of the book the reader is told the facts, hitherto concealed from him, from which the action springs ; with the result, not that he is at last enlightened, but that he falls into a state of complete bewilderment. The author has piled up too much of a kind ; one's comprehension of the whole suffers as a result, though not the impression it makes. We must content ourselves with selecting those themes of uncanniness which are most prominent, and seeing whether we can fairly trace them also back to infantile sources. These themes are all concerned with the idea of a ' double ' in every shape and degree, with persons, therefore, who are to be considered identical by reason of looking alike ; Hoffmann accentuates this relation by transferring mental processes from the one person to the other—what we should call telepathy—so that the one possesses knowledge, feeling and experience in common with the other, identifies himself with another person, so that his self becomes confounded, or the foreign self is substituted for his own—in other words, by doubling, dividing and interchanging the self. And finally there is the constant recurrence of similar situations, a same face, or character-trait, or twist of fortune, or a same crime, or even a same name recurring throughout several consecutive generations.

The theme of the ' double ' has been very thoroughly treated by Otto Rank.[1] He has gone into the connections the ' double ' has with reflections in mirrors, with shadows, guardian spirits, with the belief in the soul and the fear of death ; but he also lets in a flood of light on the astonishing evolution of this idea. For the ' double ' was originally an insurance against destruction to the ego, an ' energetic denial of the power of death ', as Rank says ; and probably the ' immortal ' soul was the first ' double ' of the body. This invention of doubling as a preservation against extinction has its counterpart in the language of dreams, which is fond of representing castration by a doubling or multiplication of the genital symbol ; the same desire spurred on the ancient Egyptians to the art of making images of the dead in some lasting material. Such ideas, however, have sprung from the soil of unbounded self-love, from the primary narcissism which holds sway in the mind of the child as in that of primitive man ; and when this stage has been left behind the double takes on a different aspect. From having been an assurance of immortality, he becomes the ghastly harbinger of death.

The idea of the ' double ' does not necessarily disappear with the passing of the primary narcissism, for it can receive fresh meaning from the later stages of development of the ego. A special faculty is slowly

[1] ' Der Doppelgänger.'

formed there, able to oppose the rest of the ego, with the function of observing and criticizing the self and exercising a censorship within the mind, and this we become aware of as our ' conscience '. In the pathological case of delusions of being watched this mental institution becomes isolated, dissociated from the ego, and discernible to a physician's eye. The fact that a faculty of this kind exists, which is able to treat the rest of the ego like an object—the fact, that is, that man is capable of self-observation—renders it possible to invest the old idea of a ' double ' with a new meaning and to ascribe many things to it, above all, those things which seem to the new faculty of self-criticism to belong to the old surmounted narcissism of the earliest period of all.[1]

But it is not only this narcissism, offensive to the ego-criticizing faculty, which may be incorporated in the idea of a double. There are also all those unfulfilled but possible futures to which we still like to cling in phantasy, all those strivings of the ego which adverse external circumstances have crushed, and all our suppressed acts of volition which nourish in us the illusion of Free Will.[2]

But, after having thus considered the manifest motivation of the figure of a ' double ', we have to admit that none of it helps us to understand the extraordinarily strong feeling of something uncanny that pervades the conception ; and our knowledge of

[1] I cannot help thinking that when poets complain that two souls dwell within the human breast, and when popular psychologists talk of the splitting of the ego in an individual, they have some notion of this division (which relates to the sphere of ego-psychology) between the critical faculty and the rest of the ego, and not of the antithesis discovered by psycho-analysis between the ego and what is unconscious and repressed. It is true that the distinction is to some extent effaced by the circumstance that derivatives of what is repressed are foremost among the things reprehended by the ego-criticizing faculty.

[2] In Ewers' *Der Student von Prag*, which furnishes the starting-point of Rank's study on the ' double ', the hero has promised his beloved not to kill his antagonist in a duel. But on his way to the duelling-ground he meets his ' double ', who has already killed his rival.

pathological mental processes enables us to add that nothing in the content arrived at could account for that impulse towards self-protection which has caused the ego to project such a content outward as something foreign to itself. The quality of uncanniness can only come from the circumstance of the ' double ' being a creation dating back to a very early mental stage, long since left behind, and one, no doubt, in which it wore a more friendly aspect. The ' double' has become a vision of terror, just as after the fall of their religion the gods took on daemonic shapes.[1]

It is not difficult to judge, on the same lines as his theme of the ' double ', the other forms of disturbance in the ego made use of by Hoffmann. They are a harking-back to particular phases in the evolution of the self-regarding feeling, a regression to a time when the ego was not yet sharply differentiated from the external world and from other persons. I believe that these factors are partly responsible for the impression of the uncanny, although it is not easy to isolate and determine exactly their share of it.

That factor which consists in a recurrence of the same situations, things and events, will perhaps not appeal to everyone as a source of uncanny feeling. From what I have observed, this phenomenon does undoubtedly, subject to certain conditions and combined with certain circumstances, awaken an uncanny feeling, which recalls that sense of helplessness sometimes experienced in dreams. Once, as I was walking through the deserted streets of a provincial town in Italy which was strange to me, on a hot summer afternoon, I found myself in a quarter the character of which could not long remain in doubt. Nothing but painted women were to be seen at the windows of the small houses, and I hastened to leave the narrow street at the next turning. But after having wandered about for a while without being directed, I suddenly found myself back in the same street, where my

[1] Heine, *Die Götter im Exil.*

presence was now beginning to excite attention. I hurried away once more, but only to arrive yet a third time by devious paths in the same place. Now, however, a feeling overcame me which I can only describe as uncanny, and I was glad enough to abandon my exploratory walk and get straight back to the piazza I had left a short while before. Other situations having in common with my adventure an involuntary return to the same situation, but which differ radically from it in other respects, also result in the same feeling of helplessness and of something uncanny. As, for instance, when one is lost in a forest in high altitudes, caught, we will suppose, by the mountain mist, and when every endeavour to find the marked or familiar path ends again and again in a return to one and the same spot, recognizable by some particular landmark. Or when one wanders about in a dark, strange room, looking for the door or the electric switch, and collides for the hundredth time with the same piece of furniture —a situation which, indeed, has been made irresistibly comic by Mark Twain, through the wild extravagance of his narration.

Taking another class of things, it is easy to see that here, too, it is only this factor of involuntary repetition which surrounds with an uncanny atmosphere what would otherwise be innocent enough, and forces upon us the idea of something fateful and unescapable where otherwise we should have spoken of 'chance' only. For instance, we of course attach no importance to the event when we give up a coat and get a cloak-room ticket with the number, say, 62 ; or when we find that our cabin on board ship is numbered 62. But the impression is altered if two such events, each in itself indifferent, happen close together, if we come across the number 62 several times in a single day, or if we begin to notice that every-thing which has a number—addresses, hotel-rooms, compartments in railway-trains—always has the same one, or one which at least contains the same figures.

We do feel this to be ' uncanny ', and unless a man is
utterly hardened and proof against the lure of superstition he will be tempted to ascribe a secret meaning
to this obstinate recurrence of a number, taking it,
perhaps, as an indication of the span of life allotted to
him.   Or take the case that one is engaged at the time
in reading the works of Hering, the famous physiologist,
and then receives within the space of a few days two
letters from two different countries, each from a person
called Hering ; whereas one has never before had any
dealings with anyone of that name.   Not long ago an
ingenious scientist attempted to reduce coincidences
of this kind to certain laws, and so deprive them of
their uncanny effect.[1]   I will not venture to decide
whether he has succeeded or not.

How exactly we can trace back the uncanny effect
of such recurrent similarities to infantile psychology is
a question I can only lightly touch upon in these pages ;
and I must refer the reader instead to another pamphlet,[2]
now ready for publication, in which this has been gone
into in detail, but in a different connection.   It must
be explained that we are able to postulate the principle
of a *repetition-compulsion* in the unconscious mind, based
upon instinctual activity and probably inherent in the
very nature of the instincts—a principle powerful
enough to overrule the pleasure-principle, lending to
certain aspects of the mind their daemonic character,
and still very clearly expressed in the tendencies of
small children ; a principle, too, which is responsible
for a part of the course taken by the analyses of
neurotic patients.   Taken in all, the foregoing
prepares us for the discovery that whatever reminds
us of this inner *repetition-compulsion* is perceived as
uncanny.

Now, however, it is time to turn from these aspects
of the matter, which are in any case difficult to decide upon, and look for undeniable instances of the

[1] P. Kammerer, *Das Gesetz der Serie.*
[2] [*Beyond the Pleasure-Principle.*—Trans.]

uncanny, in the hope that analysis of them will settle whether our hypothesis is a valid one.

In the story of 'The Ring of Polycrates,' the guest turns away from his friend with horror because he sees that his every wish is at once fulfilled, his every care immediately removed by kindly fate. His host has become 'uncanny' to him. His own explanation, that the too fortunate man has to fear the envy of the gods, seems still rather obscure to us ; its meaning is veiled in mythological language. We will therefore turn to another example in a less grandiose setting. In the case history of an obsessional neurotic,[1] I have described how the patient once stayed in a hydropathic establishment and benefited greatly by it. He had the good sense, however, to attribute his improvement not to the therapeutic properties of the water, but to the situation of his room, which immediately adjoined that of a very amiable nurse. So on his second visit to the establishment he asked for the same room but was told that it was already occupied by an old gentleman, whereupon he gave vent to his annoyance in the words 'Well, I hope he'll have a stroke and die '. A fortnight later the old gentleman really did have a stroke. My patient thought this an 'uncanny' experience. And that impression of uncanniness would have been stronger still if less time had elapsed between his exclamation and the untoward event, or if he had been able to produce innumerable similar coincidences. As a matter of fact, he had no difficulty in producing coincidences of this sort, but then not only he but all obsessional neurotics I have observed are able to relate analogous experiences. They are never surprised when they invariably run up against the person they have just been thinking of, perhaps for the first time for many months. If they say one day 'I haven't had news of so-and-so for a long time ', they will be sure to get a letter from him the next morning. And an accident

[1] Freud, 'Notes upon a Case of Obsessional Neurosis', COLLECTED PAPERS, vol. iii.

or a death will rarely take place without having cast
its shadow before on their minds. They are in the
habit of mentioning this state of affairs in the most
modest manner, saying that they have ' presentiments '
which ' usually ' come true.

One of the most uncanny and wide-spread forms of
superstition is the dread of the evil eye.[1] There never
seems to have been any doubt about the source of this
dread. Whoever possesses something at once valuable
and fragile is afraid of the envy of others, in that he
projects on to them the envy he would have felt in
their place. A feeling like this betrays itself in a look
even though it is not put into words ; and when a man
attracts the attention of others by noticeable, and
particularly by unattractive, attributes, they are ready
to believe that his envy is rising to more than usual
heights and that this intensity in it will convert it
into effective action. What is feared is thus a secret
intention of harming someone, and certain signs are
taken to mean that such an intention is capable of
becoming an act.

These last examples of the uncanny are to be
referred to that principle in the mind which I have
called ' omnipotence of thoughts ', taking the name
from an expression used by one of my patients. And
now we find ourselves on well-known ground. Our
analysis of instances of the uncanny has led us back to
the old, animistic conception of the universe, which
was characterized by the idea that the world was
peopled with the spirits of human beings, and by the
narcissistic overestimation of subjective mental processes (such as the belief in the omnipotence of thoughts,
the magical practices based upon this belief, the carefully proportioned distribution of magical powers or
' mana ' among various outside persons and things), as
well as by all those other figments of the imagination
with which man, in the unrestricted narcissism of that

[1] Seligmann, the Hamburg ophthalmologist, has made a thorough
study of this superstition in his *Der böse Blick und Verwandtes*.

stage of development, strove to withstand the inexorable laws of reality. It would seem as though
each one of us has been through a phase of individual
development corresponding to that animistic stage in
primitive men, that none of us has traversed it without
preserving certain traces of it which can be re-activated,
and that everything which now strikes us as ‘uncanny’ fulfils the condition of stirring those vestiges
of animistic mental activity within us and bringing
them to expression.[1]

This is the place now to put forward two considerations which, I think, contain the gist of this short study.
In the first place, if psycho-analytic theory is correct in
maintaining that every emotional affect, whatever its
quality, is transformed by repression into morbid
anxiety, then among such cases of anxiety there must
be a class in which the anxiety can be shown to come
from something repressed which *recurs*. This class
of morbid anxiety would then be no other than what is
uncanny, irrespective of whether it originally aroused
dread or some other affect. In the second place, if
this is indeed the secret nature of the uncanny, we can
understand why the usage of speech has extended *das
Heimliche* into its opposite *das Unheimliche* ;[2] for this
uncanny is in reality nothing new or foreign, but something familiar and old-established in the mind that
has been estranged only by the process of repression.
This reference to the factor of repression enables us,
furthermore, to understand Schelling’s definition of the
uncanny as something which ought to have been kept
concealed but which has nevertheless come to light.

It only remains for us to test our new hypothesis on
one or two more examples of the uncanny.

---

[1] Cf. my book *Totem und Tabu*, part iii., ‘ Animismus, Magie und
Allmacht der Gedanken ’; also the footnote on p. 7 of the same book : ‘ It
would appear that we invest with a feeling of uncanniness those impressions which lend support to a belief in the omnipotence of thoughts,
and to the animistic attitude of mind, at a time when our judgement
has already rejected these same beliefs ’.

[2] Cf. abstract on p. 377.

Many people experience the feeling in the highest
degree in relation to death and dead bodies, to the
return of the dead, and to spirits and ghosts. As we
have seen, many languages in use to-day can only
render the German expression ' an *unheimliches* house '
by ' a *haunted* house '. We might indeed have begun
our investigation with this example, perhaps the most
striking of all, of something uncanny, but we refrained
from doing so because the uncanny in it is too much
mingled with and in part covered by what is purely
gruesome. There is scarcely any other matter, however, upon which our thoughts and feelings have
changed so little since the very earliest times, and in
which discarded forms have been so completely
preserved under a thin disguise, as that of our relation
to death. Two things account for our conservatism :
the strength of our original emotional reaction to it,
and the insufficiency of our scientific knowledge about
it. Biology has not yet been able to decide whether
death is the inevitable fate of every living being or
whether it is only a regular but yet perhaps avoidable
event in life. It is true that the proposition ' All men are
mortal ' is paraded in text-books of logic as an example
of a generalization, but no human being really grasps
it, and our unconscious has as little use now as ever
for the idea of its own mortality. Religions continue
to dispute the undeniable fact of the death of each one
of us and to postulate a life after death ; civil govern-
ments still believe that they cannot maintain moral
order among the living if they do not uphold this
prospect of a better life after death as a recompense
for earthly existence. In our great cities, placards
announce lectures which will tell us how to get into
touch with the souls of the departed ; and it cannot
be denied that many of the most able and penetrating
minds among our scientific men have come to the
conclusion, especially towards the close of their lives,
that a contact of this kind is not utterly impossible.
Since practically all of us still think as savages do on

this topic, it is no matter for surprise that the primitive fear of the dead is still so strong within us and always ready to come to the surface at any opportunity. Most likely our fear still contains the old belief that the deceased becomes the enemy of his survivor and wants to carry him off to share his new life with him. Considering our unchanged attitude towards death, we might rather inquire what has become of the repression, that necessary condition for enabling a primitive feeling to recur in the shape of an uncanny effect. But repression is there, too. All so-called educated people have ceased to believe, officially at any rate, that the dead can become visible as spirits, and have hedged round any such appearances with improbable and remote circumstances; their emotional attitude towards their dead, moreover, once a highly dubious and ambivalent one, has been toned down in the higher strata of the mind into a simple feeling of reverence.[1]

We have now only a few more remarks to add, for animism, magic and witchcraft, the omnipotence of thoughts, man's attitude to death, involuntary repetition and the castration-complex comprise practically all the factors which turn something fearful into an uncanny thing.

We also call a living person uncanny, usually when we ascribe evil motives to him. But that is not all; we must not only credit him with bad intentions but must attribute to these intentions capacity to achieve their aim in virtue of certain special powers. A good instance of this is the 'Gettatore', that uncanny figure of Roman superstition which Schaeffer, with intuitive poetic feeling and profound psycho-analytic knowledge, has transformed into a sympathetic figure in his *Josef Montfort*. But the question of these secret powers brings us back again to the realm of animism. It is her intuition that he possesses secret power of this kind that makes Mephistopheles so

[1] Cf. *Totem und Tabu* : ' Das Tabu und die Ambivalenz '.

uncanny to the pious Gretchen. ' She divines that I
am certainly a spirit, even the devil himself perchance '.[1]

The uncanny effect of epilepsy and of madness has
the same origin. The ordinary person sees in them
the workings of forces hitherto unsuspected in his
fellow-man but which at the same time he is dimly
aware of in a remote corner of his own being. The
Middle Ages quite consistently ascribed all such
maladies to daemonic influences, and in this their
psychology was not so far out. Indeed, I should not
be surprised to hear that psycho-analysis, which is
concerned with laying bare these hidden forces, has
itself become uncanny to many people for that very
reason. In one case, after I had succeeded—though
none too rapidly—in effecting a cure which had lasted
many years in a girl who had been an invalid, the
patient's own mother confessed to this attitude long
after the girl's recovery.

Dismembered limbs, a severed head, a hand cut
off at the wrist,[2] feet which dance by themselves[3]—
all these have something peculiarly uncanny about
them, especially when, as in the last instance, they
prove able to move of themselves in addition. As we
already know, this kind of uncanniness springs from
its association with the castration-complex. To many
people the idea of being buried alive while appearing
to be dead is the most uncanny thing of all. And yet
psycho-analysis has taught us that this terrifying
phantasy is only a transformation of another phantasy
which had originally nothing terrifying about it at
all, but was filled with a certain lustful pleasure—the
phantasy, I mean, of intra-uterine existence.

*   *   *   *

There is one more point of general application I
should like to add, though, strictly speaking, it has

---

[1] ' Sie ahnt, dass ich ganz sicher ein Genie,
        Vielleicht sogar der Teufel bin.'
[2] Cf. a fairy-tale of Hauff's.
[3] As in Schaeffer's book mentioned above.

been included in our statements about animism and mechanisms in the mind that have been surmounted ; for I think it deserves special mention. This is that an uncanny effect is often and easily produced by effacing the distinction between imagination and reality, such as when something that we have hitherto regarded as imaginary appears before us in reality, or when a symbol takes over the full functions and significance of the thing it symbolizes, and so on. It is this element which contributes not a little to the uncanny effect attaching to magical practices. The infantile element in this, which also holds sway in the minds of neurotics, is the over-accentuation of psychical reality in comparison with physical reality—a feature closely allied to the belief in the omnipotence of thoughts. In the midst of the isolation of war-time a number of the English *Strand Magazine* fell into my hands ; and, amongst other not very interesting matter, I read a story about a young married couple, who move into a furnished flat in which there is a curiously shaped table with carvings of crocodiles on it. Towards evening they begin to smell an intolerable and very typical odour that pervades the whole flat ; things begin to get in their way and trip them up in the darkness ; they seem to see a vague form gliding up the stairs—in short, we are given to understand that the presence of the table causes ghostly crocodiles to haunt the place, or that the wooden monsters come to life in the dark, or something of that sort. It was a thoroughly silly story, but the uncanny feeling it produced was quite remarkable.

To conclude this collection of examples, which is certainly not complete, I will relate an instance taken from psycho-analytical experience ; if it does not rest upon mere coincidence, it furnishes a beautiful confirmation of our theory of the uncanny. It often happens that male patients declare that they feel there is something uncanny about the female genital organs. This *unheimlich* place, however, is the entrance to the former *heim* [home] of all human beings, to the place where everyone dwelt once upon a time and in the beginning. There is a humorous saying : ' Love is home-sickness ' ; and whenever a man dreams of a place or a country and says to himself, still in the dream, ' this place is familiar to me, I have been there before ', we may interpret the place as being his mother's genitals or her body. In this case, too, the *unheimlich* is what was once *heimisch*, home-like, familiar ; the prefix ' un ' is the token of repression.

III

Having followed the discussion as far as this the reader will have felt certain doubts arising in his mind about much that has been said ; and he must now have an opportunity of collecting them and bringing them forward.

It may be true that the uncanny is nothing else than a hidden, familiar thing that has undergone repression and then emerged from it, and that everything that is uncanny fulfils this condition. But these factors do not solve the problem of the uncanny. For our proposition is clearly not convertible. Not everything that fulfils this condition—not everything that is connected with repressed desires and archaic forms of thought belonging to the past of the individual and of the race—is therefore uncanny.

Nor would we, moreover, conceal the fact that for almost every example adduced in support of our hypothesis some other analogous one may be found which rebuts it. The story of the severed hand in Hauff's fairy-tale certainly has an uncanny effect, and we have derived that effect from the castration-complex. But in the story in Herodotus of the treasure of Rhampsenitus, where the master-thief leaves his brother's severed hand behind him in that of the princess who wants to hold him fast, most readers will agree with me that the episode has no trace

of uncanniness.   Again, the instant fulfilment of the
king's wishes in ' The Ring of Polycrates ' undoubtedly
does affect us in the same uncanny way as it did the
king of Egypt.   Yet our own fairy-tales are crammed
with instantaneous wish-fulfilments which produce no
uncanny effect whatever.   In the story of ' The Three
Wishes ', the woman is tempted by the savoury smell
of a sausage to wish that she might have one too,
and immediately it lies on a plate before her.   In his
annoyance at her forwardness her husband wishes it
may hang on her nose.   And there it is, dangling from
her nose.   All this is very vivid but not in the least
uncanny.   Fairy-tales quite frankly adopt the animistic standpoint of the omnipotence of thoughts and
wishes, and yet I cannot think of any genuine fairy-
story which has anything uncanny about it.   We have
heard that it is in the highest degree uncanny when
inanimate objects—a picture or a doll—come to life ;
nevertheless in Hans Andersen's stories the household
utensils, furniture and tin soldiers are alive and nothing
could perhaps be more remote from the uncanny.
And we should hardly call it uncanny when Pygmalion's
beautiful statue comes to life.

Catalepsy and the re-animation of the dead have
been represented as most uncanny themes.   But things
of this sort again are very common in fairy-stories.
Who would be so bold as to call it an uncanny moment,
for instance, when Snow-White opens her eyes once
more ?   And the resuscitation of the dead in miracles,
as in the New Testament, elicits feelings quite unrelated
to the uncanny.   Then the theme that achieves such
an indubitably uncanny effect, the involuntary recurrence of the like, serves, too, other and quite
different purposes in another class of cases.   One case
we have already heard about in which it is employed
to call forth a feeling of the comic ; and we could
multiply instances of this kind.   Or again, it works
as a means of emphasis, and so on.   Another consideration is this : whence come the uncanny influences

of silence, darkness and solitude ?   Do not these factors point to the part played by danger in the aetiology of what is uncanny, notwithstanding that they are also the most frequent accompaniment of the expression of fear in infancy ? And are we in truth justified in entirely ignoring intellectual uncertainty as a factor, seeing that we have admitted its importance in relation to death ?

It is evident that we must be prepared to admit that there are other elements besides those set down here determining the production of uncanny feelings. We might say that these preliminary results have satisfied psycho-analytic interest in the problem of the uncanny, and that what remains probably calls for an aesthetic valuation. But that would be to open the door to doubts about the exact value of our general contention that the uncanny proceeds from something familiar which has been repressed.

One thing we may observe which may help us to resolve these uncertainties : nearly all the instances which contradict our hypothesis are taken from the realm of fiction and literary productions. This may suggest a possible differentiation between the uncanny that is actually experienced, and the uncanny as we merely picture it or read about it.

Something uncanny in *real experience* is conditioned much more simply, but is limited to much fewer occasions. We shall find, I think, that it fits in perfectly with our attempt at solution, and can be traced back without exception to something familiar that has been repressed. But here, too, we must make a certain important and psychologically significant differentiation in our material, best illustrated by turning to suitable examples.

Let us take the uncanny in connection with the omnipotence of thoughts, instantaneous wish-fulfil-ments, secret power to do harm and the return of the dead. The condition under which the feeling of uncanniness arises here is unmistakable. We—or our primitive forefathers—once believed in the possibility of these things and were convinced that they really happened. Nowadays we no longer believe in them, we have *surmounted* such ways of thought; but we do not feel quite sure of our new set of beliefs, and the old ones still exist within us ready to seize upon any confirmation. As soon as something actually happens in our lives which seems to support the old, discarded beliefs we get a feeling of the uncanny ; and it is as though we were making a judgement something like this : ' So, after all, it is true that one can kill a person by merely desiring his death ! ' or, ' Then the dead do continue to live and appear before our eyes on the scene of their former activities ! ', and so on. And con- versely, he who has completely and finally dispelled animistic beliefs in himself, will be insensible to this type of the uncanny. The most remarkable coin- cidences of desire and fulfilment, the most mysterious recurrence of similar experiences in a particular place or on a particular date, the most deceptive sights and suspicious noises—none of these things will take him in or raise that kind of fear which can be described as ' a fear of something uncanny '. For the whole matter is one of ' testing reality ', pure and simple, a question of the material reality of the phenomena.[1]

---

[1] Since the uncanny effect of a ' double ' also belongs to this class, it is interesting to observe what the effect is of suddenly and un- expectedly meeting one's own image. E. Mach has related two such observations in his *Analyse der Empfindungen* (1900, p. 3). On the first occasion he started violently as soon as he realized that the face before him was his own. The second time he formed a very unfavour- able opinion about the supposed stranger who got into the omnibus, and thought ' What a shabby-looking school-master that is getting in now '.—I can supply a similar experience. I was sitting alone in my *wagon-lit* compartment when a more than usually violent jerk of the train swung back the door of the adjoining washing-cabinet, and an elderly gentleman in a dressing-gown and a travelling cap came in. I assumed that he had been about to leave the washing- cabinet which divides the two compartments, and had taken the wrong direction and come into my compartment by mistake. Jumping up with the intention of putting him right, I at once realized to my dismay that the intruder was nothing but my own reflection in the looking-glass of the open door. I can still recollect that I thoroughly disliked his appearance. Instead, therefore, of being terrified by our doubles, both Mach and I simply failed to recognize them as such. Is it not possible, though, that our dislike of them was a vestigial trace of that older reaction which feels the double to be something uncanny ?

The state of affairs is somewhat different when the uncanny proceeds from repressed infantile complexes, from the castration-complex, womb-phantasies, etc. ; but experiences which arouse this kind of uncanny feeling are not of very frequent occurrence in real life. Actual occurrences of the uncanny belong for the most part to the first group ; nevertheless the distinction between the two is theoretically very important. Where the uncanny comes from infantile complexes the question of external reality is quite irrelevant ; its place is taken by psychical reality. What is concerned is an actual repression of some definite material and a return of this repressed material, not a removal of the *belief* in its objective reality. We might say that in the one case what had been repressed was a particular ideational content and in the other the belief in its physical existence. But this last way of putting it no doubt strains the term ' repression ' beyond its legitimate meaning. It would be more correct to respect a perceptible psychological difference here, and to say that the animistic beliefs of civilized people have been *surmounted*—more or less. Our conclusion could then be stated thus : An uncanny experience occurs either when repressed infantile complexes have been revived by some impression, or when the primitive beliefs we have surmounted seem once more to be confirmed. Finally, we must not let our predilection for smooth solution and lucid exposition blind us to the fact that these two classes of uncanny experience are not always sharply distinguishable. When we consider that primitive beliefs are most intimately connected with infantile complexes, and are, in fact, based upon them, we shall not be greatly astonished to find the distinction often rather a hazy one.

The uncanny as it is depicted in *literature*, in stories and imaginative productions, merits in truth a separate discussion. To begin with, it is a much more fertile province than the uncanny in real life, for it contains the whole of the latter and something more besides, something that cannot be found in real life. The distinction between what has been repressed and what has been surmounted cannot be transposed on to the uncanny in fiction without profound modification ; for the realm of phantasy depends for its very existence on the fact that its content is not submitted to the reality - testing faculty. The somewhat paradoxical result is that *in the first place a great deal that is not uncanny in fiction would be so if it happened in real life ; and in the second place that there are many more means of creating uncanny effects in fiction than there are in real life.*

The story-teller has this licence among many others, that he can select his world of representation so that it either coincides with the realities we are familiar with or departs from them in what particulars he pleases. We accept his ruling in every case. In fairy-tales, for instance, the world of reality is left behind from the very start, and the animistic system of beliefs is frankly adopted. Wish-fulfilments, secret powers, omnipotence of thoughts, animation of lifeless objects, all the elements so common in fairy-stories, can exert no uncanny influence here ; for, as we have learnt, that feeling cannot arise unless there is a conflict of judgement whether things which have been ' surmounted ' and are regarded as incredible are not, after all, possible ; and this problem is excluded from the beginning by the setting of the story. And thus we see that such stories as have furnished us with most of the contradictions to our hypothesis of the uncanny confirm the first part of our proposition—that in the realm of fiction many things are not uncanny which would be so if they happened in real life. In the case of the fairy-story there are other contributory factors, which we shall briefly touch upon later.

The story-teller can also choose a setting which, though less imaginary than the world of fairy-tales, does yet differ from the real world by admitting superior spiritual entities such as daemonic influences or

departed spirits. So long as they remain within their
setting of poetic reality their usual attribute of uncanniness fails to attach to such beings. The souls in
Dante's *Inferno*, or the ghostly apparitions in *Hamlet*,
Macbeth or *Julius Caesar*, may be gloomy and terrible
enough, but they are no more really uncanny than is
Homer's jovial world of gods. We order our judgement
to the imaginary reality imposed on us by the writer,
and regard souls, spirits and spectres as though their
existence had the same validity in their world as our
own has in the external world. And then in this case
too we are spared all trace of the uncanny.

The situation is altered as soon as the writer pretends
to move in the world of common reality. In this case
he accepts all the conditions operating to produce
uncanny feelings in real life ; and everything that
would have an uncanny effect in reality has it in his
story. But in this case, too, he can increase his effect
and multiply it far beyond what could happen in
reality, by bringing about events which never or very
rarely happen in fact. He takes advantage, as it were,
of our supposedly surmounted superstitiousness ; he
deceives us into thinking that he is giving us the sober
truth, and then after all oversteps the bounds of
possibility. We react to his inventions as we should
have reacted to real experiences ; by the time we have
seen through his trick it is already too late and the
author has achieved his object ; but it must be added
that his success is not unalloyed. We retain a feeling
of dissatisfaction, a kind of grudge against the attempted
deceit ; I have noticed this particularly after reading
Schnitzler's *Die Weissagung* and similar stories which
flirt with the supernatural. The writer has then one
more means he can use to escape our rising vexation
and at the same time to improve his chances of success.
It is this, that he should keep us in the dark for a long
time about the precise nature of the conditions he has
selected for the world he writes about, or that he should
cunningly and ingeniously avoid any definite informa-

tion on the point at all throughout the book.   Speaking generally, however, we find a confirmation of the second part of our proposition—that fiction presents more opportunities for creating uncanny sensations than are possible in real life.

Strictly speaking, all these complications relate only to that class of the uncanny which proceeds from forms of thought that have been surmounted.   The class which proceeds from repressed complexes is more irrefragable and remains as powerful in fiction as in real experience, except in one point.   The uncanny belonging to the first class—that proceeding from forms of thought that have been surmounted—retains this quality in fiction as in experience so long as the setting is one of physical reality ; but as soon as it is given an arbitrary and unrealistic setting in fiction, it is apt to lose its quality of the uncanny.

It is clear that we have not exhausted the possibilities of poetic licence and the privileges enjoyed by story-writers in evoking or in excluding an uncanny feeling.   In the main we adopt an unvarying passive attitude towards experience and are acted upon by our physical environment.   But the story-teller has a peculiarly directive influence over us ; by means of the states of mind into which he can put us and the expectations he can rouse in us, he is able to guide the current of our emotions, dam it up in one direction and make it flow in another, and he often obtains a great variety of effects from the same material.   All this is nothing new, and has doubtless long since been fully taken into account by professors of aesthetics. We have drifted into this field of research half involuntarily, through the temptation to explain certain instances which contradicted our theory of the causes of the uncanny.   And accordingly we will now return to the examination of a few instances.

We have already asked why it is that the severed hand in the story of the treasure of Rhampsenitus has no uncanny effect in the way that Hauff's story of the severed hand has. The question seems to us to have gained in importance now that we have recognized that class of the uncanny which proceeds from repressed complexes to be the more durable of the two. The answer is easy. In the Herodotus story our thoughts are concentrated much more on the superior cunning of the master-thief than on the feelings of the princess. The princess may well have had an uncanny feeling, indeed she very probably fell into a swoon ; but we have no such sensations, for we put ourselves in the thief's place, not in hers. In Nestroy's farce, *Der Zerrissene,* another means is used to avoid any impression of the uncanny in the scene in which the fleeing man, convinced that he is a murderer, lifts up one trap-door after another and each time sees what he takes to be the ghost of his victim rising up out of it. He calls out in despair, ' But I've only killed *one* man. Why this horrid multiplication ? ' We know the truth and do not share the error of the *Zerrissener,* so what must be uncanny to him has an irresistibly comic effect on us. Even a ' real ' ghost, as in Oscar Wilde's *Canterville Ghost,* loses all power of arousing at any rate an uncanny horror in us as soon as the author begins to amuse himself at its expense and allows liberties to be taken with it. Thus we see how independent emotional effects can be of the actual subject-matter in the world of fiction. In fairy-stories feelings of fear—including uncanny sensations—are ruled out altogether. We understand this, and that is why we ignore the opportunities we find there for any development of a feeling of this kind.

Concerning the factors of silence, solitude and darkness, we can only say that they are actually elements in the production of that infantile morbid anxiety from which the majority of human beings have never become quite free. This problem has been discussed from a psycho-analytical point of view in another place.

CONTRIBUTIONS TO THE PSYCHOLOGY OF LOVE

A Special Type of Choice of Object made by Men [1]

(1910)

HITHERTO we have left it to poets and imaginative writers to depict for us the 'conditions of love' under which men and women make their choice of an object, and the way in which they reconcile the demands expressed in their phantasy with the exigencies of real life. Writers indeed have certain qualities which fit them for such a task ; more especially, a sensitiveness of perception in regard to the hidden feelings of others, and the courage to give voice to their own unconscious minds. But from the point of view of knowledge one circumstance lessens the value of what they tell us. Writers are bound to certain conditions ; they have to evoke intellectual and aesthetic pleasure as well as certain effects on the emotions. For this reason they cannot reproduce reality unchanged ; they have to isolate portions of it, detach them from their connection with disturbing elements, fill up gaps and soften the whole. This is the privilege of what is called 'poetic licence'. They can display no great interest, moreover, in the origin and growth of those conditions of mind which they portray in being. It is inevitable, therefore, that science should lay hands on the stuff which poets have fashioned so as to give pleasure to mankind for thousands of years, although its touch must be clumsier and the result in pleasure less. These considerations may serve to

[1] First published in *Jahrbuch*, Bd. II., 1910 ; reprinted in *Sammlung*, Vierte Folge. [Translated by Joan Riviere.]

vindicate our handling of the loves of men and women
as well as other things in a strictly scientific way. For
science betokens the most complete renunciation of the
pleasure-principle of which our minds are capable.

During psycho-analytic treatment one has plenty of
opportunity for collecting impressions about the erotic
life of neurotics, and when this happens one also
recalls having noticed or heard of similar behaviour on
the part of ordinary healthy persons or even in people
of exceptional qualities. When by a lucky chance any
such impressions are multiplied in the material that
comes under observation, distinct types clearly emerge.
I shall first describe one type of this kind relating to a
choice of object effected by men, because it is characterized by a series of ' conditions of love ' the juxta-
position of which is unintelligible or indeed disconcert-
ing, and because it admits of a simple psycho-analytic
explanation.
    1. The first of these conditions of love must be
described as quite specific ; wherever one discovers it
one may look out for the presence of the other features
belonging to the type. It may be termed the ' need for
an injured third party ' ; its effect is that the person in
question never chooses as an object of love a woman
who is unattached, that is, a girl or an independent
woman, but only one in regard to whom another man
has some right of possession, whether as husband,
betrothed, or near friend. In some cases this condition
is so peremptory that a given woman can be ignored
or even treated with contempt so long as she belongs
to no other man, but instantly becomes the object of
feelings of love as soon as she comes into a relationship
of the kind described with another man.
    2. The second condition is perhaps a less constant
one, but it is no less remarkable. The type I am
speaking of is only built up by the two conditions in
combination ; the first condition seems also to occur

very frequently by itself. The second condition is thus constituted : a virtuous and reputable woman never possesses the charm required to exalt her to an object of love ; this attraction is exercised only by one who is more or less sexually discredited, whose fidelity and loyalty admit of some doubt. This last element may vary within the limits of a significant series, from the faint breath of scandal attaching to a married woman who is not averse to flirtation up to the openly polygamous way of life of a prostitute, or of a *grande amoureuse*—but the man who belongs to the type in question will never dispense with something of the kind. By a rough characterization this condition could be called that of ' love for a harlot '.

While the first condition provides an opportunity for gratification of the feelings of enmity against the man from whom the loved woman is wrested, the second, that of the woman's infidelity, is connected with feelings of jealousy, which seem to be a necessity to lovers of this type. Not until they have some occasion for jealousy does their passion reach its height and the woman acquire her full value to them, and they never fail to seize upon some incident by which this intensity of feeling may thus be called out. Strange to say, it is not the lawful possessor of the loved one against whom this jealousy is directed, but new acquaintances or strangers in regard to whom she may be brought under suspicion. In pronounced cases the lover shows no desire to possess her for himself alone and seems altogether contented with the triangular situation. One of my patients, who had suffered torments from his lady's escapades, had no objection to her marrying, doing all he could to bring it about ; and after, throughout several years, he never showed a trace of jealousy against the husband. Another typical case had, it is true, in his first love-affair been very jealous of the husband and had insisted on the lady ceasing marital relations ; but in his numerous later relationships he behaved like the others and no longer regarded the lawful husband as any disturbance.

So much for the conditions required in the loved object ; the following points relate to the lover's behaviour towards the object of his choice.

3. In normal love between the sexes the value of the woman is measured according to her sexual integrity and sinks with any approach to the character of a ' light woman '. It seems to be a striking departure from the normal, therefore, that men of this type should set the *highest value* upon women of this character as their love-objects. Their love-relationships with such women absorb the whole of their mental energy, to the exclusion of all other interests ; such women are ' the only ones it is possible to love ' and the ideal of the lover's own fidelity is invariably set up again, however often it may be shattered in reality. A high degree of compulsion, which indeed in some measure characterizes every case of passionate love, is clearly discernible in these features of the love-relationships described. But the sincerity and intensity of the attachment in these cases is no indication that any one such relationship makes up the whole erotic life of the person concerned or happens only once in it. On the contrary, passionate attachments of this kind are repeated many times over with all the same peculiarities —each an exact replica of the others—in the lives of those belonging to this type ; indeed, in consequence of external conditions, such as changes of residence and environment, the loved objects may be so often replaced by others that it comes in the end to a long chain of such experiences being formed.

4. The trait in this type of lover that is most astonishing to the observer is the desire they express to ' rescue ' the beloved. The man is convinced that the loved woman has need of him, that without him she would lose all hold on respectability and rapidly sink to a deplorable level. He saves her from this fate, therefore, by not letting her go. The impulse to

rescue the woman is occasionally justified by her un-trustworthy temperament sexually and by the danger to her social position ; it is no less plainly marked, however, where any such real occasion for it is absent. One of the men belonging to the type, who knew how to win his ladies by the subtlety of his methods of seduction and his skill in argument, spent endless pains during the course of each of these love-relationships in composing tracts to induce the loved one to keep in the path of ' virtue '.

When we review the various features of the picture presented here—the condition that the woman should belong to another man, her ' light ' nature, the high value set on this last, the thirst for jealousy, the fidelity which is in spite of all compatible with the long chain of repetitions, and the longing to ' save '—any hope of tracing them all back to a single source will seem very remote. And yet penetrating psycho-analytic study of the lives of those concerned yields this quite easily. The choice of an object complying with these peculiar conditions and this strange way of loving her have the same source as the normal attitude in love ; they are derived from a fixation of the infantile feelings of tenderness for the mother and represent one of the forms in which this fixation expresses itself. In the normal attitude there remain only a few traces unmistakably betraying the maternal prototype behind the chosen object, for instance, the preference young men show for mature women ; the detachment of the libido from the mother is accomplished comparatively swiftly. In our type, on the contrary, the libido has dwelt so long in its attachment to the mother, even after puberty, that the maternal characteristics remain stamped on the love-objects chosen later—so long that they all become easily recognizable mother-surrogates. The comparison with the way in which the skull of a new-born child is shaped comes irresistibly to one's mind ; after a protracted labour it always bears the form of a cast of the maternal pelvis.

It is now obligatory on us to show some probable grounds for the statement that the characteristic features of this type, both as to conditions of love and behaviour in love, actually derive from the group of feelings relating to the mother. This is most easily accomplished in reference to the first condition, that the woman should belong to another man, the 'need for an injured third party'. One sees at once that the fact of the mother belonging to the father would come to be an inseparable part of the mother's nature to the child growing up in the family circle, also that the 'injured third party' is none other than the father himself. The feature of overestimation by which the loved one becomes the unique, the irreplaceable one, fits just as readily into the infantile set of ideas, for no one possesses more than one mother, and the relation to her rests on an experience which is assured beyond all doubt and can never be repeated again.

If the love-objects chosen by our type are above everything mother-surrogates, then the formation of a long series of them, which seems so directly to contradict the condition of fidelity to the woman, becomes comprehensible as well. We learn through other examples which psycho-analysis has brought to light that the pressing desire in the unconscious for some irreplaceable thing often resolves itself into an endless series in actuality—endless for the very reason that the satisfaction longed for is in spite of all never found in any surrogate. The insatiable questioning which children are given to at a certain age is explicable in this way—they have one single question to ask, the words of which they cannot bring their lips to form ; and in the same way, too, the garrulity of many neurotically crippled persons may be explained—what makes them talk is the burden of a secret pressing for disclosure, which in spite of all temptation they never reveal.

The second condition of love, that of the 'loose' character of the object chosen, seems on the other hand to stand in sharp opposition to a derivation from the mother-complex. The grown man's conscious mind likes to regard the mother as a personification of impeccable moral purity, and few suggestions from without are so insulting, or from within so painful, as those which cast doubt on the mother's character in this respect. This very relation, however, of sharpest possible contrast between the ' mother ' and the ' harlot ' would prompt us to study the developmental history of the two complexes and unconscious relation between them, since we long ago discovered that a thing which in consciousness makes its appearance as two contraries is often in the unconscious a united whole. Investigation then leads us back to the period in the boy's life at which he first obtained more or less detailed knowledge of the sexual relations between adults, somewhere in the years before puberty. The secret of sexual life is revealed to him then in coarse language, undisguisedly derogatory and hostile in intent, and the effect is to destroy the authority of adults, which is irreconcilable with these revelations about their sexual activities. The greatest impression on the child who is being initiated is made by the relation the information bears to his own parents, which is often instantly repudiated in some such words as these : ' It may be true that your father and mother and other people do such things, but it is quite impossible that mine do '.

Along with this piece of ' sexual enlightenment ' there seldom fails to go, as a corollary, a further one about the existence of certain women who practise sexual intercourse as a means of livelihood and are universally despised in consequence. To the boy himself this contempt is necessarily quite foreign ; as soon as he realizes that he too can be initiated by these unfortunates into that sexual life which he has hitherto regarded as the exclusive prerogative of ' grown-ups ', his feeling for them is only a mixture of longing and shuddering. Then, when he cannot any longer maintain the doubt that claims exception for his own parents from the ugly sexual behaviour of the rest of the world, he says to himself with cynical logic that the difference between his mother and a whore is after all not so very great, since at bottom they both do the same thing. What he has been told has in fact revived the memory-traces of his early infantile impressions and desires, and thus re-activated certain feelings in his mind. In the light of this new knowledge he begins to desire the mother herself and to hate the father anew for standing in his way ; he comes, as we say, under the sway of the Oedipus complex. He does not forget that the mother has given the privilege of sexual intercourse with her to the father instead of to him, and he regards it as an act of infidelity on her part. If these feelings do not rapidly pass, there is only one way in which they can find an outlet—the way of phantasies, in which the mother is represented in sexual situations of the most manifold kind, and in which also the accompanying excitement leads particularly readily to culmination in an onanistic act. In consequence of the constant simultaneous pressure of the two currents of feeling, desire for the mother and revenge against the father, phantasies of the mother's infidelity are by far the most favoured ; the lover with whom the mother commits the act of unfaithfulness almost invariably bears the features of the boy himself, or, to be more correct, of the idealized image he forms of himself as brought to equality with his father by growing to manhood. What I have elsewhere [1] described as the ' family-romance ' comprises the manifold elaborations of this work of phantasy, which is interwoven with various egoistic interests active at this period of life. Now, however, that we have had a glimpse into this phase of mental development we can no longer regard it as contradictory or extraordinary that the condition of a ' loose ' character in the woman should derive directly from the mother-complex. The type of erotic life in

[1] In Otto Rank's *Der Mythus von der Geburt des Helden*, p. 64.

men which we are considering bears the marks of this historical development, and is easily to be understood as a fixation on the phantasies formed by the boy during puberty which have after all found their way to realization later in life. There is no difficulty in assuming that the ardent masturbation practised in the years of puberty contributed to the fixation of these phantasies.

The impulse to ' rescue ' the beloved appears to stand merely in a loose and superficial relation, founded entirely on conscious grounds, to these phantasies that have gained control of the love-experiences of real life. Her propensity to fickleness and infidelity brings the loved woman into dangerous situations, so it is natural that the lover should do all he can to protect her by watching over her virtue and opposing her evil ways. Study of the screen-memories, phantasies and nocturnal dreams of men and women shows, however, that an exceptionally felicitous ' rationalization ' of an un-conscious motive is present here, comparable to a very successful secondary elaboration of a dream. The idea of ' rescue ' actually has a significance and history of its own and is an independent derivative of the mother-complex, or, more correctly, of the parental complex. When a child hears that he owes his life to his parents, that his mother gave him life, the feelings of tenderness in him mingle with the longing to be big and independent himself, so that he forms the wish to repay the parents for this gift and requite it by one of a like value. It is as though the boy said in his defiance : ' I want nothing from father ; I shall repay him all I have cost him '. He then weaves a phantasy of saving his father's life on some dangerous occasion by which he becomes quits with him, and this phantasy is commonly enough displaced on to the Emperor, the King, or any other great man, after which it can enter consciousness and is even made use of by poets. So far as it applies to the father, the attitude of defiance in the ' saving ' phantasy far outweighs the tender feeling in it, the latter being usually directed towards the mother.   The mother gave the child his life and it is not easy to replace this unique gift with anything of equal value.   By a slight change of meaning, which is easily effected in the un-conscious—comparable to the way in which shades of meaning merge into one another in conscious concep-tions—rescuing the mother acquires the significance of giving her a child or making one for her—one like himself, of course.   The departure from the original meaning of the idea of ' saving life ' is not too great, the change in sense is no arbitrary one.   The mother gave him his own life and he gives her back another life, that of a child as like himself as possible.   The son shows his gratitude by wishing to have a son by his mother that shall be like himself ; in the rescue phantasy, that is, he identifies himself completely with the father.   All the instincts, the loving, the grateful, the sensual, the defiant, the self-assertive and independent —all are gratified in the wish to be *the father of himself.* Even the element of danger is not lost in the change of meaning ; the experience of birth itself is the danger from which he was saved by the mother's efforts. Birth is in fact the first of all dangers to life, as well as the prototype of all the later ones we fear ; and this experience has probably left its mark behind it on that expression of emotion which we call anxiety.   Thus it was that Macduff of the Scottish legend, who was not born of his mother but ' ripp'd from her womb ', knew no fear.

The ancient dream-interpreter Artemidorus was undoubtedly right in his opinion that dreams have different meanings according to the person of the dreamer.   Under the laws governing the expression of unconscious thoughts, the meaning of ' saving life ' can vary according to whether the phantasy is framed by a man or a woman.   It can mean either : making a child, bringing it to life (in a man) ; or giving birth to a child (in a woman).

These various significations of ' saving ' in dreams and phantasies are especially clearly recognizable when they occur in some connection with water.   When in a dream a man rescues a woman from the water, it means that he makes her a mother, which in view of the considerations discussed above means that he makes her his own mother.   When a woman rescues someone else (a child) out of the water, she represents herself as the mother who bore him, like Pharaoh's daughter in the Moses legend.[1]

The phantasy of rescuing the father will also occasionally have a tender meaning.   It then expresses the wish to have the father for a son, that is, to have a son like the father.   On account of all these connections between the idea of ' saving ' and the parental complex, the desire to rescue the loved woman forms an essential feature of the type under discussion.

I do not consider it necessary to advance any justification for my method of working out my observations ; here, as also in the matter of anal erotism, the aim of it is first of all to single out extreme types in sharp outline.   In both these fields there is a far greater number of persons in whom only one or two of the typical features, and even these but indistinctly traced, are recognizable ; it is evident, therefore, that it will not be possible to appreciate them correctly until the whole range of ideas to which these elements belong has been explored.

[1] Rank, *loc. cit.*

CONTRIBUTIONS TO THE PSYCHOLOGY OF LOVE

THE MOST PREVALENT FORM OF DEGRADATION IN EROTIC LIFE [1]

(1912)

I

IF a practising psycho-analyst asks himself what disorder he is most often called upon to remedy, he is obliged to reply—apart from anxiety in all its many forms—psychical impotence. This strange disorder affects men of a strongly libidinous nature, and is manifested by a refusal on the part of the sexual organs to execute the sexual act, although both before and after the attempt they can show themselves intact and competent to do so, and although a strong mental inclination to carry out the act is present. The man gets his first inkling in the direction of understanding his condition by discovering that he fails in this way only with certain women, whereas it never happens with others. He knows then that the inhibition of his masculine potency is due to some quality in the sexual object, and sometimes he describes having had a sensation of holding back, of having perceived some check within him which interfered successfully with his conscious intention. What this inner opposition is, however, he cannot guess, or what quality in the sexual object makes it active. If the failure has been repeated several times he probably concludes, by the familiar erroneous line of argument, that a recollection of the first occasion acted as a disturbance by

[1] First published in *Jahrbuch*, Bd. IV., 1912 ; reprinted in *Sammlung*, Vierte Folge. [Translated by Joan Riviere.]

causing anxiety and brought about the subsequent failures ; the first occasion itself he refers to some ' accidental ' occurrence.

Psycho-analytic studies of psychical impotence have already been carried out and published by various writers.[1] Every analyst can, from his own experience, confirm the explanations adduced in them. The disorder is in fact due to the inhibiting influence of certain complexes in the mind that are withdrawn from the knowledge of the person in question. As the most universal feature of this pathogenic material an incestuous fixation on mother and sister which has not been surmounted stands out. In addition to this, the influence of accidental impressions of a painful kind connected with infantile sexuality comes into consideration, together with those factors which in general reduce the amount of libido available for the female sexual object.[2]

When cases of severe psychical impotence are subjected to exhaustive study by means of psycho-analysis, the following psycho-sexual processes are found to be operative. Here again—as very probably in all neurotic disorders—the root of the trouble lies in an arrest occurring during the course of development of the libido to that ultimate form which may be called normal. To ensure a fully normal attitude in love, two currents of feeling have to unite—we may describe them as the tender, affectionate feelings and the sensual feelings—and this confluence of the two currents has in these cases not been achieved.

Of these two currents affection is the older. It springs from the very earliest years of childhood, and was formed on the foundation provided by the interests of the self-preservative instinct ; it is directed towards the members of the family and those who have care of

<hr>

[1] M. Steiner, *Die funktionelle Impotenz des Mannes und ihre Behandlung* ; W. Stekel, in *Nervöse Angstzustände und ihre Behandlung* ; Ferenczi, ' Analytic Interpretation and Treatment of Psychosexual Impotence '.

[2] W. Stekel, *loc. cit.* p. 191 *et seq.*

the child. From the very beginning elements from the sexual instincts are taken up into it—component-parts of the erotic interest—which are more or less clearly visible in childhood and are invariably discovered in the neurotic by psycho-analysis in later years. This tender feeling represents the earliest childish choice of object. From this we see that the sexual instincts find their first *objects* along the path laid down by the ego-instincts and in accordance with the value set by the latter on their objects, in just the same way that the first sexual *satisfactions* are experienced, *i.e.* in connection with the bodily functions necessary for self-preservation. The ' affection ' shown to the child by its parents and attendants which seldom fails to betray its erotic character (' a child is an erotic plaything ') does a great deal to increase the erotic contributions to the cathexes that are put forth by the ego-instincts in the child, and to raise them to a level which is bound to leave its mark on future development, especially when certain other circumstances leading to the same result are present.

These fixations of the child's feelings of affection are maintained through childhood, continually absorbing erotic elements, which are thus deflected from their sexual aims. Then, when the age of puberty is reached, there supervenes upon this state of things a powerful current of ' sensual ' feeling the aims of which can no longer be disguised. It never fails, apparently, to pursue the earlier paths and to invest the objects of the primary infantile choice with currents of libido that are now far stronger. But in relation to these objects it is confronted by the obstacle of the incest-barrier that has in the meanwhile been erected ; consequently it seeks as soon as possible to pass on from these objects unsuited for real satisfaction to others in the world outside, with whom a real sexual life may be carried on. These new objects are still chosen after the pattern (imago) of the infantile ones ; in time, however, they attract to themselves the tender feeling that had been anchored to those others. A man shall leave father and mother—according to the Biblical precept—and cleave to his wife ; then are tenderness and sensuality united. The greatest intensity of sensual passion will bring with it the highest mental estimation of the object (the normal over-estimation of the sexual object characteristic of men).

Two factors will determine whether this advance in the development of the libido is accomplished successfully or otherwise. First, there is the degree of frustration in reality which is opposed to the new object-choice and reduces its value for the person concerned. For there is no sense in entering upon a choice of object if one is not to be allowed to choose at all or has no prospect of being able to choose one fit for the part. The second factor is the degree of attraction that may be exercised by the infantile objects which should be relinquished, and this is proportionate to the erotic cathexis already attaching to them in childhood. If these two factors are sufficiently powerful, the general mechanism leading to the formation of neurosis will come into operation. The libido turns away from reality, and is absorbed into the creation of phantasy (introversion), strengthens the images of the first sexual objects, and becomes fixated to them. The incest-barrier, however, necessarily has the effect that the libido attaching to these objects should remain in the unconscious. The sensual current of feeling is now attached to unconscious ideas of objects, and discharge of it in onanistic acts contributes to a strengthening of this fixation. It constitutes no change in this state of affairs if the step forward to extraneous objects which miscarried in reality is now made in phantasy, if in the phantasied situations leading up to onanistic gratification the extraneous objects are but replacements of the original ones. The phantasies become capable of entering consciousness by this replacement, but in the direction of applying the libido externally in the real world no advance has been made.

In this way it may happen that the whole current of sensual feeling in a young man may remain attached in the unconscious to incestuous objects, or, to put it in another way, may be fixated to incestuous phantasies. The result of this is then total impotence, which is perhaps even reinforced by an actual weakening, developing concurrently, of the organs destined to execute the sexual act.

Less severe conditions will suffice to bring about what is usually called psychical impotence. It is not necessary that the whole amount of sensual feeling should be fated to conceal itself behind the tender feelings ; it may remain sufficiently strong and unchecked to secure some outlet for itself in reality. The sexual activity of such people shows unmistakable signs, however, that it has not behind it the whole mental energy belonging to the instinct. It is capricious, easily upset, often clumsily carried out, and not very pleasurable. Above all, however, it avoids all association with feelings of tenderness. A restriction has thus been laid upon the object-choice. The sensual feeling that has remained active seeks only objects evoking no reminder of the incestuous persons forbidden to it ; the impression made by someone who seems deserving of high estimation leads, not to a sensual excitation, but to feelings of tenderness which remain erotically ineffectual. The erotic life of such people remains dissociated, divided between two channels, the same two that are personified in art as heavenly and earthly (or animal) love. Where such men love they have no desire and where they desire they cannot love. In order to keep their sensuality out of contact with the objects they love, they seek out objects whom they need not love ; and, in accordance with the laws of the ' sensitivity of complexes ' and the ' return of the repressed ', the strange refusal implied in psychical impotence is made whenever the objects selected in order to avoid incest possess some trait, often quite inconspicuous, reminiscent of the objects that must be avoided.

The principal means of protection used by men against this complaint consists in *lowering* the sexual object in their own estimation, while reserving for the incestuous object and for those who represent it the overestimation normally felt for the sexual object. As soon as the sexual object fulfils the condition of being degraded, sensual feeling can have free play, considerable sexual capacity and a high degree of pleasure can be developed. Another factor also contributes to this result. There is usually little refinement in the ways of obtaining erotic pleasure habitual to people in whom the tender and the sensual currents of feeling are not properly merged; they have remained addicted to perverse sexual aims which they feel it a considerable deprivation not to gratify, yet to such men this seems possible only with a sexual object who in their estimate is degraded and worth little.

The motives behind the phantasies mentioned in the preceding paper,[1] by which boys degrade the mother to the level of a prostitute, now become intelligible. They represent efforts to bridge the gulf between the two currents of erotic feeling, at least in phantasy : by degrading her, to win the mother as an object for sensual desires.

II

So far we have pursued our inquiry into psychical impotence from a medico - psychological angle which is not justified by the title of this paper. It will prove, however, that this introduction was necessary in order to provide an approach to our actual theme.

We have reduced psychical impotence to a disunion

[1] Cf. p. 169.

between the tender and sensual currents of erotic feeling, and have explained this inhibition in development itself as an effect of strong fixations in childhood and of frustration in reality later, after the incest-barrier has intervened. There is one principal objection to raise against this doctrine : it does too much, it explains why certain persons suffer from psychical impotence, but it makes it seem puzzling that others can escape the affliction. Since all the factors that appear to be involved, the strong fixation in childhood, the incest-barrier, and the frustration in the years of development after puberty, are demonstrably present in practically all civilized persons, one would be justified in expecting that psychical impotence was universally prevalent in civilized countries and not a disease of particular individuals.

It would not be difficult to escape from this conclusion by pointing to the quantitative element in the causation of disease, that greater or lesser amount of each single factor which determines whether or not recognizable disease results. But although this argument is in my opinion sound, I do not myself intend to employ it in refuting the objection advanced above. I shall, on the contrary, put forward the proposition that psychical impotence is far more widespread than is generally supposed, and that some degree of this condition does in fact characterize the erotic life of civilized peoples.

If one enlarges the meaning of the term psychical impotence, and ceases to limit it to failure to perform the act of coitus, although an intention to derive pleasure from it is present and the genital apparatus is intact, it would comprise, to begin with, all those men who are described as psycho-anaesthetic, *i.e.* who never fail in the act but who perform it without special pleasure— a state of things which is commoner than one might think. Psycho-analytic study of such cases has discovered the same aetiological factors in them as those found in psychical impotence, when employed in the narrower sense, without at first discovering any explanation of the symptomatic difference between the two. By an analogy which is easy to justify, one is led on from these anaesthetic men to consider the enormous number of frigid women, whose attitude to love can in fact not be described or understood better than by equating it with psychical impotence in men, although the latter is more conspicuous.[1]

If, however, instead of attributing a wide significance to the term psychical impotence, we look about for instances of its peculiar symptomatology in less marked forms, we shall not be able to deny that the behaviour in love of the men of present-day civilization bears in general the character of the psychically impotent type. In only very few people of culture are the two strains of tenderness and sensuality duly fused into one ; the man almost always feels his sexual activity hampered by his respect for the woman and only develops full sexual potency when he finds himself in the presence of a lower type of sexual object ; and this again is partly conditioned by the circumstance that his sexual aims include those of perverse sexual components, which he does not like to gratify with a woman he respects. Full sexual satisfaction only comes when he can give himself up wholeheartedly to enjoyment, which with his well-brought-up wife, for instance, he does not venture to do. Hence comes his need for a less exalted sexual object, a woman ethically inferior, to whom he need ascribe no aesthetic misgivings, and who does not know the rest of his life and cannot criticize him. It is to such a woman that he prefers to devote his sexual potency, even when all the tenderness in him belongs to one of a higher type. It is possible, too, that the tendency so often observed in men of the highest rank in society to take a woman of a low class as a permanent mistress, or even as a wife,

[1] At the same time I willingly admit that the frigidity of women is a complicated subject which can also be approached from another angle.

is nothing but a consequence of the need for a lower type of sexual object on which, psychologically, the possibility of complete gratification depends.

I do not hesitate to lay the responsibility also for this very common condition in the erotic life of civilized men on the two factors operative in absolute psychical impotence, namely, the very strong incestuous fixation of childhood and the frustration by reality suffered during adolescence. It has an ugly sound and a paradoxical as well, but nevertheless it must be said that whoever is to be really free and happy in love must have overcome his deference for women and come to terms with the idea of incest with mother or sister. Anyone who in the face of this test subjects himself to serious self-examination will indubitably find that at the bottom of his heart he too regards the sexual act as something degrading, which soils and contaminates not only the body. And he will only be able to look for the origin of this attitude, which he will certainly not willingly acknowledge, in that period of his youth in which his sexual passions were already strongly developed but in which gratification of them with an object outside the family was almost as completely prohibited as with an incestuous one.

The women of our civilized world are similarly affected by their up-bringing and further, too, by the reaction upon them of this attitude in men. Naturally the effect upon a woman is just as unfavourable if the man comes to her without his full potency as if, after overestimating her in the early stages of falling in love, he then, having successfully possessed himself of her, sets her at naught. Women show little need to degrade the sexual object ; no doubt this has some connection with the circumstance that as a rule they develop little of the sexual overestimation natural to men. The long abstinence from sexuality to which they are forced and the lingering of their sensuality in phantasy have in them, however, another important consequence. It is often not possible for them later on to undo the connection thus formed in their minds between sensual activities and something forbidden, and they turn out to be psychically impotent, *i.e.* frigid, when at last such activities do become permissible. This is the source of the desire in so many women to keep even legitimate relations secret for a time ; and of the appearance of the capacity for normal sensation in others as soon as the condition of prohibition is restored by a secret intrigue—untrue to the husband, they can keep a second order of faith with the lover.

In my opinion the necessary condition of forbiddenness in the erotic life of women holds the same place as the man's need to lower his sexual object. Both are the consequence of the long period of delay between sexual maturity and sexual activity which is demanded by education for social reasons. The aim of both is to overcome the psychical impotence resulting from the lack of union between tenderness and sensuality. That the effect of the same causes differs so greatly in men and in women is perhaps due to another difference in the behaviour of the two sexes. Women belonging to the higher levels of civilization do not usually transgress the prohibition against sexual activities during the period of waiting, and thus they acquire this close association between the forbidden and the sexual. Men usually overstep the prohibition under the condition of lowering the standard of object they require, and so carry this condition on into their subsequent erotic life.

In view of the strenuous efforts being made in the civilized world at the present day to reform sexual life, it is not superfluous to remind the reader that psychoanalytic investigations have no more bias in any direction than has any other scientific research. In tracing back to its concealed sources what is manifest, psycho-analysis has no aim but that of disclosing connections. It can but be satisfied if what it has brought to light is of use in effecting reforms by substituting more advantageous for injurious conditions. It cannot, however, predict whether other, perhaps even greater, sacrifices may not result from other institutions.

III

The fact that the restrictions imposed by cultural education upon erotic life involve a general lowering of the sexual object may prompt us to turn our eyes from the object to the instincts themselves. The injurious results of the deprivation of sexual enjoyment at the beginning manifest themselves in lack of full satisfaction when sexual desire is later given free rein in marriage. But, on the other hand, unrestrained sexual liberty from the beginning leads to no better result. It is easy to show that the value the mind sets on erotic needs instantly sinks as soon as satisfaction becomes readily obtainable. Some obstacle is necessary to swell the tide of the libido to its height; and at all periods of history, wherever natural barriers in the way of satisfaction have not sufficed, mankind has erected conventional ones in order to be able to enjoy love. This is true both of individuals and of nations. In times during which no obstacles to sexual satisfaction existed, such as, may be, during the decline of the civilizations of antiquity, love became worthless, life became empty, and strong reaction-formations were necessary before the indispensable emotional value of love could be recovered. In this context it may be stated that the ascetic tendency of Christianity had the effect of raising the psychical value of love in a way that heathen antiquity could never achieve ; it developed greatest significance in the lives of the ascetic monks, which were almost entirely occupied with struggles against libidinous temptation.

One's first inclination undoubtedly is to see in this difficulty a universal characteristic of our organic instincts. It is certainly true in a general way that the importance of an instinctual desire is mentally increased by frustration of it. Suppose one made the experiment of exposing a number of utterly different human beings to hunger under the same conditions. As the imperative need for food rose in them all their individual differences would be effaced, and instead the uniform manifestations of one unsatisfied instinct would appear. But is it also true, conversely, that the mental value of an instinct invariably sinks with gratification of it ? One thinks, for instance, of the relation of the wine-drinker to wine. Is it not a fact that wine always affords the drinker the same toxic satisfaction—one that in poetry has so often been likened to the erotic and that science as well may regard as comparable ? Has one ever heard of a drinker being forced constantly to change his wine because he soon gets tired of always drinking the same ? On the contrary, habit binds a man more and more to the particular kind of wine he drinks. Do we ever find a drinker impelled to go to another country where the wine is dearer or where alcohol is prohibited, in order to stimulate his dwindling pleasure in it by these obstacles ? Nothing of the sort. If we listen to what our great lovers of alcohol say about their attitude to wine, for instance, B. Böcklin,[1] it sounds like the most perfect harmony, a model of a happy marriage. Why is the relation of the lover to his sexual object so very different ?

However strange it may sound, I think the possibility must be considered that something in the nature of the sexual instinct itself is unfavourable to the achievement of absolute gratification. When we think of the long and difficult evolution the instinct goes through, two factors to which this difficulty might be ascribed at once emerge. First, in consequence of the two ' thrusts ' of sexual development impelling towards choice of an object, together with the intervention of the incest-barrier between the two, the ultimate object selected is never the original one but only a surrogate for it. Psycho-analysis has shown us, however, that

[1] G. Floerke, *Zehn Jahre mit Böcklin*, 2 Aufl., 1902, p. 16.

when the original object of an instinctual desire becomes lost in consequence of repression, it is often replaced by an endless series of substitute-objects, none of which ever give full satisfaction. This may explain the lack of stability in object-choice, the ' craving for stimulus ', which is so often a feature of the love of adults.

Secondly, we know that at its beginning the sexual instinct is divided into a large number of components— or, rather, it develops from them—not all of which can be carried on into its final form ; some have to be suppressed or turned to other uses before the final form results. Above all, the coprophilic elements in the instinct have proved incompatible with our aesthetic ideas, probably since the time when man developed an upright posture and so removed his organ of smell from the ground ; further, a considerable proportion of the sadistic elements belonging to the erotic instinct have to be abandoned. All such developmental processes, however, relate only to the upper layers of the complicated structure. The fundamental processes which promote erotic excitation remain always the same. Excremental things are all too intimately and inseparably bound up with sexual things ; the position of the genital organs—*inter urinas et faeces*—remains the decisive and unchangeable factor. One might say, modifying a well-known saying of the great Napoleon's, ' Anatomy is destiny '. The genitals themselves have not undergone the development of the rest of the human form in the direction of beauty ; they have retained their animal cast ; and so even to-day love, too, is in essence as animal as it ever was. The erotic instincts are hard to mould ; training of them achieves now too much, now too little. What culture tries to make out of them seems attainable only at the cost of a sensible loss of pleasure ; the persistence of the impulses that are not enrolled in adult sexual activity makes itself felt in an absence of satisfaction.

So perhaps we must make up our minds to the idea

that altogether it is not possible for the claims of the sexual instinct to be reconciled with the demands of culture, that in consequence of his cultural development renunciation and suffering, as well as the danger of his extinction at some far future time, are not to be eluded by the race of man. This gloomy prognosis rests, it is true, on the single conjecture that the lack of satisfaction accompanying culture is the necessary consequence of certain peculiarities developed by the sexual instinct under the pressure of culture. This very incapacity in the sexual instinct to yield full satisfaction as soon as it submits to the first demands of culture becomes the source, however, of the grandest cultural achievements, which are brought to birth by ever greater sublimation of the components of the sexual instinct. For what motive would induce man to put his sexual energy to other uses if by any disposal of it he could obtain fully satisfying pleasure? He would never let go of this pleasure and would make no further progress. It seems, therefore, that the irreconcilable antagonism between the demands of the two instincts—the sexual and the egoistic—have made man capable of ever greater achievements, though, it is true, under the continual menace of danger, such as that of the neuroses to which at the present time the weaker are succumbing.

The purpose of science is neither to alarm nor to reassure. But I myself freely admit that such far-reaching conclusions as those drawn here should be built up on a broader foundation, and that perhaps developments in other directions will enable mankind to remedy the effects of these, which we have here been considering in isolation.

CONTRIBUTIONS TO THE PSYCHOLOGY OF LOVE

THE TABOO OF VIRGINITY [1]

(1918)

THERE are few details of the sexual life of primitive races which seem so strange to our feeling as their attitude towards virginity, the condition in a woman of being sexually untouched. The high value set upon her virginity by a man wooing a woman seems to us so deeply planted and self-evident that we become almost perplexed if called upon to give reasons for it. The demand that the girl shall bring with her into marriage with one man no memory of sexual relations with another is after all nothing but a logical consequence of the exclusive right of possession over a woman which is the essence of monogamy—it is but an extension of this monopoly on to the past.

From this it is not difficult to go on and justify what at first appeared to be a prejudice by referring to our ideas concerning the character of the erotic life in women. The maiden whose desire for love has for so long and with such difficulty been held in check, in whom the influences of environment and education have formed resistances, will take the man who gratifies her longing, and thereby overcomes her resistances, into a close and lasting relationship which will never again be available to any other man. This experience brings about a state of ' thraldom ' in the woman that assures the man lasting and undisturbed possession of her and makes her able to withstand new impressions and temptations from without.

[1] First published in *Sammlung*, Vierte Folge, 1918. [Translated by Joan Riviere.]

The expression ' sexual thraldom '[1] was adopted by von Krafft-Ebing in 1892 to denote the fact that one person may develop an unusually high degree of dependence and helplessness towards another with whom he has a sexual relationship. This ' thraldom ' can at times go to great lengths, even to the total loss of independent will and the heaviest sacrifices of personal interests ; the author has not failed to observe, however, that a certain degree of this dependence is ' absolutely necessary if the relationship is to have any permanence '. Some measure of sexual thraldom is indeed indispensable in maintaining civilized marriage and restraining the polygamous tendencies that threaten to undermine it, and in our social communities this factor is regularly taken into account.

Krafft-Ebing derives the origin of sexual thraldom from the conjunction of ' an unusual degree of development of love and of weakness of character ' in the one partner with unbounded egoism in the other. Analytic experience, however, makes it impossible for us to be content with this simple explanation. On the contrary, one can clearly see that the decisive factor is the strength of the sexual resistances that are surmounted, together with the extent to which this conquest is concentrated in one single act and carried out once and for all. For this reason sexual thraldom is incomparably more frequent and more intense in women than in men, though it is nowadays much commoner in the latter than it was in antiquity. Where we have been able to study sexual thraldom in men it has proved to be the result of a victory over psychical impotence in respect of one particular woman, to whom the man in question thenceforward remained bound. Many a surprising marriage and many a tragic fate—even some of far-reaching consequences—seem to find their explanation in this course of events.

The attitude of primitive races which I shall now

---

[1] Von Krafft-Ebing, ' Bemerkungen über " geschlechtliche Hörigkeit " und Masochismus '.

discuss would be incorrectly described by saying that they set no value on virginity and by seeking to prove this from the circumstance that the defloration of girls is performed apart from marriage and before the first act of marital intercourse. On the contrary, it appears that the act of defloration has great significance for them also, but it has become the subject of a taboo, of what may be called a religious prohibition. Instead of reserving it for the bridegroom and future husband of the girl, custom demands that he should abstain from the performance of it.[1]

It is not my intention to reproduce in full the evidence in the literature concerning the existence of this prohibition, to follow out its geographical distribution or to enumerate the various forms in which it is expressed. I shall content myself with the statement that the custom of rupturing the hymen in this way apart from subsequent marriage is a very widespread one among primitive races. Thus Crawley says : [2] ' This marriage ceremony consists in perforation of the hymen by some appointed person other than the husband ; it is most common in the lowest stages of culture, especially in Australia.'

If, however, defloration is not to be effected through the first act of marital intercourse, it must, in some way or other and by some person or other, be performed beforehand. I shall quote some passages from Crawley's *Mystic Rose* which give some information on this point, but also give ground for some critical remarks.

P. 191. ' Thus in the Dieri and neighbouring tribes (in Australia) it is the universal custom when a girl reaches puberty to rupture the hymen ' (*Journal of the Royal Anthropological Institute*, xxiv. 169). In the Portland and Glenelg tribes this is done to the bride

---

[1] Crawley, *The Mystic Rose : a Study of Primitive Marriage*, 1902 ; Ploss-Bartels, *Das Weib in der Natur- und Völkerkunde*, 1891 ; various passages in Frazer's *Taboo and the Perils of the Soul* ; and Havelock Ellis, *Studies in the Psychology of Sex*.

[2] *Loc. cit.* p. 347.

by an old woman ; and sometimes white men are asked for this reason to deflower maidens (Brough Smith, *op. cit.* ii. 319).

P. 307. ' The artificial rupture of the hymen sometimes takes place in infancy, but generally at puberty. . . . It is often combined, as in Australia, with a ceremonial act of intercourse.'

P. 348. (In communications made by Spencer and Gillen about Australian tribes in which the well-known exogamic restrictions in regard to marriage are customary.) ' The hymen is artificially perforated, and then the men who are assisting have access (ceremonial, be it observed) to the girl in a stated order. . . . The act is in two parts, perforation and intercourse.'

P. 349. ' An important preliminary of marriage amongst the Masai (in Equatorial Africa) is the performance of this operation on the girl (J. Thomson, *op. cit.* ii. 258). This defloration is performed by the father of the bride amongst the Sakais (Malay), Battas (Sumatra), and Alfoers of Celebes (Ploss und Bartels, *op. cit.* ii. 490). In the Philippines there were certain men whose profession it was to deflower brides, in case the hymen had not been ruptured in childhood by an old woman who was sometimes employed for this (Featherman, *op. cit.* ii. 474). The defloration of the bride was amongst some Eskimo tribes entrusted to the *angekok*, or priest (*id.* iii. 406).'

The critical remarks to which I alluded refer to two points. First, it is unfortunate that in these accounts a closer distinction is not drawn between mere rupture of the hymen without coitus and coitus for the purpose of rupturing the hymen. Only in one place is it expressly stated that the process was divided into two actions, *i.e.* defloration (by manual or instrumental means) followed by an act of intercourse. The material collected by Ploss-Bartels, which is in other respects most fruitful, is almost useless for our purpose, because in their account the psychological significance of the act of defloration is entirely displaced by interest in its anatomical result. Secondly, one would like to hear more about the difference between the ' ceremonial ' (purely formal, ritual, official) coitus performed on these occasions and ordinary sexual intercourse. The writers of such works as I could obtain were either too much ashamed to mention such things or else they again underestimated the psychological importance of these sexual details. It is to be hoped that the first-hand reports of travellers and missionaries may be fuller and less equivocal, but in view of the inaccessibility at the present time of publications of this nature,[1] which are mostly foreign, I cannot speak with any certainty upon the matter. In any event one is entitled to pass over the doubt arising on the second point, in view of the consideration that a ceremonial mock-coitus would only be a substitute for the complete act and perhaps a commutation of the act itself performed in earlier times.[2]

Various factors, which I shall now briefly discuss, can be adduced in explanation of this taboo of virginity. Defloration of a maiden usually causes a flow of blood ; the first attempt at explanation refers therefore to the dread of shedding blood among primitive races who regard blood as the seat of life. This blood-taboo is expressed in many different regulations which have nothing to do with sexuality ; it is clearly connected with the prohibition against murder and represents a defensive measure against the primordial blood-thirstiness, primitive man's lust to kill. This conception of it brings the taboo of virginity into relation with the taboo of menstruation that is almost universally observed. The primitive cannot help connecting the mysterious phenomenon of the monthly flow of blood with sadistic ideas. Thus he interprets menstruation, especially at its onset, as the bite of a spirit-animal, or possibly as the token of sexual intercourse with this

---

[1] [Owing to the European War.—Trans.]

[2] There can be no doubt that in a large number of other forms of wedding-ceremony other persons beside the bridegroom, *i.e.* his friends and companions (the ' best man ' of our custom), were accorded full sexual access to the bride.

spirit. Occasionally the reports reveal this spirit as one of an ancestor and then from other knowledge we have gained [1] we understand that it is in virtue of her being the property of this spirit-ancestor that the menstruating girl is taboo.

Other considerations, however, warn us not to exaggerate the influence of a factor such as the horror of blood. After all, the latter does not suffice to suppress customs like the circumcision of boys and the still more cruel extirpation of the clitoris and labia minora in girls, which are practised to some extent by the same races, nor to abolish the prevalence of other ceremonies at which blood is shed. It would not have been surprising, therefore, if this taboo had been relaxed in favour of the husband on the occasion of the first cohabitation.

The second explanation is also unconnected with sexuality ; it is even more general, however, and less specific than the first. It suggests that primitive man is a prey to a perpetual ' anxious expectation ', to a lurking sense of apprehension, just like those suffering from the anxiety-neurosis classified by us in the psycho-analytical theory of the neuroses. This ' anxious expectation ' shows itself most intensely on all occasions that depart from what is usual, in regard to anything that involves something novel, unexpected, unexplained, uncanny. It is also the origin of the ritual, so widely adopted in later religions, that is observed in connection with beginning any new undertaking, with the commencement of each new period of time, or with the first-fruits of human, animal and plant life. The dangers which in his imagination menace the fearful are never expected to be more terrible than at the beginning of a perilous enterprise, and it is consequently only at that point that protective measures can avail him. The first act of intercourse in marriage certainly has sufficient importance to justify its being preceded by precautionary measures of this kind. These two

[1] Cf. Freud, *Totem und Tabu.*

attempts at explanation, by reference to the horror of blood and the dread of what is novel, do not gainsay each other ; on the contrary, they reinforce each other. The first act of intercourse is certainly a critical matter and all the more if it causes blood to flow.

A third explanation—it is that preferred by Crawley —points out that the taboo of virginity belongs to a range of ideas that includes the whole of sexual life. Not only is the first act of coitus with any woman taboo, but sexual intercourse in general ; it might almost be said that woman is altogether taboo. Not merely is woman taboo in special situations connected with her sexual life, such as during menstruation, pregnancy, child-birth and lying-in ; but quite apart from these occasions intercourse with a woman is subject to such heavy and numerous restrictions that we have every reason to question the apparent sexual liberty of savages. It is true that on special occasions the sexuality of primitive man sets all these restraints at naught ; ordinarily, however, it seems to be more strictly circumscribed than it is in higher levels of civilization. As soon as a man sets about any special undertaking, such as an expedition, a hunt, a campaign, he must avoid women, and especially abstain from sexual intercourse with them ; otherwise his strength will be paralysed and the result of the enterprise disaster. Also in the customs relating to daily life there exists an unmistakable tendency to keep the sexes apart. Women live with women and men with men ; family life as we know it is said to be hardly known in many primitive tribes. At times the separation goes so far that one sex may not speak the names of the other sex, and the women develop a special vocabulary. These dividing barriers may be broken through from time to time by sexual need, but in many tribes even intercourse between married couples must take place outside the house in secret.

Wherever primitive man institutes a taboo, there he fears a danger ; and it cannot be disputed that the general principle underlying all these regulations and avoidances is a dread of woman.   Perhaps this fear is founded on the difference of woman from man, on her eternally inexplicable, mysterious and strange nature, which thus seems hostile.   Man fears that his strength will be taken from him by woman, dreads becoming infected with her femininity and then proving himself a weakling.   The effect of coitus in discharging tensions and inducing flaccidity may be a prototype of what these fears represent ; and realization of the influence gained by the woman over a man as a result of sexual relations, and the favours she extorts by this means, may all conduce to justify the growth of these fears. There is nothing in all this which is extinct, which is not still alive in the heart of man to-day.

Many observers of primitive races existing at the present time have formed the opinion that the erotic instinct in them is comparatively weak and never reaches the intensity usually found in civilized man. Others again contradict this statement ; but in any event the taboos described are evidence of the existence of a force which, by rejecting woman as strange and hostile, sets itself against love.

Crawley, in terms that are hardly distinguishable from those employed by psycho-analysis, sets forth, how each individual is separated from the others by a ' taboo of personal isolation ' and that it is precisely the little dissimilarities in persons who are otherwise alike that arouse feelings of strangeness and enmity between them.   It would be tempting to follow up this idea and trace back to this ' narcissism of small differences ' the antagonism which in all human rela-tions we see successfully combating feelings of fellow-ship and the commandment of love towards all men. Psycho-analysis believes that, in pointing out the castration complex and its influence on the estimation in which women are held, it has discovered one of the chief factors underlying the narcissistic rejection of women by men that is so liberally mingled with disdain.

We perceive, however, that these later considerations go far beyond the subject under discussion. The universal taboo of women throws no light on special regulations for the first sexual act with a virgin. As regards this, we have got no further than the two first explanations relating to the dread of blood and the dread of what is novel, and even these, we must object, do not touch the core of the taboo-ordinance in question. The purpose underlying the latter is quite clearly that of denying to the future husband in particular, or of relieving him from, something inseparably connected with the first sexual act ; although, according to the statements with which this paper opened, this very relation would give rise to a specially close attachment in the woman to this one man.

Our present task is not that of examining the origin and ultimate significance of taboo-ordinances in general. In my book *Totem und Tabu* I have done so, and have gone into the question of an innate ambivalence inherent in taboo and argued the genesis of taboo from prehistoric conditions and events leading up to the foundation of the human family. This earlier significance pertaining to taboo is no longer recognizable in the ceremonies of those primitive men we can observe to-day. Any such expectation shows how easily we forget that the conditions of life under which even the most primitive peoples live are a complicated development far removed from the primeval state and just as old as our own, representing a later, if different, stage of development just as our own civilization does.

We find the taboos of primitive races to-day already elaborated into intricate systems, just like those constructed by our neurotics in their phobias ; the original motives in them are replaced by newer ones which harmonize with the others. Leaving these genetic problems on one side, however, we will return to the point of view that where primitive man fears a danger there he institutes a taboo. This danger that he fears is, taken altogether, a psychical one, for the primitive is not constrained to make the distinctions which to us seem so necessary. He does not separate physical danger from psychical, nor real from imaginary danger. In his animistic view of life, logically worked out as it is, every danger proceeds from a hostile impulse on the part of some being with a soul like his own, just as much if the menace comes from some force of nature as from other human beings or animals. On the other hand, however, he has the habit of projecting his own inner feelings of hostility on to the outside world, that is, of ascribing them to whatever objects he dislikes or even is merely unfamiliar with. Now woman is also looked upon as a source of such dangers and the first sexual act with a woman stands out as a specially perilous one.

I think now we shall obtain some light on the question of what this specially intense danger consists in, and why it menaces the future husband in particular, by examining the behaviour of present-day civilized women in the same circumstances. I will anticipate the result of such an examination by saying that a danger of the kind does really exist, so that with his taboo primitive man is protecting himself from a danger—a psychical one, it is true—which his intuition had quite correctly divined.

We regard it as the normal reaction to coitus for a woman to hold the man closely in her arms and press him to her at the climax of gratification, and this seems to us an expression of her gratitude and an assurance of lasting thraldom to him. We know, however, that the first act of intercourse is by no means always followed by this behaviour ; very often the experience merely signifies a disappointment to the woman, who remains cold and unsatisfied ; usually it takes some time and frequent repetition of the sexual act before satisfaction in it for her too sets in. From these cases of merely initial and quite temporary frigidity there proceeds a gradation up to the unsatisfactory extreme case of permanent and unremitting frigidity, which not

THE TABOO OF VIRGINITY

the utmost tenderness and eagerness on the part of the husband is able to overcome. In my opinion this frigidity in women is not yet sufficiently understood ; wherever the insufficient potency of the husband is not to blame, it demands explanation, which must be sought, if necessary, in other phenomena of a similar nature.

I shall not here consider the frequent attempts of women to escape the first sexual act, because they can have more than one meaning, and in the main, if not entirely, are to be construed as expressions of the general female tendency to ward off sexuality. I believe, on the other hand, that certain pathological cases throw a light on the riddle of female frigidity ; these are women who after the first act of intercourse —and, indeed, after every renewed act—openly express their enmity against the man by reviling him, threatening to strike him or even actually striking him. In one very pronounced case of this kind, which I was able to subject to thorough analysis, this animosity displayed itself although the woman loved the man deeply, used to demand intercourse and unquestionably obtained great satisfaction in it. I believe this strangely self-contradictory reaction is due to the very feelings that generally attain to expression only in the form of frigidity, *i.e.* that are then capable of preventing the tender reaction though unable to break through to expression themselves. That which in the far more common type of frigid woman unites to form an inhibition in the pathological case fell into its two components ; just as happens in what are called the ' two-movement ' symptoms of the obsessional neurosis which were long ago recognized. The danger which is thus aroused through defloration of a woman would consist in drawing down upon oneself this animosity, and the future husband would be the very man with most reason to avoid so doing.

Now analysis enables us easily to discover what those impulses in women are that bring about this paradoxical behaviour, and which, as I expect, explain frigidity.   The first act of coitus stirs up a number of impulses which can find no place in the womanly attitude proper to the situation, some of which, moreover, do not necessarily arise during subsequent intercourse.   First of all one thinks of the pain inflicted on a virgin at defloration ; indeed, one might be inclined to regard this factor as the decisive one and give up looking for any others.   But so much importance cannot well be attributed to pain ; we must set in its place the narcissistic wound which follows the destruction of an organ, and which even finds rationalized expression in the realization of a diminished sexual value after virginity is lost.   The marriage-ceremonies of primitives warn us, however, not to overestimate this. We have seen that often the rite consists of two parts ; after the rupture of the hymen has been carried out (with the hand or some instrument) there follows an official act of intercourse, or a mock-coitus, with certain persons who take the husband's place ; this is evidence that the purpose of the taboo-ordinance is not fully achieved by avoidance of the anatomical defloration and that the husband is to be spared something else beside the woman's reaction to the painful injury.

A further ground for disappointment on experiencing the first sexual act is found to lie in its failure to fulfil expectations, at least so far as civilized women are concerned.   Until this moment sexual intercourse has been closely associated with a heavy prohibition ; lawful and permissible intercourse is apprehended consequently as a quite different thing.   How fundamental this association can be is illustrated in an almost comic manner by the behaviour of so many young women about to be married, who try to keep the new experience of a love-relationship secret from everyone, including even their parents, where there is no sort of need to do so and no objection is anticipated.   Girls openly declare that love loses its value to them if others know about it.   This feeling can sometimes outweigh all others and totally prevent any development of the capacity to love in marriage. The woman then recovers her feelings of tenderness only in an illicit relationship which must be kept secret, and in which she feels certain of being actuated by her own will alone.

Not even this motive goes deep enough, however ; it is bound up, moreover, with civilized conditions and lacks sufficient connection with primitive states of culture. The next factor, therefore, which depends on the evolution of the libido, is all the more important. Analytic researches have discovered how universal and how powerful the first attachments of the libido are. It is a question of sexual wishes active in childhood and never relinquished—in women generally a fixation of the libido upon the father, or upon a brother taking his place—wishes that often enough were directed to things other than coitus, or that included it among others only as a vaguely conceived aim. A husband is, so to speak, never anything but a proxy, never the right man ; the first claim upon the feeling of love in a woman belongs to someone else, in typical cases to her father ; the husband is at best a second. Now whether the husband is rejected as unsatisfying depends upon the strength of this fixation and the tenacity with which it is upheld. The same conditioning factors thus lead to the development of frigidity as to neurosis. The more powerful the mental element in a woman's sexual life, the more her libido-distribution will resist the shock involved in the first sexual act and the less overwhelming will be the effect of a man taking bodily possession of her. Frigidity may establish itself thenceforth as a neurotic inhibition or become the soil from which other neuroses can spring, and even a quite moderate diminution of potency in the man contributes appreciably to this.

Primitive custom appears to accord some recognition to the existence of the early sexual wish by assigning the duty of defloration to an elder, a priest, or a holy man, that is, to a father-substitute (*vide supra*). This seems to lead directly to the much-contested *jus primae noctis* of mediaeval feudal lords. A. J. Storfer [1] has expressed the same view of this matter, and, further, has construed the widespread custom of the ' Tobias nights ' (the custom of continence during the first three nights) to be an acknowledgement of the prerogative of the patriarch, as C. G. Jung had done before him. [2] It is only in accord with our expectations, therefore, to find divine figures, too, among the father-surrogates to whom defloration is entrusted. In many districts in India the bride was obliged to sacrifice the hymen as an offering to the wooden lingam ; and according to St. Augustine the same custom obtained in Roman marriage-ceremonies (of his time ?), though toned down to the extent that the young wife had only to seat herself upon the gigantic stone phallus of Priapus. [3]

There is another motive reaching down into yet deeper strata, on which can be seen to rest the chief blame for the paradoxical reaction towards the man, and the influence of which in my opinion is still at work in female frigidity. The first coitus stirs yet other, older impulses in the woman besides those described—impulses which in their whole tendency oppose the female function and the female part.

From the analyses of many neurotic women we have learnt that women go through an early phase in which they envy their brothers the token of maleness and feel themselves handicapped and ill-treated on account of the lack of it (really, on account of its diminutive form). In our view this ' penis-envy ' forms part of the castration complex. If ' masculine ' is to include the connotation of ' wishing to be masculine ', the term ' masculine protest ' fits this attitude ; this term was coined by Alfred Adler for the purpose of proclaiming this factor as

---

[1] *Zur Sonderstellung des Vatermordes.*
[2] ' Die Bedeutung des Vaters für das Schicksal des Einzelnen.'
[3] Ploss und Bartels, *Das Weib*, I., XII., and Dulaure, *Des Divinités génératrices*, p. 142 *et seq.*

the foundation of all neurosis in general. During this early phase little girls often make no secret of their envy of the favoured brother, and the animosity it gives rise to against him ; they even try to urinate standing upright like the brother, thus asserting the equality with him that they claim. In the case mentioned of unbridled aggressiveness after coitus against the man who was otherwise greatly loved, I was able to establish that this phase had existed before object-choice had set in. Only later did the libido of the little girl turn towards the father and then her desire was, instead of the penis—a child.[1]

I should not wonder if in other cases this sequence were found to be reversed, this element of the castration complex becoming operative only after object-choice had been effected. But the masculine phase in woman during which she envies the boy his penis is at all events developmentally the earlier and more closely allied to primal narcissism than to object-love.

Not long ago chance gave me an opportunity of obtaining insight into a dream of a newly married woman, which revealed itself as a reaction to the loss of her virginity. It betrayed unmistakably the wish to castrate the young husband and keep his penis for herself. There was room, to be sure, for the more harmless interpretation that it was prolongation and repetition of the act that she wanted ; unfortunately, however, some details of the dream overstepped this possibility, and both the character and subsequent behaviour of the dreamer were evidence for the graver view of it. Now, upon this penis-envy follows that hostile embitterment displayed by women against men, never entirely absent in the relations between the sexes, the clearest indications of which are to be found in the writings and ambitions of ' emancipated ' women. Ferenczi, in a palaeo-biological speculation, traces this enmity in women back to the era when differentiation between the sexes

[1] Cf. ' On the Transformation of Instincts with Special Reference to Anal Erotism ', COLLECTED PAPERS, vol. ii.

took place—I do not know whether the priority for it is his. First of all, he believes, copulation was effected between two single organisms of the same kind, one of which, however, developed until it was stronger and then forced the weaker to submit to sexual union ; and the embitterment on account of this subjection is still an active predisposition in women to-day. I see no harm in such speculations, so long as one does not overestimate their value.

After this enumeration of the motives underlying the paradoxical reaction of women to defloration and traceable in frigidity, one may sum up and say that it is the immature sexuality of the woman which discharges itself upon the man who first introduces her to sexual intercourse. With this, the taboo of virginity becomes intelligible enough, and we understand a regulation which enjoins avoidance of these dangers on the very man who is entering upon life in company with this woman. In higher levels of culture the importance attaching to this danger has given way before the promise of the woman's thraldom, and certainly too for other reasons and inducements ; the virginity of the woman is looked upon as an asset which the man should not resign. Analysis of the causes of unhappy marriage, however, shows that the motives impelling the woman to revenge herself for her defloration are not entirely extinguished even in the minds of civilized women. The surprisingly large number of women who remain anaesthetic and unhappy throughout their first marriage and then, after this is dissolved, become a loving wife, able to make another man happy, must, I think, strike any observer. The archaic reaction has exhausted itself, so to speak, on the first object.

But elsewhere too in our civilized life the taboo of virginity is not extinct. The soul of the people knows it, and poets have at times made use of this material. In one of Anzengruber's comedies, a simple peasant youth refuses to marry his intended bride, because she

is ' a girl who'll cost her first his life '. He agrees to
her marrying another man, and then when she is
a widow and no longer dangerous he will have her.
The title of the piece, *Das Jungferngift* (The Virgin's
Poison), reminds one of the practice of snake-charmers
who first make the snake bite a rag so that they can
afterwards handle it safely.[1]

The taboo of virginity and some part of its motivation has been portrayed most powerfully of all in the
well-known figure of Judith in Hebbel's tragedy, *Judith
und Holofernes*. Judith is one of those women whose
virginity is protected by a taboo. Her first husband
was paralysed on the wedding-night by an inexplicable
fear and never again dared to touch her. ' My beauty
is like deadly nightshade,' she says, ' enjoyment of it
brings madness and death'. When the Assyrian
general is besieging the city, she conceives the plan of
enticing him with her beauty and destroying him, thus
using a patriotic motive to mask a sexual one. After
being deflowered by the masterful man who makes a
boast of his might and his ruthlessness, she in her fury
finds strength to strike off his head and so becomes the
saviour of her people. Decapitation is to us a well-
known symbolic substitute for castration ; so Judith
is a woman who castrates the man by whom she was
deflowered, just as the newly married woman wished
to do in the dream I mentioned. Hebbel deliberately
sexualized the patriotic narrative in the Apocrypha,
for there Judith boasts after her return to the city of
not having been polluted, nor is there any mention in

---

[1] A masterly short story of Arthur Schnitzler's (*Das Schicksal des
Freiherrn von Leisenbogh*) deserves to be mentioned in this connection,
in spite of a departure in it from the situation under discussion. The
lover of an actress who had had great experience in love is dying as the
result of an accident ; and he creates a new virginity for her, as it
were, by uttering a curse of death upon the next man to possess her
after him. For a time the woman who is thus placed under a taboo
does not venture to have intercourse with anyone. Then she falls in
love with a singer, and resorts to the plan of first granting a night with
her to Freiherr von Leisenbogh, who has for years tried in vain to win
her. And the curse fulfils itself on him ; he dies of a stroke on hearing
the reason of his unexpected good fortune.

the Biblical text of her uncanny nuptials. But with the sensitive intuition of a poet Hebbel probably divined the primordial theme that had been lost in the tendentious story, and only gave back to the content its earlier currency.

Sadger has worked out in an excellent analysis the way in which Hebbel's choice of material was determined by his own parental complex, and how it was that in a struggle between the sexes he invariably took the part of woman and knew intuitively the most hidden feelings of her soul.[1] He quotes also the reasons the poet himself gave for his alterations of the material, and rightly finds them factitious and apparently designed superficially to justify the poet's own unconscious to himself, but ultimately to conceal it. I will not touch Sadger's explanation of why the widowed Judith of the Bible had to become a virgin widow. He adduces the motive in the infantile phantasy of denying the sexual intercourse of the parents, so that the mother becomes an untouched virgin. But I will continue : after the poet has duly established his heroine's virginity, his phantasy probes into and dwells upon the resentful reaction let loose after maidenhood has been violated.

In conclusion, then, we may say that the act of defloration has not merely the socially useful result of binding the woman closely to the man ; it also liberates an archaic reaction of enmity towards the man, which may assume pathological forms, and often enough expresses itself by inhibitions in the erotic life of the pair, and to which one may ascribe the fact that second marriages so often turn out better than first. The strange taboo of virginity—the fear which among primitive peoples induces the husband to avoid the performance of defloration—finds its full justification in this hostile turn of feeling.

It is interesting now to find that psycho-analysts come across women in whom the two contrary attitudes

[1] Sadger, ' Von der Pathographie zur Psychographie '.

—thraldom and enmity—both come to expression and remain in close association. There are women who appear to be utterly alienated from their husbands and who can yet make only vain attempts to separate from them. As often as they try to turn their love to some other man, the image of the first, who is nevertheless not loved, comes as a barrier between. Analysis then shows that these women still cling to their first husbands, in thraldom, truly, but no longer from affection. They cannot free themselves from him because their revenge upon him is not yet complete ; and, indeed, in extreme cases they have never even let the vengeful impulse reach their conscious minds.

THOUGHTS FOR THE TIMES ON WAR AND DEATH [1]

(1915)

I

THE DISILLUSIONMENT OF THE WAR

SWEPT as we are into the vortex of this war-time, our information one-sided, ourselves too near to focus the mighty transformations which have already taken place or are beginning to take place, and without a glimmering of the inchoate future, we are incapable of apprehending the significance of the thronging impressions, and know not what value to attach to the judgements we form. We are constrained to believe that never has any event been destructive of so much that is valuable in the common wealth of humanity, nor so misleading to many of the clearest intelligences, nor so debasing to the highest that we know. Science herself has lost her passionless impartiality ; in their deep embitterment her servants seek for weapons from her with which to contribute towards the defeat of the enemy. The anthropologist is driven to declare the opponent inferior and degenerate ; the psychiatrist to publish his diagnosis of the enemy's disease of mind or spirit. But probably our sense of these immediate evils is disproportionately strong, and we are not entitled to compare them with the evils of other times of which we have not undergone the experience.

The individual who is not himself a combatant—and so a wheel in the gigantic machinery of war—feels

---

[1] First published early in 1915 in *Imago*, Bd. V. ; reprinted in *Sammlung*, Vierte Folge. [Translated by E. Colburn Mayne.]

conscious of disorientation, and of an inhibition in his powers and activities. I believe that he will welcome any indication, however slight, which may enable him to find out what is wrong with himself at least. I propose to distinguish two among the most potent factors in the mental distress felt by non-combatants, against which it is such a heavy task to struggle, and to treat of them here: the disillusionment which this war has evoked; and the altered attitude towards death which this—like every other war—imposes on us.

When I speak of disillusionment, everyone at once knows what I mean. One need not be a sentimentalist; one may perceive the biological and psychological necessity of suffering in the economics of human life, and yet condemn war both in its means and in its aims, and devoutly look forward to the cessation of all wars. True, we have told ourselves that wars can never cease so long as nations live under such widely differing conditions, so long as the value of individual life is in each nation so variously computed, and so long as the animosities which divide them represent such powerful instinctual forces in the mind. And we were prepared to find that wars between the primitive and the civilized peoples, between those races whom a colour-line divides, nay, wars with and among the undeveloped nationalities of Europe or those whose culture has perished—that for a considerable period such wars would occupy mankind. But we permitted ourselves to have other hopes. We had expected the great ruling powers among the white nations upon whom the leadership of the human species has fallen, who were known to have cultivated world-wide interests, to whose creative powers were due our technical advances in the direction of dominating nature, as well as the artistic and scientific acquisitions of the mind—peoples such as these we had expected to succeed in discovering another way of settling misunderstandings and conflicts of interest. Within each of these nations there pre-vailed high standards of accepted custom for the individual, to which his manner of life was bound to conform if he desired a share in communal privileges. These ordinances, frequently too stringent, exacted a great deal from him, much self-restraint, much renunciation of instinctual gratification. He was especially forbidden to make use of the immense advantages to be gained by the practice of lying and deception in the competition with his fellow-men. The civilized state regarded these accepted standards as the basis of its existence ; stern were its proceedings when an impious hand was laid upon them ; frequent the pronouncement that to subject them even to examination by a critical intelligence was entirely impracticable. It could be assumed, therefore, that the state itself would respect them, nor would contemplate undertaking any infringement of what it acknowledged as the basis of its own existence. To be sure, it was evident that within these civilized states were mingled remnants of certain other races who were universally unpopular and had therefore been only reluctantly, and even so not to the fullest extent, admitted to participation in the common task of civilization, for which they had shown themselves suitable enough. But the great nations themselves, it might have been supposed, had acquired so much comprehension of their common interests, and enough tolerance for the differences that existed between them, that ' foreigner ' and ' enemy ' could no longer, as still in antiquity, be regarded as synonymous.

Relying on this union among the civilized races, countless people have exchanged their native home for a foreign dwelling-place, and made their existence dependent on the conditions of intercourse between friendly nations. But he who was not by stress of circumstances confined to one spot, could also confer upon himself, through all the advantages and attractions of these civilized countries, a new, a wider fatherland, wherein he moved unhindered and unsuspected. In this way he enjoyed the blue sea, and the grey ; the beauty of the snow-clad mountains and of the green pasture-lands ; the magic of the northern forests and the splendour of the southern vegetation ; the emotion inspired by landscapes that recall great historical events, and the silence of nature in her inviolate places. This new fatherland was for him a museum also, filled with all the treasures which the artists among civilized communities had in the successive centuries created and left behind. As he wandered from one gallery to another in this museum, he could appreciate impartially the varied types of perfection that miscegenation, the course of historical events, and the special character-istics of their mother-earth had produced among his more remote compatriots. Here he would find a cool inflexible energy developed to the highest point ; there, the gracious art of beautifying existence ; else-where, the sense of order and fixed law—in short, any and all of the qualities which have made mankind the lords of the earth.

Nor must we forget that each of these citizens of culture had created for himself a personal ' Parnassus ' and ' School of Athens '. From among the great thinkers and artists of all nations he had chosen those to whom he conceived himself most deeply indebted for what he had achieved in enjoyment and compre-hension of life, and in his veneration had associated them with the immortals of old as well as with the more familiar masters of his own tongue. None of these great figures had seemed to him alien because he had spoken another language—not the incomparable investigator of the passions of mankind, nor the intoxicated worshipper of beauty, nor the vehement and threatening prophet, nor the subtle mocking satirist ; and never did he on this account rebuke himself as a renegade towards his own nation and his beloved mother-tongue.

The enjoyment of this fellowship in civilization was from time to time disturbed by warning voices, which declared that as a result of long-prevailing differences

wars were unavoidable, even among the members of a
fellowship such as this. We refused to believe it ; but
if such a war indeed must be, what was our imaginary
picture of it ? We saw it as an opportunity for
demonstrating the progress of mankind in communal
feeling since the era when the Greek Amphictyones
had proclaimed that no city of the league might be
demolished, nor its olive-groves hewn down, nor its
water cut off. As a chivalrous crusade, which would
limit itself to establishing the superiority of one side
in the contest, with the least possible infliction of dire
sufferings that could contribute nothing to the decision,
and with complete immunity for the wounded who
must of necessity withdraw from the contest, as well
as for the physicians and nurses who devoted themselves to the task of healing. And of course with the
utmost precautions for the non-combatant classes of the
population—for women who are debarred from war-
work, and for the children who, grown older, should be
enemies no longer but friends and co-operators. And
again, with preservation of all the international undertakings and institutions in which the mutual civilization of peace-time had been embodied.

Even a war like this would have been productive
of horrors and sufferings enough ; but it would not
have interrupted the development of ethical relations
between the greater units of mankind, between the
peoples and the states.

Then the war in which we had refused to believe
broke out, and brought—disillusionment. Not only is
it more sanguinary and more destructive than any war
of other days, because of the enormously increased
perfection of weapons of attack and defence ; but it is
at least as cruel, as embittered, as implacable as any
that has preceded it. It sets at naught all those
restrictions known as International Law, which in
peace-time the states had bound themselves to observe ;
it ignores the prerogatives of the wounded and the
medical service, the distinction between civil and

military sections of the population, the claims of private property. It tramples in blind fury on all that comes in its way, as though there were to be no future and no goodwill among men after it has passed. It rends all bonds of fellowship between the contending peoples, and threatens to leave such a legacy of embitterment as will make any renewal of such bonds impossible for a long time to come.

Moreover, it has brought to light the almost un-believable phenomenon of a mutual comprehension between the civilized nations so slight that the one can turn with hate and loathing upon the other. Nay, more—that one of the great civilized nations is so universally unpopular that the attempt can actually be made to exclude it from the civilized community as ' barbaric ', although it long has proved its fitness by the most magnificent co-operation in the work of civilization. We live in the hope that the impartial decision of history will furnish the proof that precisely this nation, this in whose tongue we now write, this for whose victory our dear ones are fighting, was the one which least transgressed the laws of civilization—but at such a time who shall dare present himself as the judge of his own cause ?

Nations are in a measure represented by the states which they have formed ; these states, by the govern-ments which administer them. The individual in any given nation has in this war a terrible opportunity to convince himself of what would occasionally strike him in peace-time—that the state has forbidden to the individual the practice of wrong-doing, not because it desired to abolish it, but because it desires to monopolize it, like salt and tobacco. The warring state permits itself every such misdeed, every such act of violence, as would disgrace the individual man. It practises not only the accepted stratagems, but also deliberate lying and deception against the enemy ; and this, too, in a measure which appears to surpass the usage of former wars. The state exacts the utmost degree of obedience and sacrifice from its citizens, but at the same time treats them as children by maintaining an excess of secrecy, and a censorship of news and expressions of opinion that renders the spirits of those thus intellectually oppressed defenceless against every unfavourable turn of events and every sinister rumour. It absolves itself from the guarantees and contracts it had formed with other states, and makes unabashed confession of its rapacity and lust for power, which the private individual is then called upon to sanction in the name of patriotism.

Nor may it be objected that the state cannot refrain from wrong-doing, since that would place it at a disadvantage. It is no less disadvantageous, as a general rule, for the individual man to conform to the customs of morality and refrain from brutal and arbitrary conduct ; and the state but seldom proves able to indemnify him for the sacrifices it exacts. It cannot be a matter for astonishment, therefore, that this relaxation of all the moral ties between the greater units of mankind should have had a seducing influence on the morality of individuals ; for our conscience is not the inflexible judge that ethical teachers are wont to declare it, but in its origin is ' dread of the community ' and nothing else. When the community has no rebuke to make, there is an end of all suppression of the baser passions, and men perpetrate deeds of cruelty, fraud, treachery and barbarity so incompatible with their civilization that one would have held them to be impossible.

Well may that civilized cosmopolitan, therefore, of whom I spoke, stand helpless in a world grown strange to him—his all-embracing patrimony disintegrated, the common estates in it laid waste, the fellow-citizens embroiled and debased !

In criticism of his disillusionment, nevertheless, certain things must be said. Strictly speaking, it is not justified, for it consists in the destruction of—an illusion ! We welcome illusions because they spare us emotional distress, and enable us instead to indulge in gratification. We must not then complain if now and again they come into conflict with some portion of reality, and are shattered against it.

Two things in this war have evoked our sense of disillusionment : the destitution shown in moral relations externally by the states which in their interior relations pose as the guardians of accepted moral usage, and the brutality in behaviour shown by individuals, whom, as partakers in the highest form of human civilization, one would not have credited with such a thing.

Let us begin with the second point and endeavour to formulate, as succinctly as may be, the point of view which it is proposed to criticize. How do we imagine the process by which an individual attains to a higher plane of morality ? The first answer is sure to be : He is good and noble from his very birth, his very earliest beginnings. We need not consider this any further. A second answer will suggest that we are concerned with a developmental process, and will probably assume that this development consists in eradicating from him the evil human tendencies and, under the influence of education and a civilized environment, replacing them by good ones. From that standpoint it is certainly astonishing that evil should show itself to have such power in those who have been thus nurtured.

But this answer implies the thesis from which we propose to dissent. In reality, there is no such thing as ' eradicating ' evil tendencies. Psychological—more strictly speaking, psycho-analytic—investigation shows instead that the inmost essence of human nature consists of elemental instincts, which are common to all men and aim at the satisfaction of certain primal needs. These instincts in themselves are neither good nor evil. We but classify them and their manifestations in that fashion, according as they meet the needs and demands of the human community. It is admitted that all those instincts which society condemns as evil—let us take as representatives the selfish and the cruel—are of this primitive type.

These primitive instincts undergo a lengthy process of development before they are allowed to become active in the adult being. They are inhibited, directed towards other aims and departments, become commingled, alter their objects, and are to some extent turned back upon their possessor. Reaction-formations against certain instincts take the deceptive form of a change in content, as though egoism had changed into altruism, or cruelty into pity. These reaction-formations are facilitated by the circumstance that many instincts are manifested almost from the first in pairs of opposites, a very remarkable phenomenon—and one strange to the lay public—which is termed the ' ambivalence of feeling '. The most easily observable and comprehensible instance of this is the fact that intense love and intense hatred are so often to be found together in the same person. Psycho-analysis adds that the conflicting feelings not infrequently have the same person for their object.

It is not until all these ' vicissitudes to which instincts are subject ' have been surmounted that what we call the character of a human being is formed, and this, as we know, can only very inadequately be classified as ' good ' or ' bad '. A human being is seldom altogether good or bad ; he is usually ' good ' in one relation and ' bad ' in another, or ' good ' in certain external circumstances and in others decidedly ' bad '. It is interesting to learn that the existence of strong ' bad ' impulses in infancy is often the actual condition for an unmistakable inclination towards ' good ' in the adult person. Those who as children have been the most pronounced egoists may well become the most helpful and self-sacrificing members of the community ; most of our sentimentalists, friends of humanity, champions of animals, have been evolved from little sadists and animal-tormentors.

The transformation of ' bad ' instincts is brought about by two co-operating factors, an internal and an external. The internal factor consists in an influence on the bad—say, the egoistic—instincts exercised by erotism, that is, by the human need for love, taken in its widest sense. By the admixture of *erotic* components the egoistic instincts are transmuted into *social* ones. We learn to value being loved as an advantage for which we are willing to sacrifice other advantages. The external factor is the force exercised by up-bringing, which advocates the claims of our cultural environment, and this is furthered later by the direct pressure of that civilization by which we are surrounded. Civilization is the fruit of renunciation of instinctual satisfaction, and from each new-comer in turn it exacts the same renunciation. Throughout the life of the individual there is a constant replacement of the external compulsion by the internal. The influences of civilization cause an ever-increasing transmutation of egoistic trends into altruistic and social ones, and this by an admixture of erotic elements. In the last resort it may be said that every internal compulsion which has been of service in the development of human beings was originally, that is, in the evolution of the human race, nothing but an external one. Those who are born to-day bring with them as an inherited constitution some degree of a tendency (disposition) towards transmutation of egoistic into social instincts, and this disposition is easily stimulated to achieve that effect. A further measure of this transformation must be accomplished during the life of the individual himself. And so the human being is subject not only to the pressure of his immediate environment, but also to the influence of the cultural development attained by his forefathers.

If we give the name of *cultural adaptability* to a man's personal capacity for transformation of the egoistic impulses under the influence of the erotic, we may further affirm that this adaptability is made up of two parts, one innate and the other acquired through experience, and that the relation of the two to each other and to that portion of the instinctual life which remains untransformed is a very variable one.

Generally speaking, we are apt to attach too much importance to the innate part, and in addition to this we run the risk of overestimating the general adaptability to civilization in comparison with those instincts which have remained in their primitive state—by which I mean that in this way we are led to regard human nature as ' better ' than it actually is. For there is, besides, another factor which obscures our judgement and falsifies the issue in too favourable a sense.

The impulses of another person are naturally hidden from our observation. We deduce them from his actions and behaviour, which we trace to motives born of his instinctual life. Such a conclusion is bound to be, in many cases, erroneous. This or that action which is ' good ' from the civilized point of view may in one instance be born of a ' noble ' motive, in another not so. Ethical theorists class as ' good ' actions only those which are the outcome of good impulses ; to the others they refuse their recognition. But society, which is practical in its aims, is little troubled on the whole by this distinction ; it is content if a man regulates his behaviour and actions by the precepts of civilization, and is little concerned with his motives.

We have seen that the external compulsion exercised on a human being by his up-bringing and environment produces a further transformation towards good in his instinctual life—a turning from egoism towards altruism. But this is not the regular or necessary effect of the external compulsion. Education and environment offer benefits not only in the way of love, but also employ another kind of premium system, namely, reward and punishment. In this way their effect may turn out to be that he who is subjected to their influence will choose to ' behave well ' in the civilized sense of the phrase, although no ennoblement of instinct, no transformation of egoistic into altruistic inclinations, has taken place within. The result will, roughly speaking, be the same ; only a particular concatenation of circumstances will reveal that one man always acts rightly because his instinctual inclination compels him so to do, and the other is ' good ' only in so far and for so long as such civilized behaviour is advantageous for his own egoistic purposes. But superficial acquaintance with an individual will not enable us to distinguish between the two cases, and we are certainly misled by our optimism into grossly exaggerating the number of human beings who have been transformed in a civilized sense.

Civilized society, which exacts good conduct and does not trouble itself about the impulses underlying it, has thus won over to obedience a great many people who are not thereby following the dictates of their own natures. Encouraged by this success, society has suffered itself to be led into straining the moral standard to the highest possible point, and thus it has forced its members into a yet greater estrangement from their instinctual dispositions. They are consequently subjected to an unceasing suppression of instinct, the resulting strain of which betrays itself in the most remarkable phenomena of reaction and compensation formations. In the domain of sexuality, where such suppression is most difficult to enforce, the result is seen in the reaction-phenomena of neurotic disorders. Elsewhere the pressure of civilization brings in its train no pathological results, but is shown in malformations of character, and in the perpetual readiness of the inhibited instincts to break through to gratification at any suitable opportunity. Anyone thus compelled to act continually in the sense of precepts which are not the expression of instinctual inclinations, is living, psychologically speaking, beyond his means, and might objectively be designated a hypocrite, whether this difference be clearly known to him or not. It is undeniable that our contemporary civilization is extraordinarily favourable to the production of this form of hypocrisy. One might venture to say that it is based upon such hypocrisy, and that it would have to submit to far-reaching modifications if people were to undertake to live in accordance with the psychological truth. Thus there are very many more hypocrites than truly civilized persons—indeed, it is a debatable point whether a certain degree of civilized hypocrisy be not indispensable for the maintenance of civilization, because the cultural adaptability so far attained by those living to-day would perhaps not prove adequate to the task. On the other hand, the maintenance of civilization even on so questionable a basis offers the prospect of each new generation achieving a farther-reaching transmutation of instinct, and becoming the pioneer of a higher form of civilization.

From the foregoing observations we may already derive this consolation—that our mortification and our grievous disillusionment regarding the uncivilized behaviour of our world-compatriots in this war are shown to be unjustified. They were based on an illusion to which we had abandoned ourselves. In reality our fellow-citizens have not sunk so low as we feared, because they had never risen so high as we believed. That the greater units of humanity, the peoples and states, have mutually abrogated their moral restraints naturally prompted these individuals to permit themselves relief for a while from the heavy pressure of civilization and to grant a passing satisfaction to the instincts it holds in check. This probably caused no breach in the relative morality within their respective national frontiers.

We may, however, obtain insight deeper than this into the change brought about by the war in our former compatriots, and at the same time receive a warning against doing them an injustice. For the evolution of the mind shows a peculiarity which is present in no other process of development. When a village grows into a town, a child into a man, the village and the child become submerged in the town and the man. Memory alone can trace the earlier features in the new image ; in reality the old materials or forms have been superseded and replaced by new ones. It is otherwise with the development of the mind. Here one can describe the state of affairs, which is a quite peculiar one, only by saying that in this case every earlier stage of development persists alongside the later stage which has developed from it ; the successive stages condition a co-existence, although it is in reference to the same materials that the whole series of transformations has been fashioned. The earlier mental state may not have manifested itself for years, but none the less it is so far present that it may at any time again become the mode of expression of the forces in the mind, and that exclusively, as though all later developments had been annulled, undone. This extraordinary plasticity of the evolution that takes place in the mind is not unlimited in its scope ; it might be described as a special capacity for retroversion—for regression—since it may well happen that a later and higher stage of evolution, once abandoned, cannot be reached again. But the primitive stages can always be re-established ; the primitive mind is, in the fullest meaning of the word, imperishable.

What are called mental diseases inevitably impress the layman with the idea of destruction of the life of mind and soul. In reality, the destruction relates only to later accretions and developments. The essence of mental disease lies in a return to earlier conditions of affective life and functioning. An excellent example of the plasticity of mental life is afforded by the state of sleep, which every night we desire. Since we have learnt to interpret even absurd and chaotic dreams, we know that whenever we sleep we cast off our hard-won morality like a garment, only to put it on again next morning. This divestiture is naturally unattended by any danger because we are paralysed, condemned to inactivity, by the state of sleep. Only through a dream can we learn of the regression of our emotional life to one of the earliest stages of development. For instance, it is noteworthy that all our dreams are governed by purely egoistic motives. One of my English friends put forward this proposition at a scientific meeting in America, whereupon a lady who was present remarked that that might be the case in Austria, but she could maintain for herself and her friends that *they* were altruistic even in their dreams. My friend, although himself of English race, was obliged to contradict the lady emphatically on the ground of his personal experience in dream-analysis, and to declare that in their dreams high-minded American ladies were quite as egoistical as the Austrians.

Thus the transformations of instinct on which our cultural adaptability is based, may also be permanently or temporarily undone by the experiences of life. Undoubtedly the influences of war are among the forces that can bring about such regression ; therefore we need not deny adaptability for culture to all who are at the present time displaying uncivilized behaviour, and we may anticipate that the refinement of their instincts will be restored in times of peace.

There is, however, another symptom in our world-compatriots which has perhaps astonished and shocked us no less than the descent from their ethical nobility which has so greatly distressed us. I mean the narrow-mindedness shown by the best intellects, their obduracy, their inaccessibility to the most forcible arguments, their uncritical credulity for the most disputable assertions. This indeed presents a lamentable picture, and I wish to say emphatically that in this I am by no means a blind partisan who finds all the intellectual shortcomings on one side. But this phenomenon is much easier to account for and much less disquieting than that which we have just considered. Students of human nature and philosophers have long taught us that we are mistaken in regarding our intelligence as an independent force and in overlooking its dependence upon the emotional life. Our intelligence, they teach us, can function reliably only when it is removed from the influences of strong emotional impulses ; otherwise it behaves merely as an instrument of the will and delivers the inference which the will requires. Thus, in their view, logical arguments are impotent against affective interests, and that is why reasons, which in Falstaff's phrase are ' as plenty as blackberries ', produce so few victories in the conflict with interests. Psycho-analytic experience has, if possible, further confirmed this statement. It daily shows that the shrewdest persons will all of a sudden behave like imbeciles as soon as the needful insight is confronted by an emotional resistance, but will completely regain their wonted acuity once that resistance has been overcome. The logical infatuations into which this war has deluded our fellow-citizens, many of them the best of their kind, are therefore a secondary phenomenon, a consequence of emotional excitement, and are destined, we may hope, to disappear with it.

Having in this way come to understand once more our fellow-citizens who are now so greatly alienated from us, we shall the more easily endure the disillusionment which the nations, those greater units of the human race, have caused us, for we shall perceive that the demands we make upon them ought to be far more modest. Perhaps they are reproducing the course of individual evolution, and still to-day represent very primitive phases in the organization and formation of higher unities. It is in agreement with this that the educative factor of an external compulsion towards morality, which we found to be so effective for the individual, is barely discernible in them. True, we had hoped that the extensive community of interests established by commerce and production would constitute the germ of such a compulsion, but it would seem that nations still obey their immediate passions far more readily than their interests. Their interests serve them, at most, as rationalizations for their passions ; they parade their interests as their justification for satisfying their passions. Actually why the national units should disdain, detest, abhor one another, and that even when they are at peace, is indeed a mystery. I cannot tell why it is. It is just as though when it becomes a question of a number of people, not to say millions, all individual moral acquirements were obliterated, and only the most primitive, the oldest, the crudest mental attitudes were left. Possibly only future stages in development will be able in any way to alter this regrettable state of affairs. But a little more truthfulness and upright dealing on all sides, both in the personal relations of men to one another and between them and those who govern them, should also do something towards smoothing the way for this transformation.

II

Our Attitude towards Death

The second factor to which I attribute our present sense of estrangement in this once lovely and congenial world is the disturbance that has taken place in our attitude towards death, an attitude to which hitherto we have clung so fast.

This attitude was far from straightforward. We were of course prepared to maintain that death was the necessary outcome of life, that everyone owes a debt to Nature and must expect to pay the reckoning—in short, that death was natural, undeniable and unavoidable. In reality, however, we were accustomed to behave as if it were otherwise. We displayed an unmistakable tendency to ' shelve ' death, to eliminate it from life. We tried to hush it up ; indeed we even have the saying, ' To think of something as we think of death '.[1] That is our own death, of course. Our

---

[1] [The German saying is used as an equivalent for ' incredible ' or ' unlikely '.—Trans.]

own death is indeed unimaginable, and whenever we make the attempt to imagine it we can perceive that we really survive as spectators. Hence the psycho-analytic school could venture on the assertion that at bottom no one believes in his own death, or to put the same thing in another way, in the unconscious every one of us is convinced of his own immortality.

As to the death of another, the civilized man will carefully avoid speaking of such a possibility in the hearing of the person concerned. Children alone disregard this restriction ; unabashed they threaten one another with the eventuality of death, and even go so far as to talk of it before one whom they love, as for instance : ' Dear Mamma, it will be a pity when you are dead but then I shall do this or that.' The civilized adult can hardly even entertain the thought of another's death without seeming to himself hard or evil-hearted ; unless, of course, as a physician, lawyer or something of the sort, he has to deal with death professionally. Least of all will he permit himself to think of the death of another if with that event some gain to himself in freedom, means or position is connected. This sensitiveness of ours is of course impotent to arrest the hand of death ; when it has fallen, we are always deeply affected, as if we were prostrated by the overthrow of our expectations. Our habit is to lay stress on the fortuitous causation of the death—accident, disease, infection, advanced age ; in this way we betray our endeavour to modify the significance of death from a necessity to an accident. A multitude of simultaneous deaths appears to us exceedingly terrible. Towards the dead person himself we take up a special attitude, something like admiration for one who has accomplished a very difficult task. We suspend criticism of him, overlook his possible misdoings, issue the command : *De mortuis nil nisi bene*, and regard it as justifiable to set forth in the funeral-oration and upon the tombstone only that which is most favourable to his memory. Consideration for the dead, who no longer need it, is dearer to us than the truth, and certainly, for most of us, is dearer also than consideration for the living.

The culmination of this conventional attitude towards death among civilized persons is seen in our complete collapse when death has fallen on some person whom we love—a parent or a partner in marriage, a brother or sister, a child, a dear friend. Our hopes, our pride, our happiness, lie in the grave with him, we will not be consoled, we will not fill the loved one's place. We behave then as if we belonged to the tribe of the Asra, who must die too when those die whom they love.

But this attitude of ours towards death has a powerful effect upon our lives. Life is impoverished, it loses in interest, when the highest stake in the game of living, life itself, may not be risked. It becomes as flat, as superficial, as one of those American flirtations in which it is from the first understood that nothing is to happen, contrasted with a Continental love-affair in which both partners must constantly bear in mind the serious consequences. Our ties of affection, the unbearable intensity of our grief, make us disinclined to court danger for ourselves and for those who belong to us. We dare not contemplate a great many undertakings which are dangerous but quite indispensable, such as attempts at mechanical flight, expeditions to far countries, experiments with explosive substances. We are paralysed by the thought of who is to replace the son with his mother, the husband with his wife, the father with his children, if there should come disaster. The tendency to exclude death from our calculations brings in its train a number of other renunciations and exclusions. And yet the motto of the Hanseatic League declared : ' *Navigare necesse est, vivere non necesse* ' ! (It is necessary to sail the seas, it is not necessary to live.)

It is an inevitable result of all this that we should seek in the world of fiction, of general literature and

of the theatre compensation for the impoverishment of
life.   There we still find people who know how to die,
indeed, who are even capable of killing someone else.
There alone too we can enjoy the condition which
makes it possible for us to reconcile ourselves with
death—namely, that behind all the vicissitudes of life
we preserve our existence intact.   For it is indeed too
sad that in life it should be as it is in chess, when
one false move may lose us the game, but with the
difference that we can have no second game, no return-
match.   In the realm of fiction we discover that
plurality of lives for which we crave.   We die in the
person of a given hero, yet we survive him, and are
ready to die again with the next hero just as safely.

It is evident that the war is bound to sweep away
this conventional treatment of death.   Death will no
longer be denied ; we are forced to believe in him.
People really are dying, and now not one by one, but
many at a time, often ten thousand in a single day.
Nor is it any longer an accident.   To be sure, it still
seems a matter of chance whether a particular bullet
hits this man or that ; but the survivor may easily be
hit by another bullet ; and the accumulation puts an
end to the impression of accident.   Life has, in truth,
become interesting again ; it has regained its full
significance.

Here a distinction should be made between two
groups—those who personally risk their lives in battle,
and those who have remained at home and have only
to wait for the loss of their dear ones by wounds,
disease, or infection.   It would indeed be very interesting to study the changes in the psychology of the
combatants, but I know too little about it.   We must
stop short at the second group, to which we ourselves
belong.   I have said already that in my opinion the
bewilderment and the paralysis of energies, now so
generally felt by us, are essentially determined in part
by the circumstance that we cannot maintain our
former attitude towards death, and have not yet dis-

covered a new one. Perhaps it will assist us to do this
if we direct our psychological inquiry towards two
other relations with death—the one which we may
ascribe to primitive, prehistoric peoples, and that other
which in every one of us still exists, but which conceals
itself, invisible to consciousness, in the deepest-lying
strata of our mental life.

The attitude of prehistoric man towards death is
known to us, of course, only by inferences and reconstruction, but I believe that these processes have
furnished us with tolerably trustworthy information.

Primitive man assumed a very remarkable attitude
towards death. It was far from consistent, was indeed
extremely contradictory. On the one hand, he took
death seriously, recognized it as the termination of life
and used it to that end ; on the other hand, he also
denied death, reduced it to nothingness. This contradiction arose from the circumstance that he took up
radically different attitudes towards the death of
another man, of a stranger, of an enemy, and towards
his own. The death of the other man he had no
objection to ; it meant the annihilation of a creature
hated, and primitive man had no scruples against
bringing it about. He was, in truth, a very violent
being, more cruel and more malign than other animals.
He liked to kill, and killed as a matter of course. That
instinct which is said to restrain the other animals
from killing and devouring their own species we need
not attribute to him.

Hence the primitive history of mankind is filled
with murder. Even to-day, the history of the world
which our children learn in school is essentially a series
of race-murders. The obscure sense of guilt which has
been common to man since prehistoric times, and
which in many religions has been condensed into the
doctrine of original sin, is probably the outcome of a
blood-guiltiness incurred by primitive man. In my
book *Totem und Tabu* (1913) I have, following clues
given by W. Robertson Smith, Atkinson and Charles

Darwin, attempted to surmise the nature of this primal guilt, and I think that even the contemporary Christian doctrine enables us to deduce it. If the Son of God was obliged to sacrifice his life to redeem mankind from original sin, then by the law of the talion, the requital of like for like, that sin must have been a killing, a murder. Nothing else could call for the sacrifice of a life in expiation. And if the original sin was an offence against God the Father, the primal crime of mankind must have been a parricide, the killing of the primal father of the primitive human horde, whose image in memory was later transfigured into a deity.[1]

His own death was for primitive man certainly just as unimaginable and unreal as it is for any one of us to-day. But there was for him a case in which the two opposite attitudes towards death came into conflict and joined issue ; and this case was momentous and productive of far-reaching results. It occurred when primitive man saw someone who belonged to him die— his wife, his child, his friend, whom assuredly he loved as we love ours, for love cannot be much younger than the lust to kill. Then, in his pain, he had to learn that one can indeed die oneself, an admission against which his whole being revolted ; for each of these loved ones was, in very truth, a part of his own beloved ego. But even so, on the other hand, such deaths had a rightfulness for him, since in each of the loved persons something of the hostile stranger had resided. The law of ambivalence of feeling, which to this day governs our emotional relations with those whom we love most, had assuredly a very much wider validity in primitive periods. Thus these beloved dead had also been enemies and strangers who had aroused in him a measure of hostile feeling.[2]

Philosophers have declared that the intellectual enigma presented to primitive man by the picture of death was what forced him to reflection, and thus that

[1] Cf. ' Die infantile Wiederkehr des Totemismus ', *Totem und Tabu*.
[2] Cf. ' Tabu und Ambivalenz ', *Totem und Tabu*.

it became the starting-point of all speculation. I believe that here the philosophers think too philosophically, and give too little consideration to the primarily effective motives. I would therefore limit and correct this assertion : By the body of his slain enemy primitive man would have triumphed, without racking his brains about the enigma of life and death. Not the intellectual enigma, and not every death, but the conflict of feeling at the death of loved, yet withal alien and hated persons was what disengaged the spirit of inquiry in man. Of this conflict of feeling psychology was the direct offspring. Man could no longer keep death at a distance, for he had tasted of it in his grief for the dead ; but still he did not consent entirely to acknowledge it, for he could not conceive of himself as dead. So he devised a compromise ; he conceded the fact of death, even his own death, but denied it the significance of annihilation, which he had had no motive for contesting where the death of his enemy had been concerned. During his contemplation of his loved one's corpse he invented ghosts, and it was his sense of guilt at the satisfaction mingled with his sorrow that turned these new-born spirits into evil, dreaded demons. The changes wrought by death suggested to him the disjunction of the individuality into a body and a soul—first of all into several souls ; in this way his train of thought ran parallel with the process of disintegration which sets in with death. The enduring remembrance of the dead became the basis for assuming other modes of existence, gave him the conception of life continued after apparent death.

These subsequent modes of existence were at first no more than appendages to that life which death had brought to a close—shadowy, empty of content, and until later times but slightly valued ; they showed as yet a pathetic inadequacy. We may recall the answer made to Odysseus by the soul of Achilles :

Erst in the life on the earth, no less than a god we revered thee,
We the Achaeans ; and now in the realm of the dead as a monarch

Here dost thou rule ; then why should death thus grieve thee,
    Achilles ?
Thus did I speak : forthwith then answering thus he addressed me,
Speak not smoothly of death, I beseech, O famous Odysseus,
Better by far to remain on the earth as the thrall of another ;
E'en of a portionless man that hath means right scanty of living,
Rather than reign sole king in the realm of the bodiless phantoms.[1]

Or in the powerful, bitterly burlesque rendering by
Heine, where he makes Achilles say that the most insignificant little Philistine at Stuckert-on-the-Neckar,
in being alive, is far happier than he, the son of Peleus,
the dead hero, the prince of shadows in the nether world.

It was not until much later that the different
religions devised the view of this after-life as the more
desirable, the truly valid one, and degraded the life
which is ended by death to a mere preparation. It
was then but consistent to extend life backward into
the past, to conceive of former existences, transmigra-
tions of the soul and reincarnation, all with the purpose
of depriving death of its meaning as the termination of
life. So early did the denial of death, which above
we designated a convention of civilization, actually
originate.

Beside the corpse of the beloved were generated not
only the idea of the soul, the belief in immortality, and
a great part of man's deep-rooted sense of guilt, but
also the earliest inkling of ethical law. The first and
most portentous prohibition of the awakening conscience was : Thou shalt not kill. It was born of the
reaction against that hate-gratification which lurked
behind the grief for the loved dead, and was gradually
extended to unloved strangers and finally even to
enemies.

This final extension is no longer experienced by
civilized man. When the frenzied conflict of this war
shall have been decided, every one of the victorious
warriors will joyfully return to his home, his wife and
his children, undelayed and undisturbed by any thought

[1] *Odyssey*, xi. 484-491 ; translated by H. B. Cotterill.

of the enemy he has slain either at close quarters or by distant weapons of destruction. It is worthy of note that such primitive races as still inhabit the earth, who are undoubtedly closer than we to primitive man, act differently in this respect, or did so act until they came under the influence of our civilization. The savage— Australian, Bushman, Tierra del Fuegan—is by no means a remorseless murderer ; when he returns victorious from the war-path he may not set foot in his village nor touch his wife until he has atoned for the murders committed in war by penances which are often prolonged and toilsome. This may be presumed, of course, to be the outcome of superstition ; the savage still goes in fear of the avenging spirits of the slain. But the spirits of the fallen enemy are nothing but the expression of his own conscience, uneasy on account of his blood-guiltiness ; behind this superstition lurks a vein of ethical sensitiveness which has been lost by us civilized men.[1]

Pious souls, who cherish the thought of our remoteness from whatever is evil and base, will be quick to draw from the early appearance and the urgency of the prohibition of murder gratifying conclusions in regard to the force of these ethical stirrings, which must consequently have been implanted in us. Unfortunately this argument proves even more for the opposite contention. So powerful a prohibition can only be directed against an equally powerful impulse. What no human soul desires there is no need to prohibit ;[2] it is automatically excluded. The very emphasis of the commandment *Thou shalt not kill* makes it certain that we spring from an endless ancestry of murderers, with whom the lust for killing was in the blood, as possibly it is to this day with ourselves. The ethical strivings of mankind, of which we need not in the least depreciate the strength and the significance, are an acquisition accompanying evolution ; they have

[1] Cf. *Totem und Tabu.*
[2] Cf. the brilliant argument of Frazer quoted in *Totem und Tabu.*

then become the hereditary possession of those human beings alive to-day, though unfortunately only in a very variable measure.

Let us now leave primitive man, and turn to the unconscious in our own mental life. Here we depend entirely upon the psycho-analytic method of investigation, the only one which plumbs such depths. We ask what is the attitude of our unconscious towards the problem of death. The answer must be : Almost exactly the same as primitive man's. In this respect, as in many others, the man of prehistoric ages survives unchanged in our unconscious. Thus, our unconscious does not believe in its own death ; it behaves as if immortal. What we call our ' unconscious ' (the deepest strata of our minds, made up of instinctual impulses) knows nothing whatever of negatives or of denials—contradictories coincide in it—and so it knows nothing whatever of our own death, for to that we can give only a negative purport. It follows that no instinct we possess is ready for a belief in death. This is even perhaps the secret of heroism. The rational explanation for heroism is that it consists in the decision that the personal life cannot be so precious as certain abstract general ideals. But more frequent, in my view, is that instinctive and impulsive heroism which knows no such motivation, and flouts danger in the spirit of Anzengruber's Hans the Road - Mender : ' Nothing can happen to *me*.' Or else that motivation serves but to clear away the hesitation which might delay an heroic reaction in accord with the unconscious. The dread of death, which dominates us oftener than we know, is on the other hand something secondary, being usually the outcome of the sense of guilt.

On the other hand, for strangers and for enemies, we do acknowledge death, and consign them to it quite as readily and unthinkingly as did primitive man. Here there does, indeed, appear a distinction which in practice shows for a decisive one. Our unconscious does not carry out the killing ; it merely thinks it and

wishes it.   But it would be wrong entirely to depreciate
this psychical reality as compared with actual reality.
It is significant and pregnant enough.   In our unconscious we daily and hourly deport all who stand in
our way, all who have offended or injured us.   The
expression : ' Devil take him ! ' which so frequently
comes to our lips in joking anger, and which really
means ' Death take him ! ' is in our unconscious an
earnest deliberate death-wish.   Indeed, our unconscious
will murder even for trifles ; like the ancient Athenian
law of Draco, it knows no other punishment for crime
than death ; and this has a certain consistency, for
every injury to our almighty and autocratic ego is at
bottom a crime of *lèse-majesté*.

And so, if we are to be judged by the wishes in our
unconscious, we are, like primitive man, simply a gang
of murderers.   It is well that all these wishes do not
possess the potency which was attributed to them by
primitive men ; [1] in the cross-fire of mutual maledic-
tions mankind would long since have perished, the best
and wisest of men and the loveliest and fairest of women
with the rest.

Psycho-analysis finds little credence among laymen
for assertions such as these.   They reject them as
calumnies which are confuted by conscious experience,
and adroitly overlook the faint indications through
which the unconscious is apt to betray itself even to
consciousness.   It is therefore relevant to point out
that many thinkers who could not have been influenced
by psycho-analysis have quite definitely accused our
unspoken thoughts of a readiness, heedless of the
murder-prohibition, to get rid of anyone who stands
in our way.   From many examples of this I will choose
one very famous one :

In *Le Père Goriot*, Balzac alludes to a passage in the
works of J. J. Rousseau where that author asks the
reader what he would do if—without leaving Paris and
of course without being discovered—he could kill, with

[1] Cf. ' Allmacht der Gedanken ', *Totem und Tabu*.

great profit to himself, an old mandarin in Peking by a mere act of the will. Rousseau implies that he would not give much for the life of this dignitary. ' *Tuer son mandarin* ' has passed into a proverb for this secret readiness even on the part of ourselves to-day.

There is as well a whole array of cynical jests and anecdotes which testify in the same sense, such as, for instance, the remark attributed to a husband : ' If one of us dies, I shall go and live in Paris.' Such cynical jokes would not be possible unless they contained an unacknowledged verity which could not be countenanced if seriously and baldly expressed. In joke, as we know, even the truth may be told.

As for primitive man, so also for us in our unconscious, there arises a case in which the two contrasted attitudes towards death, that which acknowledges it as the annihilation of life and the other which denies it as ineffectual to that end, conflict and join issue—and this case is the same as in primitive ages— the death, or the endangered life, of one whom we love, a parent or partner in marriage, a brother or sister, a child or dear friend. These loved ones are on the one hand an inner possession, an ingredient of our personal ego, but on the other hand are partly strangers, even enemies. With the exception of only a very few situations, there adheres to the tenderest and closest of our affections a vestige of hostility which can excite an unconscious death-wish. But this conflict of ambivalence does not now, as it did then, find issue in theories of the soul and of ethics, but in neuroses, which afford us deep insight into normal mental life as well. How often have those physicians who practise psychoanalysis had to deal with the symptom of an exaggeratedly tender care for the well-being of relatives, or with entirely unfounded self-reproaches after the death of a loved person. The study of these cases has left them in no doubt about the extent and the significance of unconscious death-wishes.

The layman feels an extraordinary horror at the

possibility of such feelings, and takes this repulsion as a legitimate ground for disbelief in the assertions of psycho-analysis. I think, mistakenly. No depreciation of our love is intended, and none is actually contained in it. It is indeed foreign to our intelligence as also to our feelings thus to couple love and hate, but Nature, by making use of these twin opposites, contrives to keep love ever vigilant and fresh, so as to guard it against the hate which lurks behind it. It might be said that we owe the fairest flowers of our love-life to the reaction against the hostile impulse which we divine in our breasts.

To sum up : Our unconscious is just as inaccessible to the idea of our own death, as murderously minded towards the stranger, as divided or ambivalent towards the loved, as was man in earliest antiquity But how far we have moved from this primitive state in our conventionally civilized attitude towards death !

It is easy to see the effect of the impact of war on this duality. It strips us of the later accretions of civilization, and lays bare the primal man in each of us. It constrains us once more to be heroes who cannot believe in their own death ; it stamps the alien as the enemy, whose death is to be brought about or desired ; it counsels us to rise above the death of those we love. But war is not to be abolished ; so long as the conditions of existence among the nations are so varied, and the repulsions between peoples so intense, there will be, must be, wars. The question then arises : Is it not we who must give in, who must adapt ourselves to them ? Is it not for us to confess that in our civilized attitude towards death we are once more living psychologically beyond our means, and must reform and give truth its due ? Would it not be better to give death the place in actuality and in our thoughts which properly belongs to it, and to yield a little more prominence to that unconscious attitude towards death which we have hitherto so carefully suppressed ? This hardly seems indeed a greater achievement, but rather a backward step in more than one direction, a regression ; but it has the merit of taking somewhat more into account the true state of affairs, and of making life again more endurable for us. To endure life remains, when all is said, the first duty of all living beings. Illusion can have no value if it makes this more difficult for us.

We remember the old saying : *Si vis pacem, para bellum.* If you desire peace, prepare for war.

It would be timely thus to paraphrase it : *Si vis vitam, para mortem.* If you would endure life, be prepared for death.

DREAMS AND TELEPATHY [1]

(1922)

AT the present time, when such great interest is felt in what are called 'occult' phenomena, very definite anticipations will doubtless be aroused by the announcement of a paper with this title. I will therefore hasten to explain that there is no ground for any such anticipations. You will learn nothing from this paper of mine about the enigma of telepathy; indeed, you will not even gather whether I believe in the existence of 'telepathy' or not. On this occasion I have set myself the very modest task of examining the relation of telepathic occurrences, whatever their origin may be, to dreams, more exactly, to our theory of dreams. You will know that the connection between dreams and telepathy is commonly held to be a very intimate one; I shall propound the view that the two have little to do with each other, and that if the existence of telepathic dreams were established there would be no need to alter our conception of dreams in any way.

The material on which the present communication is based is very slight. In the first place, I must express my regret that I could make no use of my own dreams, as I did when I wrote the *Traumdeutung* (1900). But I have never had a 'telepathic' dream. Not that I have been without dreams that conveyed an impression of a certain definite occurrence taking place at some distant place, leaving it to the dreamer to decide whether the occurrence is taking place at that moment or will do so at some later time. In

[1] Paper read before the Vienna Psycho-Analytical Society; published in *Imago*, Bd. viii., 1922. [Translated by C. J. M. Hubback.]

waking life, too, I have often become aware of presentiments of distant events. But these hints, fore-
tellings and forebodings have none of them ' come
true ', as we say ; there proved to be no external
reality corresponding to them, and they had therefore
to be regarded as purely subjective anticipations.

For example, I once dreamt during the war that
one of my sons then serving at the front had fallen.
This was not directly stated in the dream, but was
expressed in an unmistakable manner, by means of
the well-known death-symbolism of which an account
was first given by W. Stekel. (Let us not omit here
to fulfil the duty, often felt to be inconvenient, of
making literary acknowledgements !) I saw the young
soldier standing on a landing-stage, between land and
water, as it were ; he looked to me very pale ; I spoke
to him but he did not answer. There were other
unmistakable indications. He was not wearing military
uniform, but a ski-ing costume that he had worn when
a serious ski-ing accident had happened to him several
years before the war. He stood on something like a
footstool with a chest in front of him ; a situation
always closely associated in my mind with the idea of
' falling ', through a memory of my own childhood.
As a child of little more than two years old I had
myself climbed on such a footstool to get something
off the top of a chest—probably something good to eat—
whereupon I fell and gave myself an injury, of which I
can even now show the scar. My son, however, whom
the dream pronounced to be dead, came home from
the war unscathed.

Only a short time ago, I had another dream an-
nouncing misfortune ; it was, I think, just before I
decided to put together these few remarks. This time
there was not much attempt at disguise : I saw my two
nieces who live in England ; they were dressed in black
and said to me ' We buried her on Thursday '. I knew the
reference was to the death of their mother, now eighty-
seven years of age, the widow of my eldest brother.

A time of disagreeable anticipation followed ; there would of course be nothing surprising in so aged a woman suddenly passing away, yet it would be very unpleasant for the dream to coincide exactly with the occurrence. The next letter from England, however, dissipated this fear. For the benefit of those who are concerned for the wish-fulfilment theory of dreams I may interpolate a reassurance by saying that there was no difficulty in detecting by analysis the unconscious motives that might be presumed to exist in these death-dreams just as in others.

Do not now urge the objection that what I have just related is valueless because negative experiences prove as little here as they do in less occult matters. I am well aware of that and have not adduced these instances with any intention whatever of proving anything or of surreptitiously influencing you in any particular way. My sole purpose was to explain the paucity of my material.

Another fact certainly seems to me of more significance, namely, that during my twenty-seven years of work as an analyst I have never been in a position to observe a truly telepathic dream in any of my patients. The people among whom my practice lay certainly formed a good collection of very neurotic and ' highly sensitive ' temperaments ; many of them have related to me most remarkable incidents in their previous life on which they based a belief in mysterious occult influences. Events such as accidents or illnesses of near relatives, in particular the death of one of the parents, have often enough happened during the treatment and interrupted it ; but not on one single occasion did these occurrences, eminently suitable as they were, afford me the opportunity of registering a single telepathic dream, although treatment extended over several months or even years. Anyone may explain this fact as he likes ; in any event it again limits the material at my disposal. You will see that any such explanation would not affect the subject of this paper.

Nor does it embarrass me to be asked why I have made no use of the abundant supply of telepathic dreams that have been published. I should not have had far to seek, since the publications of the English as well as of the American Society for Psychical Research are accessible to me as a member of both societies. In all these communications no attempt is ever made to subject such dreams to analytic investigation, which would be our first interest in such cases.[1] Moreover, you will soon perceive that for the purposes of this paper one single dream will serve well enough.

My material thus consists simply and solely of two communications which have reached me from correspondents in Germany. They are not personally known to me, but they give their names and addresses: I have not the least ground for presuming any intention to mislead on the part of the writers.

I

With the first I had already been in correspondence ; he had been good enough to send me, as many of my readers do, observations of everyday occurrences and the like. He is obviously an educated and highly intelligent man ; this time he expressly places his material at my disposal if I care to turn it ' to literary account '.

His letter runs as follows :

' I consider the following dream of sufficient interest to give you some material for your researches.

' I must first state the following facts. My daughter, who is married and lives in Berlin, was expecting her first confinement in the middle of December of this year. I intended to go to Berlin about that time with my (second) wife, my daughter's stepmother. During

---

[1] In two publications by W. Stekel (mentioned above) (*Der tele-pathische Traum*, no date, and *Die Sprache des Traumes*, Zweite Auflage, 1922) there are at least attempts to apply the analytic technique to alleged telepathic dreams. The author expresses his belief in the reality of telepathy.

the night of November 16-17 I dreamt, with a vivid-
ness and clearness I have never before experienced,
that my wife had given birth to twins. I saw quite
plainly the two healthy infants with their chubby
faces lying in their cot side by side ; I was not sure
of their sex : one with fair hair had distinctly my
features and something of my wife's, the other with
chestnut-brown hair clearly resembled her with a look
of me. I said to my wife, who has red-gold hair,
"Probably 'your' child's chestnut hair will also go
red later on ". My wife gave them the breast. In
the dream she had also made some jam in a wash-
basin and the two children crept about on all fours in
the basin and licked up the contents.

   ' So much for the dream. Four or five times I had
half awaked from it, asked myself if it were true that
we had twins, but did not come to the conclusion
with any certainty that it was only a dream. The
dream lasted till I woke, and after that it was some
little time before I felt quite clear about the true state
of affairs. At breakfast I told my wife the dream,
which much amused her. She said, "Surely Ilse (my
daughter) won't have twins ? " I answered, " I should
hardly think so, as there have never been twins either
in my family or in G.'s " (her husband). On November
18, at ten o'clock in the morning, I received a telegram
from my son-in-law handed in the afternoon before,
telling me of the birth of twins, boy and girl. The
birth thus took place at the time when I was dreaming
that my wife had twins. The confinement occurred
four weeks earlier than had been expected by my
daughter and her husband.

   ' But there is a further circumstance : the next
night I dreamt that my dead wife, my daughter's own
mother, had undertaken the care of forty-eight new-
born infants. When the first dozen were being brought
in, I protested. At that point the dream ended.

   ' My dead wife was very fond of children. She
often talked about it, saying she would like a whole

troop round her, the more the better, and that she would do very well if she had charge of a Kindergarten and would be quite happy so. The noise children make was music to her. On one occasion she invited in a whole troop of children from the streets and regaled them with chocolates and cakes in the courtyard of our villa. My daughter must have thought at once of her mother after her confinement, especially because of the surprise of its coming on prematurely, the arrival of twins, and their difference in sex. She knew her mother would have greeted the event with the liveliest joy and sympathy. " Only think what mother would say, if she were by me now ! " This thought must undoubtedly have gone through her mind. And then I dream of my dead wife, of whom I very seldom dream, and had neither spoken of nor thought of since the first dream.

'Do you think the coincidence between dream and event in both cases accidental ? My daughter is much attached to me and was most certainly thinking of me during the labour, particularly because we had often exchanged letters during the pregnancy and I had constantly given her advice.'

It is easy to guess what my answer to this letter was. I was sorry to find that my correspondent's interest in analysis had been so completely killed by that in telepathy ; I therefore avoided his direct question, and, remarking that the dream contained a good deal besides its connection with the birth of the twins, I asked him to let me know what information or incidents could give me a clue to the meaning of the dream.

Thereupon I received the following second letter which certainly did not give me what I wanted :

'I have not been able to answer your kind letter of the 24th until to-day. I shall be only too pleased to tell you " without omission or reserve " all the associations that occur to me. Unfortunately there is not much, more would come out in talking.

'Well then—my wife and I do not wish for any more children. We very rarely have sexual intercourse ; at any rate at the time of the dream there was certainly no " danger ". My daughter's confinement, which was expected about the middle of December, was naturally a frequent subject of conversation between us. My daughter had been examined and skiagraphed in the summer, and the doctor making the examination had made sure that the child would be a boy. My wife said at the time, " I should laugh if after all it were a girl ". At the time she also thought to herself it would be better if it were an H. rather than a G. (my son-in-law's family name) ; my daughter is handsomer and has a better figure than my son-in-law, although he has been a naval officer. I have made some study of the question of heredity and am in the habit of looking at small children to see whom they resemble. One more thing ! We have a small dog which sits with us at table in the evening to have his food and licks the plates and dishes. All this material appears in the dream.

'I am fond of small children and have often said that I should like to have the bringing up of a child once more, now that I should have so much more understanding, interest and time to devote to it, but with my wife I should not wish it, as she does not possess the necessary qualities for rearing a child judiciously. The dream makes me a present of two children—I am not sure of the sex. I see them even at this moment lying in the bed and I recognize the features, the one more like myself, the other like my wife, but each with minor traits from the other side. My wife has auburn hair, one of the children chestnut (red) brown. I say, " Yes, it will later on be red too ". Both the children crawl round a large wash-basin in which my wife has been stirring jam and lick it all over (dream). The origin of this detail is easily explicable, just as is the dream as a whole ; it would not be difficult to understand or interpret it, if it had not coincided with the unexpectedly early arrival of my grandchildren (three weeks too soon), a coincidence of time almost to the hour (I cannot exactly say when the dream began ; my grandchildren were born at nine P.M. and a quarter past ; I went to bed at about eleven and dreamed during the night). Our knowledge too that the child would be a boy adds to the difficulty, though possibly the doubt whether this had been fully established might account for the appearance of twins in the dream. Still, all the same, there is the coincidence of the dream with the unexpected and premature appearance of my daughter's twins.

' It is not the first time that distant events have become known to me before I received the actual news. To give one instance among many. In October I had a visit from my three brothers. We had not all seen one another together for thirty years (naturally one had seen another oftener), once only at my father's funeral and once at my mother's. Both deaths were expected, and I had had no " presentiments " in either case. But, when about twenty-five years ago my youngest brother died quite suddenly and unexpectedly at the age of nine, as the postman handed me the postcard with the news of his death, before I even glanced at it, the thought came to me at once, " That is to say that your brother is dead ". He was the only one left at home, a strong healthy lad, while we four elder brothers were already fully fledged and had left the parents' house. At the time of their visit to me the talk by chance came round to this experience of mine, and, as if on the word of command, all three brothers came out with the declaration that exactly the same thing had happened to them. Whether exactly in the same way I cannot say ; at all events each one said that he had felt perfectly certain of the death in advance before the quite unexpected news had been communicated, following closely as it did on the presentiment. We are all from the mother's side of a sensitive disposition, though tall, strong men, but not one of us is in the least inclined towards spiritism or occultism ; on the contrary, we disclaim adherence to either. My brothers are all three University men, two are schoolmasters, one a surveyor, all rather pedants than visionaries. That is all I can tell you in regard to the dream. If you can turn it to account in any of your writings, I am delighted to place it at your disposal.'

I am afraid that you will behave like the writer of these letters. You, too, will be primarily interested in the question whether this dream can really be regarded as a telepathic notification of the unexpected birth of the twin children, and you will not be disposed to submit this dream like any other to analysis. I foresee that it will always be so when psycho-analysis and occultism encounter each other. The former has, so to speak, all our instinctive prepossessions against it ; the latter is met half-way by powerful and mysterious sympathies. I am not, however, going to take up the position that I am nothing but a psycho-analyst, that the problems of occultism do not concern me : you would rightly judge that to be only an evasion of the problem. On the contrary, I maintain that it would be a great satisfaction to me if I could convince myself and others on unimpeachable evidence of the existence of telepathic processes, but I also consider that the data about this dream are altogether inadequate to justify any such pronouncement. You will observe that it does not once occur to this intelligent man, deeply interested as he is in the problem of his dream, to tell us when he had last seen his daughter or what news he had lately had from her ; he writes in the first letter that the birth was a month too soon, in the second, however, the month has become three weeks only, and in neither do we gain the information whether the birth was really premature, or whether, as so often happens, those concerned were out in their reckoning. But we should have to consider these and other details of the occurrence if we are to weigh the probability of the dreamer making unconscious estimates and guesses. I felt too that it would be of no use even if I succeeded in getting answers to such questions. In the course of arriving at the information new doubts would constantly arise, which could only be set at rest if one had the man in front of one and could revive all the relevant memories which he had perhaps dismissed as unessential. He is certainly right in what he says at the beginning of his second letter: more would come out if he were able to talk to me.

Consider another and similar case, in which the disturbing interest of occultism has no part. You must often have been in the position to compare the anamnesis and the information about the illness given during the first sitting by any neurotic with what you have gained from him after some months of psycho-analysis. Apart from the inevitable abbreviations of the first communication, how many essentials were left out or suppressed, how many displacements made in the relation the various facts bear to one another—in fact, how much that was incorrect or untrue was related to you that first time! You will not call me hypercritical if I refuse in the circumstances to make any pronouncement whether the dream in question is a telepathic fact or a particularly subtle achievement on the part of the dreamer's unconscious or whether it is simply to be taken as a striking coincidence. Our curiosity must be allayed with the hope of some later opportunity for detailed oral examination of the dreamer. But you cannot say that this outcome of our investigation has disappointed you, for I prepared you for it ; I said you would hear nothing which would throw any light on the problem of telepathy.

If we now pass on to the analytic treatment of this dream, we are obliged again to admit that we are not satisfied. The material that the dreamer associates with the manifest content of the dream is insufficient to make any analysis possible. The dream, for example, goes into great detail over the likeness of the children to the parents, discusses the colour of their hair and the probable change of colour at a later age, and as an explanation of this much spun-out detail we only have the dry piece of information from the dreamer that he has always been interested in questions of likeness and heredity ; we are certainly accustomed to push the matter rather further ! But at *one* point the dream does admit of an analytic interpretation, and just at this point analysis, otherwise having no connection with occultism, comes to the aid of telepathy in a remarkable way. It is only on account of this single point that I am asking for your attention to this dream at all.

Rightly viewed, this dream has no right whatever to be called ' telepathic '. It does not inform the dreamer of anything that is taking place elsewhere— apart from what is otherwise known to him. What, on the other hand, the dream does relate is something quite different from the event reported in the telegram the second day after the night of the dream. Dream and actual occurrence diverge at a particularly important point, and only agree, apart from the coincidence of time, in another very interesting element. In the dream the dreamer's *wife* has twins. The occurrence, however, is that his *daughter* has given birth to twins in her distant home. The dreamer does not overlook this difference, he does not seem to know any way of getting over it and, as according to his own account he has no leaning towards the occult, he only asks quite tentatively whether the coincidence between dream and occurrence on the point of the twin-birth can be more than an accident. The psycho-analytic interpretation of dreams, however, does away with this difference between the dream and the event, and gives to both the same content. If we consult the association-material to this dream, it proves to us, in spite of its sparseness, that an inner bond of feeling exists between this father and daughter, a bond of feeling which is so usual and so natural that we ought to cease to be ashamed of it, one that in daily life merely finds expression as a tender interest and only in dreams is pushed to its logical conclusion. The father knows that his daughter clings to him, he is convinced that she often thought of him during the labour, in his heart I think he grudges her to the son-in-law, about whom in one letter he makes a few disparaging remarks. On the occasion of her confinement (whether expected or communicated by telepathy) the unconscious though repressed wish becomes active ; ' she ought rather to be my (second) wife ' ; it is this wish that has distorted the dream-thoughts and is the cause of the difference between the manifest dream-content and the event. We are entitled to replace the second wife in the dream by the daughter. If we possessed more associations with the dream, we could undoubtedly verify and deepen this interpretation.

And now I have reached the point I wish to put before you. We have endeavoured to maintain the strictest impartiality and have allowed two conceptions of the dream to rank as equally probable and equally unproved. According to the first the dream is a reaction to the telepathic message : ' your daughter has just brought twins into the world '. According to the second an unconscious chain of thought underlies the dream, which may be reproduced somewhat as follows : ' To-day is undoubtedly the day the confinement will take place if the young people in Berlin are out in their reckoning by a month, as I strongly suspect. And if my (first) wife were still alive, she certainly would not be content with one grandchild ! To please her there would have to be at least twins.' If this second view is right, no new problems arise. It is simply a dream like any other. The (preconscious) dream-thoughts as outlined above are reinforced by the (unconscious) wish that no other than the daughter should be the second wife of the dreamer, and thus the manifest dream as described to us arises.

If you prefer to assume that a telepathic message about the daughter's confinement reached the sleeper, further questions arise of the relation of such a message to the dream and of its influence on the formation of the dream. The answer is not far to seek and is not at all ambiguous. The telepathic message has been treated as a portion of the material that goes to the formation of a dream, like any other external or internal stimulus, like a disturbing noise in the street or an insistent organic sensation in the sleeper's own body. In our example it is evident how the message, with the help of a lurking repressed wish, becomes remodelled into a wish-fulfilment ; it is unfortunately less easy to show that it blends with other material that becomes active at the same time so as to make a dream. The telepathic message—if we are justified in recognizing its existence—can thus make no alteration in the structure of the dream ; telepathy has nothing to do with the essential nature of dreams. And that I may avoid the impression that I am trying to conceal a vague notion behind an abstract and fine-sounding word, I am willing to repeat : the essential nature of dreams consists in the peculiar process of the ' dream-work ' whereby the preconscious thoughts (residue from the previous day) are worked over into the manifest dream-content by means of an unconscious wish. The problem of telepathy concerns dreams as little as the problem of anxiety.

I am hoping that you will grant this, but that you will raise the objection that there are, nevertheless, other telepathic dreams in which there is no difference between the event and the dream, and in which there is nothing else to be found but the undisguised repro-duction of the event. I have no knowledge of such dreams from my own experience, but I know they have often been reported. If we now assume that we have such an undisguised and unadulterated telepathic dream to deal with, another question arises. Ought we to call such a telepathic experience a ' dream ' at all ? You will certainly do so as long as you keep to popular usage, in which everything that takes place in mental life during sleep is called a dream. You, too, perhaps say, ' I tossed about in my dream ', and you are not conscious of anything incorrect when you say, ' I shed tears in my dream ' or ' I felt apprehensive in my dream '. But notice that in all these cases you are using ' dream ' and ' sleep ' and ' state of being asleep ' interchangeably, as if there were no distinction between them. I think it would be in the interests of scientific accuracy to keep ' dream ' and ' state of sleep ' more distinctly separate. Why should we provide a counterpart to the confusion evoked by Maeder who, by refusing to distinguish between the dream-work and the latent dream-thoughts, has discovered a new function for dreams ? Supposing, then, that we are brought face to face with a pure telepathic ' dream ', let us call it instead a telepathic experience in a state of sleep. A dream without condensation, distortion, dramatization, above all, without wish-fulfilment, surely hardly deserves the name. You will remind me that, if so, there are other mental products in sleep to which the right to be called ' dreams ' would have to be refused. Actual experiences of the day are known to be simply repeated in sleep ; reproductions of traumatic scenes in ' dreams ' have led us only lately to revise the theory of dreams. There are dreams which by certain special qualities are to be distinguished from the usual type, which are, properly speaking, nothing but night-phantasies, not having undergone additions or alterations of any kind and in all other ways similar to the well-known day-dreams. It would be awkward, certainly, to exclude these imaginings from the realm of ' dreams '. But still they all come from within, are products of our mental life, whereas the very conception of the purely ' telepathic dream ' lies in its being a perception of something external, in relation to which the mind remains passive and receptive.

II

The second case I intend to bring before your notice belongs to quite another type. This is not a telepathic dream, but a dream that has recurred from childhood onwards, in a person who has had many telepathic experiences. Her letter, which I reproduce here, contains much that is remarkable about which we cannot form any judgement. Some part of it is of interest in connection with the problem of the relation of telepathy to dreams.

1. '. . . My doctor, Herr Dr. N., advises me to give you an account of a dream that has haunted me for about thirty or thirty-two years. I am following his advice, and perhaps the dream may possess interest for you in some scientific respect. Since, in your opinion, such dreams are to be traced to an experience of a sexual nature in the first years of childhood, I relate some reminiscences of childhood, that is, experiences which even now make an impression on me and were of so marked a character as to have determined my religion for me.

' May I beg of you to send me word in what way you explain this dream and whether it is not possible to banish it from my life, for it haunts me like a ghost, and the circumstances that always accompany it—I always fall out of bed, and have inflicted on myself not inconsiderable injuries—make it particularly disagreeable and distressing.

2. ' I am thirty-seven years old, very strong and in good physical health, but in childhood I had, besides measles and scarlet fever, an attack of inflammation of the kidneys. In my fifth year I had a very severe inflammation of the eyes, which left double vision. One image slants towards the other and the edges of the image are blurred, as the scars from the ulcers affect the clearness. In the specialist's opinion there is nothing more to be done to the eyes and no chance of improvement. The left side of my face was somewhat

awry, from having screwed up my left eye to see better. By dint of practice and determination I can do the finest needlework, and similarly, when a six-year-old child, I broke myself of squinting sideways by practising in front of a looking-glass, so that now there is no external sign of the defect in vision.

'In my earliest years I was always lonely, kept apart from other children, and had visions (clairvoyance and clairaudience) ; I was not able to distinguish these from reality, and was often in consequence in embarrassing positions, with the result that I am a very reserved and shy person. Since as a quite small child I already knew far more than I could have learnt, I simply did not understand children of my own age. I am myself the eldest of a family of twelve.

'From six to ten years old I attended the parish school and up to sixteen the high-school of the Ursuline Nuns in B. At ten years old I had taken in as much French in four weeks, in eight lessons, as other children learn in two years. I had only to repeat it and it was just as if I had already learnt it and only forgotten it. I have never had any need to learn French, in contradistinction to English, which certainly gave me no trouble but was not known to me beforehand. The same thing happened to me with Latin as with French and I have never properly learnt it, only knowing it from ecclesiastical Latin, which is, however, quite familiar to me. If I read a French book to-day, then I immediately begin thinking in French, whereas this never happens to me with English, although I have more command of English.—My parents are peasant people who for generations have never spoken any languages except German and Polish.

'*Visions :* Sometimes reality vanishes for some moments and I see something quite different. In my house, for example, I often see an old couple and a child ; and the house is then differently furnished. In a sanatorium a friend once came into my room at about four in the morning ; I was awake, had the lamp

burning, and was sitting at my table reading, as I
suffer much from sleeplessness. This apparition of
her always means a trying time for me—as also on
this occasion.

' In 1914 my brother was on active service ; I was
not with my parents in B., but in C. It was ten in
the morning on August 22 when I heard my brother's
voice calling, "Mother! mother!". It came again ten
minutes later, but I saw nothing. On August 24 I
came home, found my mother greatly depressed, and
in answer to my questions she said that the boy had
appeared on August 22. She had been in the garden
in the morning, when she had heard him call, "Mother!
mother!". I tried to comfort her and said nothing
about myself. Three weeks after there came a card
from my brother, written on August 22 between nine
and ten in the morning ; shortly after that he died.

' On September 27, 1921, while in the sanatorium,
I received a message of some kind. There were violent
knockings two or three times repeated on the bed of
the patient who shared my room. We were both
awake ; I asked if she had knocked ; she had not
heard anything at all. Eight weeks later I heard
that one of my friends had died in the night of September 26-27.

' Now something which is regarded as an hallucination, a matter of opinion ! I have a friend who married
a widower with five children ; I got to know the
husband only through my friend. Nearly every time
that I have been to see her, I have seen a lady going
in and out of the house. It was natural to suppose
that this was the husband's first wife. I asked at some
convenient opportunity for a portrait of her, but could
not identify the apparition with the photograph.
Seven years later I saw a picture with the features of
the lady, belonging to one of the children. It was after
all the first wife. In the first picture she looked in
much better health : she had just been through a
feeding-up treatment and that alters the appearance

of a consumptive patient.—These are only a few examples out of many.

' *The dream :* I see a tongue of land surrounded by water. The waves are driven to and fro by the surf. On this piece of land stands a palm-tree, bent somewhat towards the water. A woman has her arm wound round the stem of the palm and is bending low towards the water, where a man is trying to reach the shore. At last she lies down on the ground, holds tightly to the palm-tree with her left hand and stretches out her right hand as far as she can towards the man in the water, but without reaching him. At that point I fall out of bed and wake. I was about fifteen or sixteen years old when I realized that this woman was myself, and from that time I not only went through all the woman's apprehensions for the man but I stood there many a time as a third who was not taking part and only looked on. I dreamed this dream too in separate scenes. As the interest in men awoke in me (eighteen to twenty years old), I tried to see the man's face ; it was never possible. The foam hid everything but the neck and the back of the head. I have twice been engaged to be married, but the head and build were not those of either of the two men.—Once, when I was lying in the sanatorium under the influence of paraldehyde, I saw the man's face, which I now always see in this dream. It was that of the doctor under whose care I was. I liked him as a doctor, but there was nothing more between us.

' *Memories :* Six to nine months old. I was in a perambulator. Quite close to me were two horses ; one, a chestnut, is looking at me very hard and in a way full of meaning. This is the most vivid experience ; I had the feeling that it was a human being.

' *One year old*. Father and I in the town-park, where a park-keeper is putting a little bird into my hand. Its eyes look into mine. I feel " That is a live creature like yourself ".

' *Animals being slaughtered*. When I heard the

pigs screaming I always called for help and cried out,
" You are killing a person " (four years old). I have
always avoided eating meat. Pork always makes me
sick. I came to eat meat during the war, but only
against my will ; now I have given it up again.

' *Five years old*. My mother was confined and I
heard her cry out. I had the feeling, " There is a
human being or an animal in the greatest distress ",
just as I had over the pig-killing.

' I was quite indifferent as a child to sexual matters ;
at ten years old I had as yet no conception of offences
against chastity. Menstruation came on at the age of
twelve. The woman first awakened in me at six-and-
twenty, after I had given birth to a child ; up to that
time (six months) I constantly had violent vomiting
after intercourse. This also came on whenever I was
at all oppressed in mood.

' I have extraordinarily keen powers of observation,
and quite exceptionally sharp hearing, also a very keen
sense of smell. I can pick out by smell people I know
from among a crowd with my eyes bandaged.

' I do not regard my abnormal powers of sight and
hearing as pathological, but ascribe them to finer
perceptions and greater quickness of thought ; but I
have only spoken of it to my pastor and doctor—very
unwillingly to the latter, as I was afraid he would tell
me that what I regarded as *plus*-qualities were *minus*-
qualities, and also because from being misunderstood
in childhood I am very reserved and shy.'

The dream which the writer of the letter asks us
to interpret is not hard to understand. It is a dream
of saving from water, a typical birth-dream. The
language of symbolism, as you are aware, knows no
grammar ; it is an extreme case of a language of
infinitives, and even the active and passive are represented by one and the same image. If in a dream a
woman pulls (or wishes to pull) a man out of the water,
that may mean she wishes to be his mother (takes
him for her son as Pharaoh's daughter did with Moses),

or equally she wishes him to make her into a mother, to have a son by him, a son who shall be as like him as a copy. The tree-trunk to which the woman clings is easily recognized as a phallic symbol, even though it is not standing straight up, but inclined towards the surface of the water—in the dream the word is ' bent '. The onrush and recoil of the surf brought to the mind of another dreamer who was relating a similar dream the comparison with the intermittent pains of labour, and when, knowing that she had not yet borne a child, I asked her how she knew of this characteristic of labour, she said that one imagined labour as a kind of colic, a quite unimpeachable description physiologically. She gave the association ' Waves of the Sea and Waves of Passion '.¹ How our dreamer at so early an age can have arrived at the finer details of the symbolism : tongue of land, palm-tree, I am naturally unable to say. We must not, however, overlook the fact that, when people maintain that they have for years been haunted by the same dream, it often turns out that the manifest content is not throughout quite the same. Only the kernel of the dream has recurred each time ; the details of the content are changed or additions are made to them.

At the end of this dream, which is evidently charged with anxiety, the dreamer falls out of bed. This is a fresh representation of child-birth ; analytic investigation of the fear of heights, of the dread of an impulse to throw oneself out of the window, has doubtless led you all to the same conclusion.

Who then is the man, by whom the dreamer wishes to have a child, or of whose very image she would like to be the mother ? She has often tried to see his face, but the dream never allows of it ; the man has to remain a mystery. We know from countless analyses what this veiling means, and the conclusion we should base on analogy is verified by another statement of

¹ [*Des Meeres und der Liebe Wellen*, the title of a play by Grillparzer.—Ed.]

the dreamer's. Under the influence of paraldehyde she once recognized the face of the man in the dream as that of the hospital physician who was treating her, and who meant nothing more to her conscious emotional life. The original thus never divulged its identity, but this impression of it in ' transference ' establishes the conclusion that earlier it must have always been the father. Ferenczi is undoubtedly perfectly right in pointing out that these ' dreams of the unsuspecting ' are valuable sources of information confirming the conjectures of analysis. Our dreamer was the eldest of twelve children ; how often must she have gone through the pangs of jealousy and disappointment when not she, but her mother, obtained from her father the longed-for child !

Our dreamer has quite correctly supposed that her first memories of childhood would be of value in the interpretation of her early and recurrent dream. In the first scene, in the first year of her life, as she sits in her perambulator she sees two horses close to her, one looking hard at her in a significant way. This she describes as her most vivid experience ; she had the feeling that it was a human being. This is a feeling which we can understand only if we assume that the two horses represent, in this case as so often, man and wife, father and mother. It is, as it were, a flash of infantile totemism. If we could, we should ask the writer whether the *brown* horse who looks at her in so human a way could not be recognized by its colouring as her father. The second recollection is associatively connected with the first through the same ' understanding ' gaze. ' Taking the little bird in her hand ' reminds the analyst, who, by the way, has prejudices of his own at times, of a feature in the dream in which the woman's hand is again in contact with another phallic symbol.

The next two memories belong together ; they make still slighter demands on the interpreter. The mother crying out during her confinement reminded the daughter directly of the pigs screaming when they were killed and put her into the same frenzy of pity. We may also conjecture, however, that this is a violent reaction against a death-wish directed at the mother.

With these indications of tenderness for the father, of contact with his genitals, and of the death-wish against the mother, the outline of the female Oedipus-complex is sketched. The ignorance of sexual matters retained so long and the frigidity at a later period bear out these suppositions. The writer of the letter has been virtually—and for a time no doubt actually—an hysterical neurotic. The life-force has, for her own happiness, carried her along with it, has awakened in her the sexual feelings of a woman and brought her the joys of motherhood, and the capacity to work, but a portion of her libido still clings to its point of fixation in childhood ; she still dreams that dream that flings her out of bed and punishes her for her incestuous object-choice by ' not inconsiderable injuries '.

And now a strange doctor's explanation, given in a letter, is to effect something that all the most important experiences of later life have failed to do. Probably a regular analysis continued for a considerable time might have some success. As things were, I was obliged to content myself with writing to her that I was convinced she was suffering from the after-effects of a strong emotional tie binding her to her father and from a corresponding identification with her mother, but that I did not myself expect that this explanation would help her at all. Spontaneous cures of neurosis usually leave scars behind, and these smart from time to time. We are very proud of our art if we achieve a cure through psycho-analysis, yet even so we cannot always prevent the formation of a painful scar in the process.

The little series of reminiscences must engage our attention for a while longer. I have on one occasion stated that such scenes of childhood are ' screen-memories ' selected at a later period, put together, and thereby not infrequently falsified. This subsequent elaboration serves a purpose that is sometimes easy to guess. In our case one can practically hear the ego of the writer glorifying or soothing itself throughout the whole series of recollections. ' I was from a tiny thing a particularly large-hearted and compassionate child. I learnt quite early that the animals have souls as we have, and could not endure cruelty to animals. The sins of the flesh were far from me and I preserved my chastity till late.' With declarations such as these she loudly contradicts the inferences that we have to make about her early childhood on the basis of our analytical experience, namely, that she had an abundance of premature sexual emotions and violent feelings of hatred for her mother and her younger brothers and sisters. (Beside the genital significance assigned to it, the little bird may also have that of a child-symbol, like all small animals ; her memory also accentuates in a very insistent way that this tiny creature had the same right to exist as she herself.) The short series of recollections in fact furnishes a very nice example of a mental structure with a twofold aspect. Viewed superficially, we may find in it the expression of an abstract idea, here, as usually, with an ethical reference. In H. Silberer's nomenclature the structure has an *anagogic* content ; on deeper investigation it reveals itself as a chain of phenomena belonging to the region of the repressed life of the instincts—it displays its *psycho-analytic* content. As you know, Silberer, who was among the first to issue a warning to us on no account to lose sight of the nobler side of the human soul, has put forward the view that all or nearly all dreams permit such a twofold interpretation, a purer, anagogic one beside the ordinary, psycho-analytic one. This is, however, unfortunately not so ; on the contrary, a further interpretation of this kind is rarely possible ; there has been no valuable example of such a dream-analysis with a double meaning published up to the present time within my knowledge. But something of the kind can often be observed within the series of associations that our patients produce during analytic treatment. The successive ideas are linked on the one hand by an obvious and coherent association, while on the other hand you become aware of an underlying theme which is kept secret and at the same time plays a part in all these ideas. The contrast between the two themes that dominate the same series of ideas is not always one between the lofty anagogic and the common psycho-analytic, but is rather that between shocking and decent or neutral ideas—a fact that easily explains how such a chain of associations with a twofold determination arises. In our present example it is of course not accidental that the anagogic and the psycho-analytic interpretations stand in such a sharp contrast to each other ; both relate to the same material, and the later tendency is the same as that seen in the reaction-formations erected against the disowned instinctual forces.

Now why did we make such a special search for the psycho-analytic interpretation instead of contenting ourselves with the more accessible anagogic one ? The answer to this is linked up with many other problems—with the existence of neurosis itself and the explanations it inevitably demands—with the fact that virtue does not reward a man with the joy and strength in life that is expected from it, as though it brought with it too much from its original source (this dreamer, too, had not been well rewarded for her virtue), and with many other things which I need not discuss before this audience.

So far, however, in this case we have completely neglected the question of telepathy, the other point of interest in it for us ; it is time to return to it. In a sense we have here an easier task than in the case of Herr G. With a person who so easily and so early in life succumbed before reality and replaced it by the world of phantasy, the temptation is irresistible

to connect her telepathic experiences and 'visions'
with her neurosis and to derive them from it, although
here too we should not allow ourselves to be deceived
as to the cogency of our own arguments. We shall
merely replace what is unknown and unintelligible by
possibilities that are at least comprehensible.

On August 22, 1914, at ten o'clock in the morning,
our correspondent experienced a telepathic impression
that her brother, who was at the time on active service,
was calling, 'Mother! mother!'; the phenomenon
was purely acoustic, it was repeated shortly after, but
nothing was seen. Two days later she sees her mother
and finds her much depressed because the boy had an-
nounced himself to her by repeatedly calling, 'Mother!
mother!'. She immediately recalls the same telepathic
message, which she had experienced at the same time,
and as a matter of fact some weeks later it was
established that the young soldier had died on that
day at the hour stated.

It cannot be proved, but also cannot be disproved,
that instead of this what happened was the following
the mother told her one day that the son had sent
this telepathic message; whereupon the conviction at
once arose in her mind that she had had the same
experience at the same time. Such delusory memories
arise in the mind with the force of an obsession, a force
derived from real sources—they have, however, substituted material for psychical reality. The strength
of the delusory memory lies in its being an excellent
way of expressing the sister's tendency to identify
herself with the mother. 'You are anxious about the
boy, but I am really his mother, and his cry was meant
for me; I had this telepathic message.' The sister
would naturally firmly decline to consider our attempt
at explanation and would hold to her belief in the
authenticity of the experience. She simply cannot do
otherwise; as long as the reality of the unconscious
basis of it in her own mind is concealed from her she
is obliged to believe in the reality of her pathological

logic. Every such delusion derives its strength and
its unassailable character from its source in unconscious
psychical reality. I note in passing that it is not
incumbent on us here to explain the mother's experience
or to investigate its authenticity.

The dead brother is, however, not only the imaginary
child of our correspondent ; he represents also a rival
regarded with hatred even at the time of his birth.
By far the greater number of all telepathic presentiments
relate to death or the possibility of death : when
patients under analysis keep telling us of the frequency
and infallibility of their gloomy forebodings, we can
with equal regularity show them that they are fostering
particularly strong death-wishes in their unconscious
against their nearest relations and have therefore long
suppressed them. The patient whose history I related
in 1909 [1] was an example to the point ; he was even
called a ' bird of ill omen ' by his relations. But when
the kindly and highly intelligent man—who has since
himself perished in the war—began to make progress
towards recovery, he himself gave me considerable
assistance in clearing up his own psychological conjuring tricks. In the same way, the account given
in our first correspondent's letter, of how he and his
three brothers had received the news of their youngest
brother's death as a thing they had long been inwardly
aware of, appears to need no other explanation. The
elder brothers would all have been equally convinced
of the superfluousness of the youngest arrival.

Another of our dreamer's ' visions ' will probably
become more intelligible in the light of analytical
knowledge ! Women friends have obviously a considerable significance in her emotional life. News of
the death of one of them is conveyed to her shortly
after the event by knocking at night on the bed of a
room-mate in the sanatorium. Another friend had
many years before married a widower with several

---

[1] ' Notes upon a Case of Obsessional Neurosis ', COLLECTED PAPERS,
vol. iii.

(five) children. On the occasion of her visits to their house she regularly saw the apparition of a lady, whom she felt constrained to suppose to be the dead first wife ; this did not at first permit of confirmation, and only became a matter of certainty with her seven years later, on the discovery of a fresh photograph of the dead woman. This achievement in the way of a vision has the same inner dependence on the family-complex already recognized in our correspondent as her presentiment of the brother's death. By identifying herself with her friend she could in her person achieve her own wish-fulfilment ; for all eldest daughters of a numerous family build up in their unconscious the phantasy of becoming the father's second wife by the death of the mother. If the mother is ill or dies, the eldest daughter takes her place as a matter of course in relation to the younger brothers and sisters, and may even in respect to the father take over some part of the functions of the wife. The unconscious wish fills in the other part.

I am now almost at the end of what I wish to say. I might, however, add the observation that the cases of telepathic messages or occurrences which have been discussed here are clearly connected with emotions belonging to the sphere of the Oedipus-complex. This may sound startling ; I do not intend to give it out as a great discovery, however. I would rather revert to the result we arrived at through investigating the dream I considered first. Telepathy has no relation to the essential nature of dreams ; it cannot deepen in any way what we already understand of them by analysis. On the other hand, psycho-analysis may do something to advance the study of telepathy, in so far as, by the help of its interpretations, many of the puzzling characteristics of telepathic phenomena may be rendered more intelligible to us ; or other, still doubtful phenomena be for the first time definitely ascertained to be of a telepathic nature.

There remains one element of the apparently

intimate connection between telepathy and dreams which is not affected by any of these considerations : namely, the incontestable fact that sleep creates favourable conditions for telepathy. Sleep is not, it is true, indispensable to the accomplishment of the process— whether it originates in messages or in an unconscious activity of some kind. If you are not already aware of this, you will learn it from the instance given by our second correspondent, of the message coming from the boy between nine and ten in the morning. We must add, however, that no one has a right to take exception to telepathic occurrences on the ground that the event and the presentiment (or message) do not exactly coincide in astronomical time. It is perfectly conceivable that a telepathic message might arrive contemporaneously with the event and yet only penetrate to consciousness the following night during sleep (or even in waking life only after a while, during some pause in the activity of the mind). We are, as you know, of opinion that dream-formation itself does not necessarily wait for the onset of sleep to begin. Often the latent dream-thoughts may have been lying ready during the whole day, till at night they find the contact with the unconscious wish that shapes them into a dream. But if the phenomenon of telepathy is only an activity of the unconscious mind, then no fresh problem lies before us. The laws of unconscious mental life may then be taken for granted as applying to telepathy.

Have I given you the impression that I am secretly inclined to support the reality of telepathy in the occult sense ? If so, I should very much regret that it is so difficult to avoid giving such an impression. In reality, however, I was anxious to be strictly impartial. I have every reason to be so, for I have no opinion ; I know nothing about it.

A NEUROSIS OF DEMONIACAL POSSESSION IN THE SEVENTEENTH CENTURY [1]

(1923)

EXPERIENCE of neuroses amongst children goes to show that in them much is clearly visible to the naked eye which at a later age can only be discovered after painstaking research. We may anticipate that the same holds true for the neurotic manifestations characteristic of earlier centuries, provided, of course, that we are prepared to recognize them as such under other names than those of our present-day neuroses. When we consider how in our present unpsychological epoch neuroses appear in a hypochondriacal guise, masked as organic diseases, we need not be surprised to find the neuroses of olden times masquerading in a demonological shape. As is known, many authors, foremost amongst them Charcot, have recognized states of demoniacal possession and ecstasy, descriptions of which have been preserved for us in the artistic productions of those periods, to be manifestations of hysteria ; had more attention been paid to the history of such cases at the time, it would have been a simple matter to find in them the same content as that of the neuroses to-day.

Despite the somatic ideology of the era of ' exact ' science, the demonological theory of these dark ages has in the long run justified itself. Cases of demoniacal possession correspond to the neuroses of the present day ; in order to understand these latter we have once

[1] First published in *Imago*, Bd. ix., 1923. [Translated by Edward Glover.]

The author wishes to add to the English translation two footnotes (which appear within square brackets), and to express his regret that they were omitted from the German version.

more had recourse to the conception of psychic forces. What in those days were thought to be evil spirits to us are base and evil wishes, the derivatives of impulses which have been rejected and repressed. In one respect only do we not subscribe to the explanation of these phenomena current in mediaeval times ; we have abandoned the projection of them into the outer world, attributing their origin instead to the inner life of the patient in whom they manifest themselves.

I. The Story of Christoph Haitzmann, the Painter

I am indebted to the friendly interest of Hofrat Dr. R. Payer-Thurn, director of the former Imperial *Fideikommissbibliothek* of Vienna for the opportunity of studying one of these demonological neuroses, which occurred in the seventeenth century. This gentleman discovered in the Imperial Library a manuscript originating from Mariazell, a place of pilgrimage, in which was described in detail how a pact with the Devil had been redeemed in a wonderful manner through the interposition of the Holy Virgin Mary. His interest was aroused by the resemblance of this story to the Faust legend, and led him to undertake a comprehensive presentation of the material. Finding, however, that the person whose redemption was described had been subject to visions and convulsive seizures, Dr. Payer-Thurn turned to me for a medical opinion on the case. In the end we agreed to publish our investigations independently and apart. I wish to take this opportunity of thanking him for his suggestion and for his assistance in various ways in studying the manuscript.

The history of this demonological neurosis leads to a really valuable discovery, which can be brought to light without much interpretative work—much as a vein of pure metal may sometimes be struck when elsewhere the ore can only be extracted after laborious smelting operations.

The manuscript, an exact duplicate of which is in

my possession, consists of two parts entirely distinct from each other : one written in Latin by a monastic author or compiler, and the other a fragment from the patient's diary written in German. The former contains a preface and a description of the actual miracle ; the latter can scarcely have been of much interest to the clerics but is all the more valuable to us. It serves in large part to confirm our otherwise tentative views on the case, and we have every reason to be grateful to the reverend fathers for having preserved the document although it contributed nothing of value from their point of view ; indeed, rather the contrary.

Before summarizing the contents of this little hand-written brochure, which bears the title *Trophaeum Mariano-Cellense*, I must narrate a part of its contents which I take from the Preface.

On September 5, 1677, the painter Christoph Haitzmann, a native of Bavaria, was brought to Mariazell bearing a letter of introduction from the Pastor of Pottenbrunn (in Lower Austria), which lies not far away.[1] For some months he had lived in Pottenbrunn pursuing his occupation of painting ; on August 29, whilst in church, he was seized with frightful convulsions and, as these recurred in the days following, he had been interrogated by the Praefectus Dominii Pottenbrunnensis, in order to discover what was oppressing him and whether he had yielded to an impulse to have illicit traffic with the Evil One.[2] Whereupon he confessed that nine years previously, in a state of despondency in regard to his art and of despair about his livelihood, he had succumbed to the nine-times-repeated temptation of the Evil One and had given his bond in writing to belong to the Devil body and soul at the end of nine years. On the twenty-fourth of that month

---

[1] No mention is anywhere made of the painter's age. One surmises from the context that he was between thirty and forty, probably nearer thirty. He died, as we shall hear, in 1700.

[2] We can only note here in passing the possibility that this cross-examination of the patient ' suggested ' to him the phantasy of a pact with the Devil.

the period would expire.[1]   The unfortunate man had
rued his bargain and was convinced that only the grace
of the Mother of God at Mariazell could save him, by
compelling the Evil One to disgorge this Bond which
was written in blood.   On these grounds he (*miserum
hunc hominem omni auxilio destitutum*) had been consigned to the benevolence of the fathers of Mariazell.

So far the story of Leopoldus Braun, Pastor of
Pottenbrunn, September 1, 1677.

To come now to the analysis of the Manuscript.
It consists of three parts :

(1) A coloured title-page representing the scenes of
the signing of the Pact and of the redemption in the
shrine of Mariazell; on the next page are eight drawings,
likewise coloured, representing subsequent appearances
of the Devil, with a brief legend in German attached
to each.   These illustrations are not original ; they
are copies—exact copies, we are solemnly assured—
from original paintings by Christoph Haitzmann.

(2) The actual *Trophaeum Mariano-Cellense* (in
Latin), the work of a reverend compiler who signs
himself at the foot P. A. E., adding four lines in verse
containing his biography.   It ends with a deposition
by the Abbot Kilian of St. Lambert, dated September
12, 1729, which is in a different handwriting, and
testifies to the exact correspondence of manuscript
and illustrations with the originals preserved in the
archives.   The year in which the *Trophaeum* was
written is not mentioned.   We are at liberty to assume
that it was done in the same year as that in which the
Abbot Kilian made his deposition, in 1729 ; or, since
1714 is the last date mentioned in the text, we may
put the work of the compiler somewhere between 1714
and 1729.   The miracle which has been rescued from
oblivion by means of this manuscript happened in the
year 1677, that is to say, from thirty-seven to fifty-
two years before.

(3) The painter's diary written in German, covering

---

[1] *Quorum et finis 24 mensis hujus futurus appropinquat.*

the period from his redemption in the shrine until January 13 in the following year, 1678. It is inserted in the text of the *Trophaeum* almost at the end.

The main part of the actual *Trophaeum* is made up of two portions, the before-mentioned letter of introduction of the Pastor of Pottenbrunn, Leopold Braun, dated September 1, 1677, and the report of the Abbot Franciscus of Mariazell and St. Lambert describing the miraculous cure, dated September 12, 1677, that is to say, only a few days after it happened. The work of the editor or compiler P. A. E. consists of a preface in which the contents of these two documents are condensed, together with some less important passages introduced to connect the two, and a report at the end on the subsequent history of the painter based on inquiries made in the year 1714.[1]

The painter's previous history is thus related three times over in the *Trophaeum* : (1) in the introductory letter from the Pastor of Pottenbrunn, (2) in the formal deposition of the Abbot Franciscus and (3) in the editorial preface. A comparison of these three sources discloses certain contradictions which it will be important for us to follow up.

I can now continue the story of the painter. After a prolonged period of expiation and prayer at Mariazell, the Devil appeared before him in the Holy Shrine at midnight on September 8, the birthday of the Virgin, in the form of a winged dragon, and gave him back the Pact, which was written in blood. Much to our surprise we learn at a later stage that two Pacts with the Devil are mentioned in the history of Christoph Haitzmann, an earlier one written in black ink and a later one written in blood. The one referred to in the scene of exorcism, which is also that illustrated on the title-page, is the Blood Pact, that is, the later one.

It might occur to us at this point to question the

---

[1] This would seem to indicate that the *Trophaeum* too was written in the year 1714.

credibility of these ecclesiastical reporters—a misgiving prompting us not to waste our energies on a mere product of monastic superstition. We are told that several clerics, each mentioned by name, assisted at the exorcism and were even present in the chapel during the Devil's appearance. Now had it been stated that they had also witnessed the dragon delivering to the painter this document inscribed in red (*schedam sibi porrigentem conspexisset*), we should be confronted by several disturbing possibilities, the least disagreeable of which would be that of a collective hallucination. The testimony of the Abbot Franciscus, however, dispels this misgiving. It is nowhere stated that the clergy present saw the Devil ; on the contrary, it is quite frankly and soberly recorded that the painter tore himself from the arms of the fathers who were supporting him, rushed into the corner of the chapel where he saw the apparition and returned with the Bond in his hand.[1]

It was a wonderful miracle ; the triumph of the Holy Mother over Satan was beyond all question, but unfortunately the cure was not a permanent one. It is again to the credit of the churchmen that they do not conceal this. After a brief interval the painter left Mariazell in good health and proceeded to Vienna, where he lived with a married sister. On October 11 fresh seizures occurred, some of them very severe, and these are reported in the Diary until January 13. They took the form of visions and of loss of consciousness, during which he saw and experienced all manner of things ; also of convulsive seizures accompanied by extremely painful sensations ; on one occasion paralysis of the lower limbs occurred ; and so on. This time it was not the Devil, however, who persecuted him ; on the contrary, these unwelcome attentions came from

---

[1] . . . *ipsumque Daemonem ad Aram Sac. Cellae per fenestrellam in cornu Epistolae Schedam sibi porrigentem conspexisset eo advolans e Religiosorum manibus, qui eum tenebant, ipsam Schedam ad manum obtinuit. . . .*

sacred personages, Christ and the Holy Virgin herself. It is remarkable that he suffered no less from the visitations of these heavenly persons and from the penances they imposed on him than from his former traffic with the Devil. We discover from the Diary that he regarded these fresh manifestations as Satanic apparitions too, and when in May 1678 he went back to Mariazell we find him bewailing these *maligni Spiritus manifestationes*.

He explained to the reverend fathers that he had come back in order to recover from the Devil a still earlier Pact written in ink.[1] Again this time the Holy Virgin and the pious fathers helped him to obtain the answer to his prayer. As to how this came about, however, the report is silent. It says briefly : *qua iuxta votum reddita*. Once again he prayed, and once again the Pact was returned to him. Afterwards he felt quite free and entered the Order of Monks Hospitallers.

We have once more to acknowledge that, despite the quite obvious tendency behind his work, the compiler has not been tempted into departing from that veracity which is a condition of a clinical history. When in 1714 inquiry is made of the Superior of the Cloister of Monks Hospitallers concerning the painter's after-history, the information obtained is not suppressed. Reverendus Pater Provincialis reports that Brother Chrysostomus had again been repeatedly tempted by the Evil One, who wished to strike a fresh Pact with him : and indeed, that this occurred only when ' he had taken somewhat more wine than usual ',[2] but by the grace of God it had always been possible for him to repulse these approaches. In the year 1700, in the cloister of the Order at Neustatt on Moldau, Brother Chrysostomus, ' meek in spirit and of good comfort ', died of a fever.

---

[1] This had been drawn up in September 1668, and in May 1678, nine and a half years after, would have been long overdue.

[2] ' *Wenn er etwas mehrers von Wein getrunken.* '

II. The Motivation of the Satanic Pact

When we come to consider this Bond with Satan as if it were the case-history of a neurotic, our interest is aroused in the first instance by the problem of its motivation, which is of course closely connected with the question of its exciting cause.   Why does one sell oneself to the Devil ?   To be sure, Dr. Faust puts the contemptuous question : What hast thou to give, thou poor Devil ?   But he erred ; the Devil, in return for the immortal soul, has much to offer that is highly treasured of man : wealth, immunity from dangers, power over mankind and over the forces of Nature, but above all these, pleasure, the enjoyment of beautiful women.   Moreover, in pacts with the Devil these terms or obligations are usually specifically mentioned.[1] What then was Christoph Haitzmann's reason for entering into his Bond ?

Remarkable to relate, it was not for any one of these very natural desires.   To put the matter beyond all doubt, one has only to read the brief remarks appended by the artist to his illustrations of the apparitions of the Devil.   For example, the legend appended to the Third Vision runs :

Zum driten ist er mir in anderthalb Jahren in disser abscheühlichen Gestalt erschinen, mit einen Buuch in der Handt, darin lauter Zauberey und schwarze Kunst war begrüffen . . .

[For the third time within one yeare and a half he hath appeared vnto me in this loathfome fhape bearing in his hand a Booke the which is full of naught but wizardrie and blacke magicke.]

We learn, however, from the legend under a later apparition that the Devil reproaches him furiously for

---

[1] Cf. *Faust*, I.   Study.

> I'll pledge myself to be your servant *here*,
> Ne'er at your call to slumber or be still ;
> But when together *yonder* we appear,
> You shall submissively obey my will.

(Translation by Anna Swanwick.)

having ' burnt his aforetold Booke ' and threatens to
tear him to pieces if he does not bring it him back.

In the Fourth Vision he shows him a large yellow
money-bag and a great ducat, promising to give him
as many of these as he cares to have : the painter,
however, can boast of his reply, ' but I would in no
wise accept of such things '.

On another occasion the Devil demands that he
should turn to pleasure and amusement, concerning
which the painter remarks, ' *welliches zwar auch auf
sein begehren geschehen aber ich yber drey Tag nit
continuirt, und gleich widerumb aussgelöst worden* '
[the which on his entreatie did come to pass, yet did
I not continue for more than three days and was
speedilie redeemed anew].

Now since he refuses magical powers, money and
pleasure when the Devil offers them, and still less
makes them a condition of the Bond, it becomes really
imperative to know what the painter desired of the
Devil when he entered into the Pact. Some motive
or other he must have had to induce him to have any
such dealings at all.

On this point, too, the *Trophaeum* provides us with
reliable information. He had become depressed, was
unable or unwilling to paint properly and was anxious
about his livelihood, that is to say, he suffered from
melancholic depression with incapacity for work and
(justified) anxiety about his future. It is clear that
we are really dealing with a morbid state of health,
and further, we are informed of the exciting cause of
the disease ; the painter himself, in the legends
appended to his illustrations, actually describes it as
a melancholia (' that I should seeke diversion and banish
Melancholy '). The first of our three sources of information, the letter of introduction from the Pastor,
to be sure, speaks only of the depression (' *dum artis
suae progressum emolumentumque secuturum* PUSILLANI-
MIS *perpenderet* ') ; the second source, however, the
report of the Abbot Franciscus, indicates the cause of

this despondency or depression : it runs thus : '*accepta aliqua pusillanimitate* EX MORTE PARENTIS', and in the compiler's introduction the same reason is advanced, merely the order of the wording being inverted : *ex morte parentis accepta aliqua pusillanimitate*. That is to say, his father had died and he had consequently fallen into a state of melancholia, whereupon the Devil had appeared before him, inquired the cause of his dejection and grief, and had promised ' to help him in every way and give him aid '.[1]

This man sold himself to the Devil, therefore, in order to be freed from a state of depression. Truly an excellent motive, in the judgement of those who can understand the torment of these states and who appreciate, moreover, how little the art of medicine can do to alleviate the malady. Yet I question if a single one of my readers who has followed the tale thus far could guess the wording of the Pact, or rather Pacts (since there are two, one written in ink and a second written about a year later in blood, both presumably still in the archives at Mariazell, and transcribed in the *Trophaeum*).

These agreements hold two great surprises in store for us. First of all there is no mention in either of them that it was for certain obligations to be fulfilled by the Devil that the painter had bartered eternal bliss : there is but one condition, which the Devil makes and the painter must observe. It strikes us as being entirely illogical and absurd that this man should barter his soul, not for something which the Devil shall afford him, but for a service which he shall himself render to the Devil. The actual agreement made by the painter sounds more extraordinary still.

The First ' Syngrapha ', written in black ink :

> *Ich Christoph Haitzmann vndterschreibe mich diesen Herrn sein leibeigener Sohn auff 9 Jahr 1669 Jahr.*

[1] ' *Auf alle Weiss zu helfen und an die Handt zu gehen.*' The first picture on the title-page, and its legend, shows the Devil in the form of an ' *ersamer Bürger* ' (honest burgher).

[*I Christoph Haitzmann sign a deede and
pledge myſelfe to be vnto this lord euen as a sonne
of his bodie for 9 yeares*   *1669 yeare*]

The Second, written in blood :

*Anno 1669 Christoph Haizmann Ich ver-
schreibe mich diſsen Satan, ich sein leibeigner Sohn
zu sein, vnd in 9 Jahr ihm mein Leib und Seel
zuzugeheren*

[*Anno 1669 Christoph Haizmann I give my
bonde and pledge myſelfe vnto this Satan for to be
vnto him euen as a sonne of his bodie and after
9 yeares to belong vnto him bodie and saule*]

Our astonishment vanishes, however, when we read
the text in the sense that what appears to be a service
demanded of the painter by Satan is instead an
obligation on the part of Satan towards the painter.
This incomprehensible Pact would then acquire a
straightforward meaning which might be expressed
thus : The Devil binds himself for a period of nine
years to take the place of his lost father to the painter.
At the end of this period the latter, as was customary
in such dealings, becomes the property of the Devil
body and soul. The train of thought motivating this
Pact seems indeed to be as follows : Owing to my
father's death I am despondent and can no longer work ;
if I can but get a father-substitute I shall be able to
regain all that I have lost.

A man who has fallen into a melancholia on account
of his father's death must have loved that father
deeply. The more curious then that he should have
come by the idea of taking the Devil as a substitute
for the loved parent.

III. The Devil as a Father-Substitute

I daresay sober-minded critics will not be prepared
to admit that by reversing the sense of this Satanic
Pact we have made the matter clear. Two objections
to this procedure might be advanced. In the first

place, it might be said that it is unnecessary to regard the Pact as a contract in which the obligations of both parties are set forth. It might contain merely the painter's obligations, without any reference in the text to the obligations of the Devil, which would remain ' understood '. The painter, however, binds himself in two ways, first to be as a son to the Devil for nine years, and secondly, to belong to him entirely after death. In this way one of the premises on which our conclusion is based would be disposed of.

The burden of the second objection would be that there is no justification for laying stress on the expression, ' the son of his body '. This is merely a phrase current at that time, which could quite well be interpreted in the way the reverend fathers understood it. The latter did not translate into Latin the kinship laid down in the Pact, but merely say that the painter ' *mancipavit* ' himself to the Evil One, surrendered himself to him, had taken upon himself to lead a life of wickedness and to deny God and the Holy Trinity. Why should we hold aloof from this obvious and natural explanation ? [1] The state of affairs would then simply be that someone in a helpless state, tortured with melancholic depression, sells himself to the Devil, in whose healing powers he reposes the greatest confidence. That the depression was caused by the father's demise would then be quite irrelevant : it could quite conceivably have been due to some other cause. This seems a forceful and reasonable objection. We hear once more the familiar criticism of psycho-analysis that it regards the simplest affairs in an unduly subtle and complicated way, discovers secrets and problems where none exist, and that it achieves this by magnifying the most insignificant

---

[1] As a matter of fact, when we come to consider when and for whom these Pacts were drawn up, we shall realize that the text had of necessity to read inoffensively and in comprehensible terms. It suffices for our purposes, however, that some ambiguity should be contained in them, which we can make the starting-point of our investigations.

trifles to support far-reaching and bizarre conclusions. It would be fruitless to assure our opponents that this rejection on their part involves the neglect of many striking analogies and the breaking of many delicate connecting-threads, such as we can point to in the present instance. Our opponent would merely reply that such analogies and connecting-links were non-existent, that they were artifacts introduced by ourselves, figments of our overweening sagacity.

Now I shall not preface my reply with the words, ' Let us be honest ' or ' Let us be sincere,' since that one must always be able to be, and without making any preliminary flourish about it. Let me say quite simply that I am well aware that any reader who does not already believe in the soundness of the psycho-analytic mode of thought will certainly not acquire this conviction by reading the case of Christoph Haitzmann, painter in the seventeenth century. Nor is it my intention to put forward this case as a proof of the validity of psycho-analytic findings : on the contrary, I presuppose their soundness and I then make use of them to explain this painter's demonological disease. My justification for so doing lies in the success of our investigations into the nature of the neuroses in general. Speaking in all modesty, we may venture to say that even the more obtuse amongst our colleagues and contemporaries are beginning to realize that no understanding of neurotic states is to be attained without the help of psycho-analysis.

With these shafts alone can Troy be taken,.

as Odysseus admits in the *Philoctetes* of Sophocles.

If we are right in regarding as a neurotic phantasy the Satanic Pact made by our painter, there is no further need to apologize for interpreting it psycho-analytically. Even trifling indications have meaning and significance, and especially as regards the causal conditions of a neurosis. To be sure, it is possible to overvalue them, just as it is to underestimate them :

it remains a matter of judgement how far one should go in relying on them. But if a person does not believe in psycho-analysis, nor even in the Devil, he must be left to make what he can of the painter's case, whether he fashion an explanation by some means of his own or whether he sees nothing at all in the case deserving of explanation.

We will come back, therefore, to our assumption that the Devil to whom the painter sells himself is a direct father-substitute. In keeping with this is the shape in which he makes his first appearance: an honest old burgher with a flowing brown beard, dressed in a red mantle with a black hat, leaning on a stick in his right hand, and beside him a black hound (Picture 1).[1] The forms he assumes after become ever more terrifying, one might almost say more mythological : he is decked out with horns, eagle's talons, and bat's wings ; finally he appears in the shrine as a flying dragon. We shall have occasion to return later to a particular detail of his bodily shape.

It does indeed sound strange that the Devil should be chosen as a substitute for a loved father, but only when we hear of this for the first time ; there are many facts at our disposal which can serve to temper our astonishment. First of all we know that God is a father-substitute, or, more correctly, an exalted father, or yet again, a reproduction of the father as seen and met with in childhood—as the individual sees him in his own childhood and as mankind saw him in prehistoric times in the father of the primal horde. Later on in life the individual acquired a different, a less exalted impression of him, but the childish image of him was preserved and it united with the inherited memory-traces of the primal father to form the idea of God. We know, too, from the inner life of individuals as disclosed in analysis, that the relation to this father was in all probability ambivalent from the outset, or at any rate it soon became so ; that is to say, it

[1] In Goethe a black dog like this turns into the Devil himself.

comprised two sets of emotional impulses, quite opposite in nature, not merely one of fondness and submission but another of hostility and defiance. We hold that this ambivalence governs the relations of mankind to its deities. From this unresolved conflict, on the one hand of longing for the father and on the other of dread and defiance, we have explained some of the important characteristics and most epoch-making vicissitudes of religion.[1]

Concerning the Evil Spirit, we know that he is regarded as the antithesis of God, yet as being somewhat akin to him in nature. His history has not been gone into so closely as has that of God : not all religions have adopted the Evil One, the enemy of God ; and his prototype in individual life remains as yet obscure. One thing, however, is certain : gods can turn into evil spirits when new gods supplant them. When one people vanquishes another, the overthrown gods of the conquered become not infrequently the evil spirits of the victors. The evil spirit of the Christian faith, the Devil of mediaeval times, was, according to Christian mythology, himself a fallen angel of godlike nature. It requires no great analytic insight to divine that God and the Devil were originally one and the same, a single figure which was later split into two bearing opposed characteristics.[2] In the prehistoric age of the religions, all those terrifying features which were afterwards merged in the form of his counterpart were still borne by the god himself.

It is an example of the process, so familiar to us, by which an idea with an opposed—ambivalent— content is split into two opposites contrasting sharply. The antitheses contained in the original idea of the nature of God are but a reflection of the ambivalence governing the relation of an individual to his personal

---

[1] Cf. Freud, *Totem and Tabu*, and, in detail, Theodor Reik, *Probleme der Religionspsychologie*, Bd. I.

[2] Cf. Theodor Reik, ' Gott und Teufel ', *Der eigene und der fremde Gott* [quoting Ernest Jones, *Der Alptraum in seiner Beziehung zu gewissen Formen des mittelälterlichen Aberglaubens*. See footnote p. 264].

father. If the benevolent and righteous God is a father-substitute, it is not to be wondered at that the hostile attitude, which leads to hate, fear and accusations against him, comes to expression in the figure of Satan. The father is thus the individual prototype of both God and the Devil. The fact that the figure of the primal father was that of a being with unlimited potentialities of evil, bearing much more resemblance to the Devil than to God, must have left an indelible stamp on all religions.

To be sure, it is by no means easy to demonstrate in the mental life of the individual traces of this satanic conception of the father. When a boy takes to drawing caricatures and grotesque figures, it may be possible to prove that he is making a mock of his father; nor is it difficult, when children of both sexes are apprehensive at night about robbers and burglars, to recognize these as derivatives of the father.[1] The animals which play a part in the animal-phobias of children are generally father-substitutes, just as the totem animal was in primitive times. But that the Devil is an image of the father and can act as an understudy for him has never been so clearly apparent as in the case of our neurotic seventeenth-century painter. It was this that, at the beginning of this paper, led me to express my belief that a demonological record of this kind would furnish that pure metal which, in the neuroses of a later age—no longer superstitious but rather hypochondriacal—can only be extracted from the raw ore of symptoms and associations by a laborious analytic process.[2]

[1] In the familiar tale of the Seven Little Goats, Father Wolf appears as a burglar.

[2] The fact that we so seldom in analyses find the Devil figuring as a father-substitute probably indicates that, in those we analyse, the rôle of this mediaeval, mythological figure has long since been outplayed. It was just as much the duty of a pious Christian in earlier centuries to believe in the Devil as to believe in God. As a matter of fact, the Devil was necessary in order to make him cling fast to God. For various reasons the increase in scepticism has affected first and foremost the person of the Devil.

Once one brings oneself to regard this idea of the Devil in the

Closer analysis of this case will in all probability
bring deeper conviction.   It is no unusual thing for a
man to develop melancholic depression and loss of
power to work after the death of his father.   We
conclude that such persons have been attached to the
father with bonds of deep affection and are reminded
how often a severe melancholia appears as a neurotic
form of grief.

So far we are undoubtedly right, but not if we
suppose further that the relation has been merely one
of love.   On the contrary, the more ambivalent the
relation had been, the more likely is the grief for the
father's loss to turn into a melancholia.   When we
bring this ambivalence into the foreground, however,
we become prepared for the possibility of the father
being denigrated in such a way as comes to expression
in the painter's demoniacal neurosis.   If only we were
in a position to learn as much about Christoph Haitzmann as we do of patients undergoing analysis, it
would be a simple matter to develop this ambivalence,
to bring into memory when and how he had cause to
fear and hate his father, above all, to discover the
accidental factors present in addition to the usual
motives for father-hate which are inevitable in the
natural father-son relation.   The inhibition of working
capacity, for example, might have had some special
explanation.   It is possible that the father had opposed
his son's wish to become a painter ; his incapacity to
paint after the father's death would then, on the one
hand, be an expression of the familiar ' deferred
obedience ' ; and, on the other, by rendering him
incapable of making a livelihood it would be bound
to increase his longing for the father to stand between
him and the cares of life.   As deferred obedience it

---

part of father-substitute as a phenomenon of cultural development,
a fresh light dawns on the witch-trials of the Middle Ages [as has already
been shown by Ernest Jones in the chapter on ' Die Hexenepidemie '
in his *Der Alptraum in seiner Beziehung zu gewissen Formen des mittelälterlichen Aberglaubens.*   See footnote p. 264].

would also constitute an expression of remorse and a successful self-punishment.

Since, however, we cannot set about the personal analysis of Christoph Haitzmann, *obiit* 1700, we must content ourselves with drawing special attention to such features in his clinical history as suggest typical exciting causes for the negative attitude to the father. There are not many such, nor are they particularly obvious, nevertheless such details as do exist are highly interesting.

Consider first of all the part played by the number Nine. The Bond with the Evil One was for nine years. On this point the entirely trustworthy report of the Pastor of Pottenbrunn is quite clear : *pro novem annis Syngraphen scriptam tradidit*. This letter, dated September 1, 1677, also informs us that the appointed term was about to expire in a few days : *quorum et finis* 24 *mensis hujus futurus appropinquat*. The Pact would therefore have been drawn up on September 24, 1668.[1] In the same report, indeed, yet another use is made of the number nine. *Nonies*—nine times— did the painter withstand the temptations of the Evil One before he fell. No mention is made of this detail in subsequent reports ; but in the Abbot's deposition the phrase ' *Post annos novem* ' is used, and the compiler also repeats ' *ad novem annos* ' in his summary, in itself a proof that the number was not regarded as unimportant.

The number Nine has become familiar to us in neurotic phantasies. Nine is the term of the months of gestation, and reference to the number Nine, whatever its connection, directs our attention to a phantasy of pregnancy. In this case, to be sure, the number refers to years, not to months, and it might be objected that the number can be of significance in other directions. But who can say whether much of the sacrosanctity of this number is not altogether due to its relation

---

[1] The contradiction disclosed by the fact that both the Pacts transcribed bear the date 1669 will be considered later.

to pregnancy ; the change from nine months to nine years need not throw dust in our eyes. Dreams have taught us how ' unconscious mental activity ' plays with numbers. If, for example, the number five occurs in a dream, this refers invariably to a five of significance in waking life ; the five may refer, however, in reality to five years' difference in age or to a company of five people, and this will appear in the dream as five pieces of money or five pieces of fruit. That is to say, the number itself is retained but the denominator is changed in accordance with the demands of condensation and displacement. Nine years in a dream could easily represent nine months in reality. The numbers of waking life are played with by the dream-work in other ways, too, as when the latter shows a lordly disregard for cyphers, not treating them as numbers at all. Five dollars in a dream may stand for fifty, five hundred, five thousand of the dollars of reality.

Another detail in the relation between the painter and the Devil also has a sexual reference. As has already been mentioned, when he first sees the Devil the latter appears in the shape of an honest burgher. On the very next occasion, however, he has already become naked, is malformed and has two pairs of breasts. Now in all of the subsequent apparitions breasts appear, sometimes singly, sometimes multiplied. On one occasion only, in addition to these breasts, the Devil has a large penis ending as a serpent. This stressing of female sexual characteristics by the intro- duction of great pendulous breasts (there is never any indication of the female genitalia) would appear to be an obvious contradiction of our assumption that the Devil was a father-substitute to the painter. Moreover, such a mode of representing the Devil is in itself quite unusual. Where devils are conceived of as a species, that is to say, where they appear in numbers, there is nothing extraordinary about the representation of female devils : but that *the* Devil, that mighty personage the Lord of Hell, the Adversary of God, should appear in any other guise but as a male, a superman indeed, with horns, tail and penis-serpent, does not seem to me to have been recorded.

These two slight indications suggest the typical factors that conditioned the negative side of the painter's attitude to his father. What he is struggling against is the feminine attitude to the father, which culminates in the phantasy of bearing him a child (nine years). We know this form of resistance very well from our analyses, where it takes many remarkable forms during the transference and is exceedingly troublesome. In his mourning for the departed father, and its intensification of the longing for him, the long-since-repressed phantasy of a pregnancy is re-awakened in our painter, which he must then defend himself against by means of a neurosis and by denigrating the father.

But why does the father, now reduced to the status of Devil, exhibit one of the bodily signs of womanhood? Here is a point which would at first seem difficult to interpret: two explanations, however, present themselves, vying with each other but at the same time mutually compatible. The feminine attitude to the father became repressed as soon as the boy realized that his rivalry with the woman for the father's love implies the loss of his own male genital, that is to say, implies castration. Repudiation of the feminine attitude is therefore a result of the struggle to avoid castration; it regularly finds its most emphatic expression in the contrasting phantasy of castrating the father and turning *him* into a woman. Hence the Devil's breasts would represent a projection of the man's own femininity on to the father-substitute. The other explanation of these female appurtenances in the Devil is in terms of tenderness, not of hostility; it sees in this female shape an indication of a transference of infantile affection from the mother to the father. The suggestion is that there had previously been a strong mother-fixation, which would in itself account in part for the hostility towards the father. The large breasts constitute the positive sexual characteristic of the mother, even at a time when the child is not familiar with the negative sign of womanhood, the absence of the penis.[1]

If it is his struggle against accepting castration which makes it impossible for the painter to yield to his longing for the father, it becomes entirely comprehensible that he should turn to the image of the mother for help and salvation. This is why he declares that he can only be released from the Pact by the Holy Mother of God at Mariazell and that he obtained his freedom on the Mother's birthday (September 8). Naturally we shall never know whether September 24, the day on which the Pact was executed, was not determined in some similar way.

Amongst all the observations concerning the mental life of children which psycho-analysis has made, there is hardly one which sounds so repugnant and incredible to the normal adult as the boy's feminine attitude to the father and the phantasy of pregnancy derived from it. Only since Daniel Paul Schreber, Senatspräsident[2] in Saxony, published the history of his psychotic illness and almost complete recovery, have we been able to speak of such things unconcernedly and with no need to apologize.[3] We learn from this invaluable book that at somewhere about the age of fifty the President became absolutely convinced that God—who incidentally had many of the characteristics of his father, the worthy physician Dr. Schreber—had formed the decision to castrate him and use him as a woman in order to produce a new race born from the spirit of Schreber. (His own marriage was childless.) In his revolt against this decision on the part of God, which seemed to him highly unjust and ' contrary to

[1] Cf. *Eine Kindheitserinnerung des Leonardo da Vinci.*
[2] [A Judge presiding over a Division in an Appeal Court.—Trans.]
[3] D. P. Schreber, *Denkwürdigkeiten eines Nervenkranken,* 1903. Cf. also ' Psycho-Analytic Notes upon an Autobiographical Account of a Case of Paranoia ', COLLECTED PAPERS, vol. iii.

the order of things ', he fell ill with symptoms of paranoia which, however, in the course of time died away, leaving only a few traces behind. The gifted writer could scarcely have guessed that in chronicling his own case-history he had brought to light a typical pathogenic factor.

This revolt against castration or the feminine attitude Alfred Adler has torn out of its organic context, has connected in a superficial or inaccurate way with the will to power and has represented as an independent trend, the ' masculine protest '. A neurosis, however, can never arise except from a conflict between two tendencies ; hence it is just as possible to regard the masculine protest as the cause of ' all ' neuroses as to regard the feminine attitude against which it protests as the cause. It is perfectly true that this masculine protest is a constant component of character-formation which in some cases plays a very large part, also that it manifests itself as a vigorous resistance during the analysis of neurotic men. Psychoanalysis has paid due attention to the masculine protest in connection with the castration - complex, but has not been able to represent it as an omnipotent or omnipresent factor in the neuroses. The most outstanding case of masculine protest, as regards manifest reactions and character-traits, which ever came to me for treatment, did so on account of an obsessional neurosis in which the unresolved conflict between a masculine and a feminine attitude (fear of and desire for castration) was quite plainly expressed. This patient, moreover, had developed masochistic phantasies which were entirely derived from the wish to experience castration ; and he had even gone beyond these phantasies to actual gratification in perverse ways. The whole of his condition was—like the Adlerian theory itself—due to a repression and repudiation of early infantile love-fixations.

President Schreber's recovery took its start from his decision to abandon all opposition to his castration and to accommodate himself to the feminine rôle designed for him by God. Following upon this, he became calm and clear in his mind, was able himself to arrange his dismissal from the asylum, and led a normal life, with the exception that he devoted some hours every day to the cultivation of his womanliness, remaining convinced that it would gradually mature to the final achievement of God's purpose.

IV. The Two Pacts

A remarkable detail in the history of our painter is the recorded circumstance that he made two separate Pacts with the Devil. The first of these, written in black ink, ran as follows [1] :

> *I, Christoph Haitzmann, sign a deede and pledge myselfe to be vnto this lord euen as a sonne of his bodie for 9 yeares   1669 yeare*

The second, written in blood, runs :

> *Anno 1669 Christoph Haizmann I give my bonde and pledge myselfe vnto this Satan for to be vnto him euen as a sonne of his bodie and after 9 yeares to belong vnto him bodie and saule*

The originals of both are said to have been in the archives at Mariazell when the *Trophaeum* was written, and both bear the date 1669.

I have already made frequent reference to both these Pacts and propose now to deal with them in greater detail, although in this connection the danger of magnifying trifles seems especially imminent.

It is unusual to find a man selling himself twice to the Devil in such a way that the second bond is substituted for the first without cancelling it. Perhaps to those who are more familiar with demonological

[1] [Cf. pp. 273-4 for original text of these documents.—Trans.]

material it may not seem so surprising. For my own part I could only regard it as something peculiar to this case, and my suspicions were aroused when I found that precisely on this point there was some lack of correspondence in the various accounts. Close examination of these points of divergence affords us, quite unexpectedly, a deeper understanding of this clinical history.

The simplest and clearest account we have is that contained in the introductory letter from the Pastor of Pottenbrunn. Here mention is made of one Pact only, written by the painter in blood nine years before, which was due to expire a few days later, on September 24, and must therefore have been written September 24, 1668 ; unfortunately this last date is not expressly mentioned, although one is entitled to make the deduction.

The deposition of the Abbot Franciscus, dated, as we know, a few days later (September 12, 1677), already describes a more complicated state of affairs. It is easy to assume that in the intervening period the painter had given more precise details. The deposition describes how the painter had made two Pacts, one in the year 1668 (a date which is in keeping with the Pastor's letter), written in black ink ; the other, however, *sequenti anno 1669*, written in blood. It was this latter Pact, written in blood in 1669, which he received back on the Birthday of the Holy Virgin. This does not arise out of the Abbot's deposition, since it merely goes on to say : *schedam redderet* and *schedam sibi porrigentem conspexisset*, as if there could be only one document. It does follow, however, from the subsequent course of the story and from the coloured title-page of the *Trophaeum*, where one can plainly see *red* script on the bond held by the Dragon. As has already been mentioned, the subsequent events were that the painter returned to Mariazell in May 1678, having been once more tempted by the Evil One in Vienna, and begged that the Holy Mother would

again have mercy upon him and cause the first Pact
written in ink to be rendered up to him. How this
came about is not so fully described as in the first
instance ; the report merely says *qua iuxta votum
reddita*, and in another place the compiler states that
this particular document was thrown to the painter
by the Devil 'all crumpled up and torn in four pieces '[1]
on May 9, 1678, at nine o'clock in the evening.

Both Pacts, however, bear the same date: the
year 1669.

This contradiction is either of no significance whatever, or else it affords us the following clue :

Starting from the Abbot's description, in which
most details are given, we are faced with various
difficulties. When Christoph Haitzmann informed the
Pastor of Pottenbrunn that he was oppressed of the
Devil and that the day of reckoning was at hand, he
must have had in mind (in 1677) the Pact drawn up
in the year 1668 : that is to say, the first, black Pact
(which in the introductory letter, by the way, is
described as the only one and a blood Pact). In
Mariazell a few days later, however, he is only concerned to get back the later blood Pact, which is not
yet due to expire (1669–1677), thus allowing the first
to become overdue. This latter is not reclaimed until
1678, *i.e.* when ten years have elapsed. We must
ask further why both Pacts are dated in the same year
1669, in face of the fact that the report expressly
attributes one to the ' *anno subsequenti* '.

The compiler must have been aware of these
difficulties, for he makes an attempt to smooth them
out. In his preface he adopts the Abbot's version,
but modifies it in one particular. The painter, he says,
made an agreement in ink with the Devil in 1669,
' *deinde vero* ', later, however, he made another in
blood. He overrides the definite statement made in
both reports that a Pact was concluded in 1668 and,
in order to agree with the date written on both the

---

[1] ' *zusammengeknäult und in vier Stücke zerrissen.* '

returned Pacts, ignores the remark in the Abbot's deposition that there was a difference in date between the Pacts.

In the Abbot's deposition a paragraph appears in brackets following the words *sequenti vero anno 1669*. This runs : *sumitur hic alter annus pro nondum completo uti saepe in loquendo fieri solet, nam eundum annum indicant Syngraphae quarum atramento scripta ante praesentem attestationem nondum habita fuit.* This is clearly an interpolation on the part of the compiler ; since the Abbot, who had only seen one Pact, could not in any case have said that both bear the same date. The placing of this passage in brackets must have been intended to show that the paragraph was by a strange hand and not part of the Abbot's evidence. It is another attempt of the compiler to reconcile conflicting evidence. His view is that whilst it is indeed correct that the first Pact was drawn up in 1668, still the year was far advanced (September), hence the painter had postdated it by a year in order that both Pacts should bear the same date. His reference to a similar custom in contracts made by word of mouth may well stamp his whole attempt at reconciliation as an ' idle prevarication '.

Now I cannot tell whether my presentation of the case will have made any impression on the reader or whether it has aroused his interest sufficiently in such minutiae. For my own part, I found it impossible to explain the case in a manner which disposed of all doubt, but in the course of my study of the situation I ventured on a surmise which has the advantage of putting the events in the most natural order, even though the documentary evidence does not entirely cover it.

My view is that during his first visit to Mariazell the painter mentioned only one regular Pact, the one which was written in blood, was about to fall due and was drawn up on September 8, 1668, precisely as described by the Pastor in his introductory letter.

In Mariazell also he produced this blood Pact as the one returned to him by the Devil under compulsion by the Holy Mother. We know what happened afterwards. The painter soon left Mariazell and went to Vienna, where until the middle of October he felt much better. Then, however, he again fell ill and the apparitions which he regarded as the work of the Evil One recommenced. He once more felt in need of redemption but was faced with the difficulty of explaining why the exorcism in the Holy Shrine had not brought about permanent relief. Returning merely as a relapsed case, he could scarcely have been welcome at Mariazell. To overcome this difficulty he invented a previous Pact, which, however, should be written in ink, so that its relative insignificance in comparison with the later blood Pact might seem more plausible. Once more at Mariazell, he brought about the return of this alleged first Pact also. Then he was at last freed from the attentions of the Evil One, though he immediately did something else which serves to indicate to us what was underlying his neurosis.

The drawings he made were certainly executed on the occasion of his second sojourn at Mariazell : the title-page is of one piece and represents both Pact scenes. The attempt to make his fresh account tally with the earlier story may well have occasioned him some embarrassment. Clearly it was inconvenient that he could only invent an earlier Pact instead of a later one. So he could not avoid the awkward result that he had redeemed the one blood Pact too soon (in the eighth year) and the other black Pact too late (in the tenth year). It then happened that in dating the Pacts he blunders, making the earlier one, too, date from the year 1669, thus betraying by this sign his twofold editing of the story. This blunder may be regarded as a piece of unintentional honesty : it enables us to guess that the alleged earlier Pact was actually fabricated at a later date. The compiler, whose work was carried out certainly not before 1714 and perhaps not till 1729, was faced with the necessity of explaining away, as best he could, this conflicting evidence about details that were far from unimportant. Finding that both the Pacts in his possession were dated 1669, he had recourse to a subterfuge, the terms of which are interpolated in the Abbot's deposition.

We can easily see wherein the weakness of this otherwise engaging speculation lies. In the Abbot's deposition reference is already made to the existence of two Pacts, one black and the other written in blood. Hence I am faced with the alternative either of insinuating that the compiler here tampered with the deposition itself, in order to make it tally with his interpolated paragraph, or of admitting frankly that I cannot unravel the tangle.[1]

I daresay the reader will consider all this discussion as superfluous and regard the issues themselves as quite too trivial. Nevertheless, if we follow the matter

[1] In my opinion the compiler found himself on the horns of a dilemma. On the one hand, he discovered that, not only in the Pastor's introductory letter but in the Abbot's deposition, the Pact (at all events, the first one) is described as having been made in 1668 ; on the other hand, both Pacts preserved in the archives bore the date 1669. That two Pacts lay before him was, in his view, conclusive evidence that two had been made. Since, however, as I believe, there was mention in the Abbot's deposition of only one Pact, he felt impelled to insert in the deposition some reference to the existence of another, subsequently reconciling any contradiction by his assumption of post-dating. This textual alteration occurs immediately before the inter-polated paragraph which he alone could have inserted. He was compelled to link up this paragraph to the textual alteration with the words *sequenti vero anno* 1669, since the painter had expressly written under the (much damaged) title-page illustrations :

> . . *Nach einem Jahr würdt Er*
> . . *schrökhliche betrohungen in ab-*
> . . *gestalt Nr. 2 bezwungen sich,*
> . . . *n Bluut zu verschreiben.*

> (A year after He was
> . . . horrid threatenings by the
> . . . . shape No. 2 compelled
> . . . to give a Pact in Bloode.)

The blunder made by the painter in writing his Syngraphae, which induced me to bring forward this attempt at explanation, appears to me to be no less interesting a product of his pen than the Pacts themselves.

up in a certain direction, it will be found to acquire fresh interest.

I have already expressed my opinion that, when the painter was disagreeably overtaken by a recurrence of his illness, he invented an earlier Pact (in ink) in order to put himself right with the fathers at Mariazell. Now since I write for those who believe in psycho-analysis and not in the Devil, my readers could point out how absurd it is to bring such an accusation against the poor fellow—*hunc miserum* he is called in the introductory letter. For the blood Pact, they might say, was just as much a product of phantasy as the alleged earlier Pact written in ink. The Devil never appeared to the painter in reality at all, and the whole Satanic Pact existed only in his imagination. I quite realize this : one cannot deny the poor fellow the right to supplement his original phantasy with a new one when occasion demands.

But the matter cannot be allowed to rest here. Unlike the apparitions of the Evil One, the two Pacts are by no means products of phantasy ; they were documents which, according to the assurance of the copyist and of the deposition of the Abbot Kilian, were preserved in the archives at Mariazell where they could be seen and handled by all and sundry. We are therefore in a dilemma. Either we must assume that the painter himself drew up, at the time when he stood in need of them, both the *Schedae* which he alleged were returned to him by the grace of God, or else we must, despite all solemn assurances, sealed testimony of witnesses and so on, discount the credibility of the ecclesiastics of Mariazell and St. Lambert. I must admit I am not inclined to take the latter course. To be sure, I incline to the view that the compiler, in the interests of conformity, has falsified part of the deposition of the first Abbot, but this ' secondary elaboration ' does not much exceed what is quite commonly perpetrated in this direction even by lay modern historians, and at all events it was done in good faith.   In other ways these reverend fathers have established good claim on our credence.   As I said before, there was nothing to prevent their suppressing the accounts of the incomplete nature of the cure and the recurrence of temptation by the Evil One : moreover, the description of the redemption-scenes in the shrine, about which one might have some anticipatory apprehensions, is in fact soberly given and inspires confidence.   So there is nothing for it but to lay the accusation at the painter's door.   The blood Pact he probably already had with him when he went to the shrine for the penitential prayer, and he produced it when he came back to the assembled company after his meeting with the Evil One.   Moreover, this need not have been the same document that was afterwards preserved in the archives, but in accordance with our surmise may have borne the date 1668 (nine years before the exorcism).

V. SUBSEQUENT COURSE OF THE NEUROSIS

But then it would all have been a ruse rather than a neurosis, the painter a malingerer and a cheat instead of a man sick of demoniacal possession ! But the transition-stages between neurosis and malingering are, as we know, very elastic.   Nor do I see any difficulty in assuming that the painter manufactured this Pact—and the later one too—and took it with him in a state comparable to that during which he saw his visions. Indeed, there was no other course open to him if he wished to realize his phantasy of a Pact with Satan and of a subsequent redemption.

The Diary written in Vienna, however, which he gave to the priests on the occasion of his second visit to Mariazell, bears the stamp of veracity.   It certainly affords us deeper insight into the motivation, or we will say rather, the utilization of the neurosis.

The entries date from his successful redemption until January 13 of the following year, 1678.   Until

October 11 he did very well in Vienna, where he lived with a married sister, but from that date he was taken with fresh seizures accompanied by visions, convulsions, loss of consciousness and painful sensations, which ultimately led to his return to Mariazell in May 1678.

This relapse can be divided into three phases. First of all temptation comes in the form of a gaily dressed cavalier, who tries to induce him to part with the document attesting his admission to the Brotherhood of the Holy Rosary. This temptation is successfully withstood, only to be repeated on the following day; the scene is laid in a marvellously decorated hall where high-born men are dancing with beautiful women. The same cavalier makes a proposal to him concerning painting,[1] promising him in return a goodly sum of money. With prayer this vision is overcome, but it is repeated a few days later in a more pressing form. On this occasion the cavalier sends one of the most beautiful of the ladies sitting at the banquet-table to persuade the painter to mingle with them, and he has some difficulty in defending himself from the wiles of the fair seducer. Most terrifying of all was the vision which occurred shortly afterwards ; it took place in a still more magnificent hall in which there stood a throne ' built verie high with pieces of golde ',[2] near which the courtiers awaited the arrival of their king. The same person who had so often importuned him now came forward and begged the painter to ascend the throne, for they ' would have him for to be their King, to honour him for ever and aye '.[3] This elaboration of his phantasy concludes the first, and entirely perspicuous, phase of the story of his temptation.

A reaction was now inevitable ; asceticism came to the fore. On October 20 a great light appeared to

---

[1] This part is unintelligible to me.
[2] *Ein von ' Goldstuckh aufgerichteter Thron '.*
[3] *' Wollten ihn für ihren König halten und in Ewigkeit verehren.'*

him, from which came the voice of Christ commanding
him to forswear this wicked world and to serve God in
a desert for a period of six years. The painter clearly
suffered more from these holy visions than from the
earlier devilish apparitions ; he came out of this
seizure only after two and a half hours. On the next
occasion the sacred figure enveloped in light was much
more hostile, upbraided him for neglecting to obey the
sacred behest, and led him into Hell that he might
be duly terrified by the fate of the damned. Evidently,
however, this had not the required effect, since visions
of a Being enveloped in light who was supposed to be
Christ recurred several times after, each seizure being
accompanied by a loss of consciousness lasting some
hours and by a state of ecstasy. During the most
impressive of all these ecstasies, this Being led him
first of all into a town whose inhabitants performed
all the works of darkness in the streets, and then for
contrast to quiet pastures wherein hermits led a godly
life and received tangible evidence of the grace and
goodness of God. There then appeared, instead of
Christ, the Holy Mother herself, who reminded the
painter of what she had already done on his behalf
and called on him to obey Her Beloved Son's behests.
' Since he coulde not resolue so to doe ', [1] Christ re-
appeared to him on the following day, rebuked him
roundly and endeavoured to prevail on him with
promises. Then at last he gave way, made up his
mind to leave the world and to do what was
required of him. The second phase ends with this
decision. The painter states that from this time
onward he saw no more apparitions and was never
again tempted.

Nevertheless, his resolution cannot have been very
strong or he must have delayed too long in carrying
it out, since in the midst of his devotions on December
26, in St. Stephen's, he caught sight of a strapping
wench accompanied by a well-dressed man and could

[1] ' *Da er sich hiezu nicht recht resolviret.*'

not help thinking that he might have filled the latter's shoes. On the same evening, like a bolt from the blue, punishment was meted out; he saw the flames swallowing him up and fell in a swoon. Attempts were made to rouse him, but he grovelled in the room till blood flowed from his nose and mouth; he became aware of the scorching heat and the foul fumes, and heard a voice declaring that this was the punishment for his vain and unprofitable thoughts. Later he was scourged by evil spirits with ropes and informed that the punishment would be repeated every day until he decided to enter the order of anchorites. These experiences continued up to the last entry (January 13).

We see how our unfortunate painter's phantasies of temptation were succeeded by ascetic ones and finally by those of punishment; the end we know already. In May he went to Mariazell, told the story of an earlier Pact written in black ink, to which he evidently ascribed his continued temptation by the Devil, received back this Pact and was finally healed.

During this second sojourn there he painted the pictures which are copied in the *Trophaeum*; next, however, he took a step which was in accord with the demands of the ascetic phase described in his Diary. To be sure, he did not go into the desert to live as a hermit but he joined the Order of Monks Hospitallers : *religiosus factus est.*

Perusal of the Diary gives us insight into another part of the narrative. We remember that the painter pledges himself to the Evil One because after his father's death he feels depressed, incapable of work and is apprehensive about his livelihood. These factors, depression, lack of working capacity and grief, have some connection with one another, whether it be a simple or a complex one. Perhaps the Devil is furnished so generously with breasts because he is to become a foster-father. This hope not being realized, the patient's condition deteriorated; he could not work properly, or perhaps he was out of luck and had not sufficient work to do. The Pastor's introductory letter speaks of him as ' *hunc miserum omni auxilio destitutum* '. He was thus not only in moral straits, he was literally in want. In the account of his later visions we find here and there remarks indicating, like the content of the scenes portrayed, that even after the first successful redemption nothing of this had changed. We come to realize that he was of the type which cannot make its way in the world and which inspires confidence in no one. In the first vision the cavalier asks him what he is going to do, since nobody takes any interest in him.[1] The first series of phantasies in Vienna corresponds entirely with the wish-phantasies of the poverty-stricken, of such as have come down in the world and hunger after pleasure : magnificent halls, high living, silver-ware and lovely women ; here we find what was missing in his traffic with the Devil. At that time he had been in the depths of a melancholia which caused him to turn from all enjoyment and to ignore the most tempting offers. After his redemption the melancholia seems to have been overcome and all the longings of a worldling rise up once more.

In one of the ascetic visions he complains to his guide (Christ) that nobody has any faith in him, hence that he is unable to carry out the commands laid upon him. The reply given is unfortunately obscure. ' So inasmuch as they will not beleeve me yet doe I know well what has happened but am vnapt to speak a worde about it.'[2] On the other hand, what happens when the celestial guide takes him amongst the hermits is very enlightening. He comes to a cave in which an old man has been sitting for

---

[1] ' *Dieweillen ich von iedermann izt verlassen, wass ich anfangen würde.*'

[2] ' *So fer man mir nit glauben, wass aber geschechen, waiss ich wol, ist mir aber selbes auszuspröchen unmöglich.*'

the last sixty years ; in answer to his question he is told that an angel from Heaven feeds this old man every day. He then sees for himself an angel bringing food : ' Three pannikins with food, one of bread, one of dumpling and wherewithall to drink '.¹ After the hermit has fed, the angel collects everything and carries it away. We realize from this the nature of the temptations presented in the pious visions : he is to be induced to adopt a mode of life in which there are no cares about sustenance. The utterances of Christ in the last vision are also worthy of note. After the threat that, should he not prove more amenable, something would come to pass (which) both he and the people would be bound (to) believe, he says directly that ' I should not heed the people even if they would persecute me or give me no succour, God would not forsake me '.²

Christoph Haitzmann was enough of an artist and a worldling to find it difficult to renounce this sinful world. Nevertheless, he did so in the end, because of the helplessness of his position. He entered a holy order, where his inner conflict as well as his material want came to an end. This outcome is reflected in the neurosis by the return of the alleged earlier Pact that puts an end to his attacks and visions. Actually, both stages of his demonological illness had the same signification. All he wanted was security in life, at first with the help of Satan but at the cost of eternal bliss ; then, when this failed and had to be abandoned, with the Church's help but at the cost of his freedom and most of the pleasures of life. Perhaps Christoph Haitzmann was only a poor devil, one of those who never have any luck ; perhaps he was too poorly gifted, too ineffective to make a living, and belonged to that well-known type, the ' eternal suckling '—to those who are unable to tear themselves away from the

¹ ' Drei Schüsserl mit Speiss, ein Brot und ein Knödl und Getränk.'
² ' Ich solle die Leith nit achten, obwollen ich von ihnen verfolgt wurdte, oder von ihnen keine hilfflaistung empfienge, Gott würde mich nit verlassen.'

joyous haven at the mother's breast, who hold fast all through their lives to their claim to be nourished by someone else. And so in his illness our painter followed the path from his own father by way of the Devil as a father-substitute to the pious Fathers.

To superficial observation his neurosis looks like a sort of jugglery covering some part of the very serious, if banal, anxiety of the struggle for existence. This aspect of it is not, of course, an invariable one, but it is by no means rare. In analytical experience we frequently find how unsatisfactory it is to treat a business man who ' in other respects healthy, has for some time shown signs of a neurosis '. The catastrophe which he knows to be threatening his business induces the neurosis as a by-product, with the advantage that behind the symptoms the man is able to conceal his real apprehensions about his livelihood. In every other respect, however, it is more than inexpedient, since it uses up energies which would be more advantageously applied in handling the threatening situation with all possible skill.

In a far greater number of cases the neurosis is more of a thing apart, more independent of the claims of self-preservation and maintenance. The interests at stake in the conflict giving rise to neurosis are either purely libidinal, or have a close libidinal relation to those of self-preservation. In all three instances the dynamics of the neurosis are identical. Libido, dammed up and unable to secure real gratification, finds discharge through the repressed unconscious by the help of regression to old fixations. In so far as the patient's ego can extract from this process a paranosic or epinosic gain, it countenances the neurosis, although there can be no manner of doubt about the economic handicap it signifies.

Not even our painter's wretched situation in life would have induced his neurosis of demoniacal possession, had not his material necessities served to intensify a longing for his father. After his melancholia and his relations with the Devil had been played out, there still remained the conflict between his libidinal pleasure in life and his recognition that in the interests of self-preservation he must become a stern anchorite and ascetic. It is interesting to see that the painter was well aware of the identity behind the two phases of his illness, since he attributed both the one and the other to Pacts which he had delivered to the Devil. On the other hand, he draws no sharp distinction between the machinations of the Evil One and those of Heavenly Powers ; he had but one characterization for both—manifestations of the Devil.

ABBREVIATIONS

The forms of citation used in the footnotes and in the subjoined list of Selected References are as follows:

Imago	*Imago,* Vienna
Jahrbuch	*Jahrbuch für psychoanalytische und psychopathologische Forschungen,* Vienna
Sammlung	Freud, *Sammlung kleiner Schriften zur Neurosenlehre,* Vienna
Zeitschrift	*Internationale Zeitschrift für ärztliche Psychoanalyse,* later called *Internationale Zeitschrift für Psychoanalyse,* Vienna
Zentralblatt	*Zentralblatt für Psychoanalyse, Vienna*

SELECTED REFERENCES

The following list comprises the main works mentioned above in the text and notes. References to additional literature and to new editions and translations of basic sources will be indicated in the annotations below.

ABEL, KARL. *Uber den Gegensinn der Urworte,* 1884.

BAIN, ALEXANDER. *Logic,* 1870.

BRANDES, G. *William Shakespeare,* 1896.

CRAWLEY, ERNEST. *The Mystic Rose; a Study of Primitive Marriage.* 2 vols. London, 1902. Rev. ed., 1927.

ELLIS, HAVELOCK. *Studies in the Psychology of Sex,* 6 vols. Philadelphia, 1897-1911.

FLOERKE, G. *Zehn Jahre mit Böcklin,* 2d ed. 1902.

FRAZER, J. G. *Taboo and the Perils of the Soul,* 3d ed. London, 1911.

FREUD, SIGMUND. *Die Traumdeutung,* Vienna, 1900.

———. *Eine Kindheitserinnerung des Leonardo da Vinci,* Vienna, 1910, 1923.

———. *Totem und Tabu.* Vienna, 1913. 3d ed. 1922.

———. *Beyond the Pleasure-Principle.* London, 1922. Translated by C. J. M. Hubback from *Jenseits des Lustprinzips.* Vienna, 1920. 3d ed. 1923.

———. *Group Psychology and the Analysis of the Ego.* London, 1922. Translated by James Strachey from *Massenpsychologie und Ichanalyse.* Vienna, 1921.

JONES, ERNEST. *Der Alptraum in seiner Beziehung zu gewissen Formen des mittelalterlichen Aberglaubens.* Vienna, 1912.

JUNG, C. G. "Die Bedeutung des Vaters fur das Schicksal des Einzelnen" *Jahrbuch,* Bd. I, 1909.

KAMMERER, P. *Das Gesetz der Serie.* Vienna, 1919.

KRAFFT-EBING, RICHARD VON. "Bemerkungen über 'geschlechtliche Hörigkeit' und Masochismus." *Jahrbücher fur Psychiatrie,* Bd. X, 1892.

LLOYD, WILLIAM WATKISS. *The Moses of Michelangelo.* London, 1863.

MACH, E., *Analyse der Empfindungen,* 1900.

PLOSS, H. H., and PAUL BARTELS. *Das Weib in der Natur-und Völkerkunde.* 1891.

RANK, OTTO. *Der Künstler.* Vienna, 1907.

——*Der Mythus von der Geburt des Helden,* Vienna, 1909. 2nd ed., 1922.

——*Das Inzestmotiv in Dichtung und Sage.* Vienna, 1912.

REIK, THEODOR. *Probleme der Religionspsychologie.* Vienna, 1919.

——. *Der eigene und der fremde Gott* (Imago-Bücher, III). Vienna, 1923.

REINACH, SALOMON. *Cultes, mythes et religions.* 1912.

SADGER, ISIDOR. "Von der Pathographie zur Psychographie." *Imago,* Bd. I. 1912.

SCHREBER, D. P. *Denkwürdigkeiten eines Nervenkranken.* Leipzig, 1903.

SCHUBERT, B. G. H. VON. *Die Symbolik des Traumes.* 4th ed. 1862.

SELIGMAN, SIEGFRIED. *Der böse Blick and Verwandtes,* 2 vols. Berlin, 1910.

STEKEL, W. *Die Sprache des Traumes.* 1911. 2d ed. 1922.

STORFER, A. J. *Zur Sonderstellung des Vatermordes.* Vienna, 1911.

STUCKEN, E. *Astralmythen.* Leipzig, 1907.

THODE, HENRY. *Michelangelo; Kritische Undersuchungen uber seine Werke.* 1908.

ANNOTATIONS

Compiled by BENJAMIN NELSON

A handy bibliography of major sources and recent literature will be found in the present editor's *Freud and the 20th Century* (New York: Meridian Books, 1957).

ONE OF THE DIFFICULTIES OF PSYCHO-ANALYSIS

P. 2-3—Freud's theories of the conflicts between the ego-instincts and the sexual instincts are everywhere receiving critical reappraisal at the present time. Drs. Heinz Hartmann, Rudolph Loewenstein, and Ernst Kris of the New York Psychoanalytical Institute and Erik Erikson and David Rapaport of the Austen Riggs Center in Stockbridge, Mass., have pioneered in the elaboration of a novel "ego Psychology." Numerous essays from their pens have appeared in professional journals, notably in the *Psychoanalytic Quarterly, Journal of the American Psychoanalytic Association* and *Psychoanalytic Study of the Child*. W. R. D. Fairbairn of Edinburgh has insisted on the importance of "object-relations" as opposed to libido theory as a point of departure for the understanding of the personality. See *Psychoanalytic Study of the Personality*. London: Tavistock Publications, 1952.

P. 5—The effects of the Copernican hypothesis on the imagination have been variously assessed. See, especially A. O. Lovejoy, *The Great Chain of Being* (Cambridge: Harvard University Press, 1936); A. Koyré, *From the Closed World to the Infinite Universe* (New York: Harper Torchbooks, 1957).

P. 6—For the response to Darwin, see William Irvine, *Apes, Angels, and Victorians* (New York: McGraw-Hill, 1951).

P. 9-10—The self-estimate of Freud allegedly implied in this essay has recently been a subject of debate between Dr. Nigel Walker of Edinburgh and Ernest Jones. See N. Walker, "A New Copernicus?" in *Freud and the 20th Century*, 22-30, 287.

THE MOSES OF MICHELANGELO

P. 11—Charles de Tolnay expresses high appreciation of Freud's essay in the last volume of his monumental study of Michelangelo. De Tolnay writes: "As a timeless character image the figure is described by Condivi Vasari, 1568, William W. Lloyd, Springer, Wolfflin, Vischer, Thode, and S. Freud. Among those perhaps the most brilliant analysis are those of Lloyd and S. Freud." The criticism of Freud by Occhini in *L'Arte*, V 1934), 123 ff, is described as "inadequate." De Tolnay, *Michelangelo*, IV (1954), 103-4; cf. illustrations 18-27 in appendix.

P. 11, n. 1—In 1933, on the occasion of the Italian publication of this essay, which was originally issued anonymously, Freud wrote to Dr. Eduardo Weiss: "My feeling for this piece of work is rather like that towards a love-child. For three lonely September weeks in 1913 I stood every day in the church in front of the statue, studied it, measured it, sketched it, until I captured the understanding for it which I ventured to express only anonymously. Only much later did I legitimatize this non-analytical child." Cited in E. Jones, *The Life and Work of Sigmund Freud*, II, 367.

P. *13-14*—The *Moses* was written at the same time that Freud was an-
nouncing his disagreements with Jung and Adler. Ernest Jones suggests
that "Freud had identified himself with Moses and was striving to
emulate the victory over passion that Michelangelo had depicted in his
stupendous achievement." Jones, *Sigmund Freud*, II, 366. "The back-
sliding mob were to him the many former supporters who had deserted
him, and gone back on his work, in the last four years—Adler and his
friend, Stekel, and now the Swiss." E. Jones, *op. cit.*, II, 366-67.

In June of 1927, Freud wrote a "Supplementary Note on the Subject
of the Moses Statue," based on a representation sent to him by Ernest
Jones of a statue of Moses made in the twelfth century by Nicholas of
Verdun, which is now in the Ashmolean Museum at Oxford. See *Gesam-
melte Werke*, XII, 321; *Standard Edition*, XIV, 321, E. Jones, II, 366;
III, 137-8.

P. *41*—The following recent studies bear on Freud's discussions of art:
Ernst Kris, *Psychoanalytic Explorations in Art*, New York: International
Universities Press, 1952; *Art and Psychoanalysis*, ed. William Phillips
(New York: Criterion Books 1957); Louis Freiberg, "Freud's Writings
on Art" *International Journal of Psycho-Analysis* (henceforth I. J. Psa.),
xxxvii. 1 (Jan-Feb 1956); E. H. Gombrich "Psychoanalysis and the
History of Art" in *Freud and the 20th Century*, ed. B. Nelson, pp.
167-206; Meyer Schapiro "Leonardo and Freud: An Art-Historical Study,"
Journal of the History of Ideas (April 1956). Dr. Richard and Editha
Sterba of Cleveland are now engaged in a documentary study of Michelangelo from the psychoanalytic point of view.

THE ANTITHETICAL SENSE OF PRIMAL WORDS

P. *55*—*Traumdeutung*. This is Freud's *Interpretation of Dreams*, originally
published in 1900; see now the splendid translation with full notes by
James Strachey. New York: Basic Books, 1953.

P. *62*—Emile Benveniste has recently written a vigorous criticism of K.
Abel and Freud's essay in *La Psychanalyse: Publication de la Société
francaise de Psychanalyse*, I (Paris: Presses Universitaires de France,
1956), 5-16.

THE THEME OF THE THREE CASKETS

P. *63*—Of this essay, Jones writes: "Most students of Freud's writings
have, apart from an estimate of their scientific value, a personal fondness
for some favorite, and I may say, that this is mine." *Sigmund Freud*, II,
361. Texts of the variants of this theme in folklore and literature will
be found in critical editions—especially the so-called Arden and Vari-
orum editions—of *The Merchant of Venice;* cf. Samuel Tannenbaum's
The Merchant of Venice: A Concise Bibliography for listing of the
studies of these variants from the philological and comparative points of
view.

THOUGHTS FOR THE TIMES ON WAR AND DEATH

P. *206 ff.*—The two parts of this paper were prepared separately. Part
Two, "Our Attitudes towards Death," was originally delivered as an
address to a Viennese lodge of the B'nai B'rith, a Jewish fraternal
society. Freud described it as an "audacious lecture containing much grim
humor." E. Jones, *op. cit.*, II, 370-7.

DREAMS AND TELEPATHY

For an account of Freud's interest in "occult" phenomena, see G. Devereux, ed., *Psychoanalysis and the Occult* (New York: International Universities Press, 1953), esp. J. Eisenbud "Psychiatric Contributions to Parapsychology: A Review," (pp. 3-15), Nandor Fodor, "Freud and the Poltergeist," *Psychoanalysis*, IV. 2 (Winter 1955-56), 22-28; *idem*, "An Unpublished Letter on Parapsychology," *Psychoanalysis and the Future*, ed. B. Nelson in collaboration with the Board of Editors of *Psychoanalysis*, New York, 1957, pp. 12-13.

A NEUROSIS OF DEMONIACAL POSSESSSION

P. 264—Freud's account of his studies under Charcot (1825-93) occur at numerous points in his letters and writings. See, now, Freud "Report of My Studies in Paris and Berlin (1886)" *I. J. Psa.*, xxxvii. 1 (Jan.-Feb., 1956), 2-7: (includes a photograph of himself given by Charcot to Freud); Josef Breuer and Sigmund Freud, "On the Psychical Mechanism of Hysterical Phenomena (1893)" *ibid*, 8-18, esp. at 8-10; *Collected Papers*, I, 9-23. See also references indicated in the indexes of Freud, *The Origins of Psychoanalysis. Letters to Wilhelm Fliess, Drafts and Notes (1887-1902)*, ed. Maria Bonaparte, Anna Freud and Ernst Kris, tr. Erich Mosbacher and James Strachey (New York: Basic Books, 1954); E. Jones, *op. cit.*, I, esp. 75, 233-35, 238, 240-1, 248-49, 273, 370.

P. 265—Discussion of the materials on Haitzmann by Rudolf Payer von Thurn was published under the title "Faust in Mariazell," in *Chronik des Wiener Goethe-Verein*, CCCIV I (1924), Payer von Thurn was editor of the *Chronik* at the time he approached Freud.

The original manuscript on which Freud's essay is based, a translation of the text and reproduction of the possessed man's Haitzmann paintings, are now available in a limited edition of 750 copies. See Ida Macalpine and Richard Hunter, *Schizophrenia 1677. A Psychiatric Study of an Illustrated Autobiographical Record of Demoniacal Possession*. London: William Dawson & Sons, Ltd., 1956. For a criticism of the interpretation of the case by the editors, see William G. Niederland, *Psychoanalytic Quarterly*, XXVII (1958), 107-11.

Many interesting insights should occur to those who read this essay in the context of the development of The Faust legend. See P. M. Palmer and R. P. Moore, *The Sources of the Faust Tradition from Simon Magus to Lessing*. (New York, 1936.)

P. 278, n. 1—The first of Reik's works mentioned is translated under the title *Ritual: Psychoanalytic Studies (The Psychoanalytic Problems of Religion, 1)*. New York: Farrar, Strauss & Cudahy, 1946.

P. 278, n. 2—See now Ernest Jones, *On The Nightmare*. New York: Liveright Publishing Co., 1951.

P. 284, n. 1—An English translation by A. A. Brill is available in Anchor Books.

P. 284, n. 2—The autobiography is now available in English. See Daniel Paul Schreber, *Memoirs of My Nervous Illness*, tr. and ed. Ida Macalpine and Richard A. Hunter (London: William Dawson & Sons, Ltd., 1955). New material on the Schreber case will be found in Franz Baumeyer, "The Schreber Case," *I. J. Psa.*, xxxvii. 1 (Jan.-Feb. 1956), 61-74.

INDEX

Abel, Karl, 55
Affect, changed into anxiety, 148
Affection and instinct of self-
    preservation, 174
Alcohol, taking of, 184
Anæsthesia, sexual, 180
Anxiety—
    and affects, 148
    and birth, 171
    morbid, 148
    of heights, 255
Anxious expectation, 192

Bain, 60
Birth, and fear, 171
Blindness, and castration, 137
Blood, taboo of, 191

Caskets, the three, 63
Castration—
    and blindness, 137
    and penis-envy, 200
Character—
    and resistances, 84
    -types, 84
    criminality from a sense of guilt,
        108
    the 'exceptions', 229
    wrecked by success, 89
Childhood—
    a recollection, 111
Children—
    and play, 44-45
    naughtiness in, 109
    Christianity and love, 183
Civilization, foundation of, 215
Community, dread of the, 212

Complex, Oedipus—
    and conscience, 49
    and sense of guilt, 109
Compulsion, in love, 165
Conscience, 142
    and Oedipus-complex, 109
Crawley, 189
Criminality from sense of guilt, 108
Criticizing faculty, 142
Cultural—
    adaptability, 215
    development, 185
Culture and component-instincts,
    185

Day-dreams, 44, 45, 46, 51
Death—
    and dumbness, 67
    and the 'uncanny', 149
    and the unconscious, 233
    attitude towards, 222
    savages and, 226
    war and, 206
Defloration, 189
Delusions, of observation, 142
Demoniacal possession, a neurosis
    of, 264
Devil, the, as a father-substitute,
    274
'Dichtung und Wahrheit', 111
Double, the, 140
Dreams—
    analysed, 77, 80
    and fairy tales, 76
    and phantasies, 49
    child-birth represented in, 255
    dumbness in, 67
    five in, 282

Menstruation, taboo of, 191
Merchant of Venice, The, 63
Monogamy, 187
Morality, attainment of, 213
Moses of Michelangelo, the, 11
Narcissism, and science, 4
Neuroses—
  and phantasy, 49
  frustration, 89, 91
  of demoniacal possession, 264

Nietzsche, 109
Nine, the number, 281
'No' and the unconscious, 55
Novels, 50-51

Obsessions, visual, 42
Oedipus-complex, *see* Oedipus
Omnipotence of thoughts, 4, 148

Payer-Thurn, R., 265
Penis-envy, 200
Phantasy—
  and neurosis, 49
  and play, 47
  and wishes, 47
  of 'saving', 170, 171
  relation to dreams, 49
  relation to time, 48
Play, 44-47
Pleasure—
  fore-, 54
  in smashing, 117
  renouncement of, 85
Poet, the, 44-54
Possession, demoniacal, 264
Pregnancy, symbolism of, 121
Priapus, 200
Psycho-analysis—
  a difficulty of, 1
  aim of, 7
  resistance to its findings, 1

Rank, Otto, 64, 141
Reality, and play, 45

Recollection, a childhood, 111
Reik, Th., 125
Repetition, and the uncanny, 144
Repetition-compulsion, 145
'Rescue', idea of, 170, 254
Resistance, and character, 84

Sachs, 115
Sadger, 204
Sand-man, the, 132
Savages—
  and danger, 195
  and death, 226
  and sexual intercourse, 188
  anxious expectation in, 192
Saving phantasy, 170, 171, 172, 254
Schreber, 284
Science, and narcissism, 4
Screen-memories, 113
Sexual—
  anæsthesia, 180
  intercourse, among savages, 188
  thralldom, 188
Sexuality, education and, 183
Silberer, 258
Smashing, pleasure in, 117
Stekel, 237
Storfer, 200
Stucken, E., 64
Success, wrecked by, 89
Symbolism, of pregnancy, 121

Taboo, 187, 189, 191, 194
Telepathy, dreams and, 236
Thoughts, omnipotence of, 4, 147

'Uncanny', the, 122
Unconscious—
  and death, 233
  and 'no', 55

Virginity, taboo of, 187
Visual obsession, 42

War and death, 206